UNLIMITED REPLAYS

THE OXFORD MUSIC / MEDIA SERIES

Daniel Goldmark, Series Editor

oxford
music/media series

Unlimited Replays

VIDEO GAMES AND CLASSICAL MUSIC

William Gibbons

OXFORD
UNIVERSITY PRESS

OXFORD
UNIVERSITY PRESS

Oxford University Press is a department of the University of Oxford. It furthers
the University's objective of excellence in research, scholarship, and education
by publishing worldwide. Oxford is a registered trade mark of Oxford University
Press in the UK and certain other countries.

Published in the United States of America by Oxford University Press
198 Madison Avenue, New York, NY 10016, United States of America.

© Oxford University Press 2018

The Lloyd Hibberd Endowment of the American Musicological Society, funded in part
by the National Endowment for the Humanities and the Andrew W. Mellon Foundation.

Library of Congress Cataloging-in-Publication Data
Names: Gibbons, William (William James), 1981– author.
Title: Unlimited replays: video games and classical music / William Gibbons.
Description: New York, NY : Oxford University Press, [2018] | Series: Oxford music/media series |
Includes bibliographical references and index.
Identifiers: LCCN 2017043127 | ISBN 9780190265250 (cloth : alk. paper) |
ISBN 9780190265267 (pbk. : alk. paper) | ISBN 9780190265304 (oxford scholarship online)
Subjects: LCSH: Video game music—History and criticism.
Classification: LCC ML3540.7 .G53 2018 | DDC 781.5/4—dc23
LC record available at https://lccn.loc.gov/2017043127

9 8 7 6 5 4 3 2 1

Paperback printed by Webcom, Inc., Canada
Hardback printed by Bridgeport National Bindery, Inc., United States of America

This volume is published with the generous support of the Lloyd Hibberd Endowment of
the American Musicological Society, funded in part by the National Endowment for the
Humanities and the Andrew W. Mellon Foundation.

Contents

Figures

Tables

Acknowledgments

WRITING A BOOK is not a single-player game. Every stage of this process has benefited from the guidance and support of family, friends, and colleagues. A number of scholars generously took the time to offer comments on earlier versions of this research. Naming all of them would be impossible, but I am particularly indebted to William Ayers, William Cheng, Karen Cook, James Deaville, Michiel Kamp, Neil Lerner, Dana Plank, Sarah Pozderac Chenevey, Steven Beverburg Reale, Douglas Shadle, Tim Summers, and Mark Sweeney. The staff at Oxford University Press and their affiliates have been a pleasure to work with. Series Editor Daniel Goldmark and OUP Senior Editor Norm Hirschy offered kind words and expert guidance throughout this process, copyeditor Susan Ecklund whipped my manuscript into shape, and the editors at Newgen ably shepherded me through the production phase. Lastly, the Lloyd Hibberd Endowment of the American Musicological Society provided much-appreciated financial support.

I'm especially grateful to the community at Texas Christian University, my academic home for the last seven years. Dean Anne Helmreich and School of Music Director Richard Gipson have both been incredibly supportive, as have many of my faculty and staff colleagues. Music librarian Cari Alexander has put up with my frequent and occasionally unusual requests for materials. And over the years, my undergraduate and graduate students have gamely let me work out these ideas in several courses on musical multimedia and music history. Special thanks are due to Kristen Queen and Martin Blessinger. As friends, musical collaborators, and traveling companions, they've been listening to me talk about this book across many years and several countries—even if I'm not sure they've ever actually let me finish a sentence.

Portions of *Unlimited Replays* have been presented or published in earlier forms. Faculty and students at universities including Denison University, the University of North Carolina at Chapel Hill, the University of Texas at Austin, Sarah Lawrence

College, the University of Southampton, Vanderbilt University, and Wesleyan University graciously invited me to their campuses and classrooms to present my research, and their thoughtful questions and comments have proved invaluable. Likewise, I am grateful to the organizers of the 2018 North American Conference on Video Game Music and the 2017 GAMuT conference at the University of North Texas for allowing me to present topics from this book as keynote addresses. Parts of chapters 6 and 7 appeared in the edited collection *Ludomusicology: Approaches to Video Game Music* (Equinox, 2016), and suggestions from editors Michiel Kamp, Tim Summers, and Mark Sweeney have enriched that material in its final form.

Introduction
PUSH START TO REPLAY

SIGNALING BOTH ENDINGS and beginnings, the idea of "replay" is at the core of the video game experience. A few years ago, I took the time to go back to an unfinished game from my childhood: Nintendo's *Zelda II: The Adventure of Link* (1987). Once I finally completed the game's quest, I was rewarded after the ending credits with what I thought was a somewhat anticlimactic message: "Thanks a million. Push start to replay" (Figure I.1). At the time, I chuckled at the quirks of 1980s games and went on about my business. Now, however, I view that option a little differently. If players follow the game's instructions, the adventure begins again—but this time they start with all the items, health, and powers they had accrued the first time through. The result is an experience at once familiar and new. Players relive the game, but with their frame of reference and mode of understanding it irrevocably altered—and hopefully enriched—by what they had already accomplished. The meaning of "replay" has evolved somewhat since the 1980s, yet the sense of simultaneously being old and new remains the same. Today, the quality of a game is often measured by its "replay value"—that is, by how many times players will enjoy playing through it. The Internet abounds with lists of the "Most Replayable Games" dedicated to identifying and praising titles that reward players for repeated playthroughs. *Zelda II*'s "replay" feature still exists in some games as a "New Game Plus" option, but more commonly "replaying" a game implies taking a favorite game off the shelf and experiencing it anew in search of unseen endings, missed opportunities, or simply a sense of nostalgia.

FIGURE 1.1 The final screen of *Zelda II: The Adventure of Link* (1987).

Replaying is equally important to music. A musician might "re-play" the same musical passage over and over during practice in an attempt to understand or master it, and our media players have "replay" buttons that allow us to set a song, album, or artist on permanent repeat. In both cases, as in *Zelda II*, our experience changes each time we play or hear the music—we carry with us everything we gained in the previous times. To extend the analogy, over significant periods of time, and through a variety of methods, music accumulates multiple layers of meaning. These complex and sometimes conflicting meanings have a profound impact on our individual interpretations of musical works—imagine, for example, a happy song that you can't bear to listen to anymore because it reminds you of a bad breakup. But through sets of shared sociocultural values, new meanings can be indelibly inscribed not just on individual works but on entire styles or genres. These meanings are present in all types of music, but they are particularly apparent in what we call "classical music," which has in many cases developed nuanced webs of intersecting references over the course of centuries of being replayed.

In this book I am interested in exploring the intersections of values and meanings in these two types of replay: where video games meet classical music, in other words, and vice versa. In a sense, my research on this project began when I was about nine years old. Like many children who grew up in the 1980s, I spent countless hours playing (and watching my parents play) games on the Nintendo Entertainment System (NES). Although I had the opportunity to experience most of the classic games of the era—*Super Mario Bros., The Legend of Zelda, Mega Man*, and so on—one of the memories that most vividly stands out in my mind comes from the relatively obscure action-adventure game *The Battle of Olympus* (1988). Although not particularly innovative from a gameplay perspective—its side-scrolling blend of item collection and combat was derived from *Zelda II* and *Castlevania II: Simon's Quest* (1987)—*The Battle of Olympus* intrigues me for several reasons even today. Chief among these is the fact that the game's protagonist is the ancient Greek hero-musician Orpheus, whose irresistible songs could charm even the gods. But what intrigued my nine-year-old self was not the game's hero, or even its plot, but rather its music—and, in fact, one particular musical moment.

To succeed in his quest, Orpheus must curry favor with the Olympian gods by offering appropriate tributes in their temples (Figure I.2). The moment I arrived at the first temple, I noticed something odd about the music: I already knew it. Instead of the game's original soundtrack (composed by Kazuo Sawa), I was greeted by the opening theme of the well-known Toccata and Fugue in D Minor (BWV 565), purportedly written by J. S. Bach. I distinctly remember my confusion at hearing this piece of music, which led me to set the controller down for a few minutes, both to listen and to think. I knew this piece from Disney's *Fantasia* (1940), and I had even played it myself in piano lessons (in a much simplified version). What on earth was this music doing in a video game? What did Bach, this particular piece, or classical music in general, have to do with Greek gods and heroes? I was sure this music *meant* something—maybe even something profound—but I just couldn't put my finger on exactly what it was. Even after I left the temple behind and continued on with the game, I couldn't shake that feeling; the bell couldn't be un-rung. Classical

FIGURE I.2 Zeus's temple in *The Battle of Olympus* (1988).

music seemed to pop up in other games with surprising frequency, and I started to relish the puzzle of uncovering it and figuring out exactly what piece it was (some things apparently never change). In the intervening decades I have not lost my sense that it *means* something when classical music intersects with games, and this book is first and foremost my attempt to explore what some of those meanings might be.

But why dedicate an entire book to this particular subject? Classical music in televisual media is nothing new, since film and television have adapted preexisting music for more than a century. And why classical music, anyway? Popular music appears much more frequently in games and has already received significantly more attention from game music scholars. But although these are valid points—and I will frequently engage with all these parallel uses of preexisting music throughout *Unlimited Replays*—I think exploring the combination of video games and classical music offers unique rewards. The cultural positioning of these two prominent media at the opposite ends of the spectrum of "high" and "low" arts creates remarkable opportunities and challenges for game designers, players, and classical music supporters. Returning to *The Battle of Olympus*, I've come to believe that Bach's Toccata and Fugue seemed so inscrutable to my younger self in that game because my frame of reference told me the music was in the wrong place. I grew up in a household that encouraged both playing video games and listening to classical music, but even at nine years old I had internalized the idea that there was a fundamental value difference between those two activities. Listening to classical music, even if enjoyable, was a serious exercise. In contrast, even the most serious video game was a form of entertainment. Although I now feel quite differently about both, I was certainly not alone in those assumptions; similar views of the value of both classical music and video games are still widely held. Because we tend to place these media in completely separate cultural categories, combining classical music with video games involves a kind of transgression, a crossing of boundaries that begs for explanation and interpretation.

In an attempt to offer some of both, I have divided *Unlimited Replays* into eleven chapters, which explore the relationship between classical music and video games from distinctive, though interlacing, perspectives. Chapter 1, "Terms and Conditions," provides an overview of the core concepts of the book, delving into the sociocultural meanings we invoke when we use the terms "classical music" and "video games," and then considering the possible ramifications of combining the two. From that point, the chapters are divided loosely into pairs. Chapter 2, "Playing with Music History," investigates how games have employed classical music to signify a particular time or place—how Tchaikovsky's music in the NES version of *Tetris* (1989) highlights the game's "Russianness," or how the changing musical selections of the strategy game *Civilization IV* (2005) reinforce the player's sense of chronological progress. Often the most interesting cases are those in which the music is the "wrong" time or place for the situation yet still provides the player with the necessary information; chapter 3, "A Requiem for Schrödinger's Cat," offers a close reading of *BioShock Infinite* (2013) to demonstrate just how complex these signifiers of time and space can become. In that case, the clever use of music paradoxically works both to orient players in particular times and places and simultaneously to destabilize their understanding of where and when they are.

The following pair of chapters deals with the often fraught relationship between video games and film. Chapter 4, "Allusions of Grandeur," considers the difference in cultural capital between games and film—the latter being more clearly established as an "art form"—and examines instances wherein game designers use classical music to draw comparisons with cinematic models. There are a number of both direct and oblique references to silent films in games, for example, particularly early on in the medium's history. More specifically, a number of video games have embraced classical music as a way to recapture the feeling of specific films, as I explore in relation to games based on the Disney classic *Fantasia* (1940), and those that refer to the influential art film *Koyaanisqatsi* (1983). Chapter 5, "A Clockwork Homage," specifically investigates several video games from the 1980s to the 2010s that use music to refer—whether parodically or earnestly (or both)—to the films of the auteur director Stanley Kubrick, particularly *2001: A Space Odyssey* (1968) and *A Clockwork Orange* (1971).

Chapters 6 and 7 deal with remixed classical music in games—situations in which the nature of the music as "classical" at all is called directly into question. Chapter 6, "Remixed Metaphors," engages with a range of these games from the 1980s to the present, including the arcade classic *Gyruss* (1983), the indie game *FEZ* (2012), and the unusual Japanese shooter *Parodius* (1988). In some cases, remixes seem to be a way of connecting games to the artistic value inherent in "classical" works, while in others the music creates a carnivalesque atmosphere in which traditional values of "high" and "low" art are, if not entirely subverted, at least challenged in meaningful ways. The following chapter, "Love in Thousand Monstrous Forms," draws on the "grotesque" in art as the irreconcilable combination of opposites, illustrating how combining "classical" and "popular" musical styles—as well as the careful selection of classical works—functions as a critical part of the game design and a form of commentary in the philosophical puzzle game *Catherine* (2011).

Chapter 8, "Violent Offenders and Violin Defenders," transitions to an entirely different method of representing classical music in games: on screen, embodied in "live" musicians. Ranging from the saintly violinist Agatha in the post-apocalyptic wasteland of *Fallout 3* (2008) to the murderously unstable composer Sander Cohen in *BioShock* (2007), these depictions of musicians offer a revealing perspective on the roles of classical music and its practitioners in contemporary society. Chapter 9, "Playing Chopin," focuses on two specific games—the role-playing game *Eternal Sonata* (2007) and the mobile music game *Frederic: Resurrection of Music* (2011)—both of which feature the nineteenth-century composer Frédéric Chopin as the protagonist. Both games carefully (if not always successfully) balance the need to adapt Chopin's historical persona to fit the practical and aesthetic needs of a video game, while still presenting the composer and his music in a positive and "authentic" light.

Up to this point in the book, the chapters have investigated instances in which classical music is incorporated in video games. The final two chapters, however, turn this formula on its head, focusing instead on how video games have been incorporated into classical music. Chapter 10, "Gamifying Classical Music," examines how classical music organizations have paired with game developers to create new educational and entertaining ways of presenting classical music to a broad audience. In particular, I consider the mobile apps *Young Person's Guide to the Orchestra* (2013)—an interactive introduction to Benjamin Britten's classical work of the same title (1945)—and *Steve Reich's Clapping Music* (2015), a gamified presentation of the titular 1972 work. In one case, the app recreates traditional notions of music appreciation for a digital-native audience; in the other, the lines between playing a game and playing a musical work are blurred to the point of invisibility. The final chapter, "Classifying Game Music," raises the question of whether game music can itself become classical. I first explore fan-centered campaigns to broaden the definition of "classical music" to encompass orchestral game music—including the push to include game music in the British radio station Classic FM's annual Hall of Fame—before considering the increasingly pervasive phenomenon of video game music performances in concert hall settings.

I make no claims that *Unlimited Replays* is a comprehensive examination of the relationship between classical music and video games. There are many intriguing examples that simply didn't fit into my overarching narrative, and I'm quite confident that there are many, many examples of classical music in games of which I remain completely unaware—not to mention the steady stream of new games, apps, and game-related concerts being developed constantly. Rather than creating an exhaustive catalog, I hope to sketch out some ways in which we might fruitfully approach this topic. My ultimate goal is to open these questions up for a larger debate, and one that extends far beyond classical music in games, contributing to an assessment of what roles of art and entertainment play in twenty-first-century culture.

1 Terms and Conditions

EARLY IN THE first episode of Netflix's political drama *House of Cards* (2013–), US representative Frank Underwood attends a lavish symphony gala. As the concert begins—with Antonio Vivaldi's Violin Concerto "Summer," from *The Four Seasons* (ca. 1723)—the camera fixates on Frank's reaction to the music. He appears mesmerized, focusing intently on the off-screen musicians—until the camera pans out, and we realize we've been duped by some clever cinematography. Although he's still wearing his tuxedo from the evening's entertainment, Frank has abandoned the luxurious surroundings and elite company of the symphony. Instead, he's sitting on a couch in his home, riveted not by Vivaldi's music but by the first-person shooter *Call of Duty*. The cut is jarring. As the action shifts from the bright, see-and-be-seen environment of the concert hall to a dark, solitary basement, the subtext is clear: classical music is socially and culturally celebrated, while video games are shameful, a guilty pleasure to be hidden away from prying eyes. Instantly, our perception of Underwood shifts drastically. How could a US congressman, a patron of the fine arts, close out his evening by trash-talking teenagers on an Xbox headset?

This scene's effectiveness depends on audiences perceiving that worlds of classical music and of video games are, if not exactly incompatible, at least starkly contrasted. The show goes to a lot of trouble, in other words, to help its viewers understand Frank as a complex and contradictory character. But *why* do we understand these pursuits—classical music and video games—as contradictory in the first place? This chapter is aimed at exploring that question, which informs the entirety of *Unlimited Replays*. How we perceive the relationship between classical music and video games is shaped by the expectations we have of each of those elements; unpacking that cultural baggage is a necessary first step to understanding what happens when they're combined. But it's not an easy first step. The utility of terms like "video games" and "classical music" depends on a shared cultural definition, yet in practice how we interpret these concepts is often deeply individualistic. Classical music in particular will reveal itself throughout this book to be a profoundly problematic, or even misleading, concept. The uncertainty hovering around these ideas in fact calls attention to my central point: although both classical music and video games are produced by artists, typically for entertainment purposes, for the most part the two media occupy radically divergent and hotly contested cultural spaces. To set the stage for the discussions to come, this chapter is devoted to exploring what it *means* to call a piece of music classical, or an interactive media object a video game. Before I can address the ramifications of combining classical music with games, I have to consider the value judgments and cultural baggage those terms carry.

Classical Music

The term "classical music" is virtually inescapable. It shapes how we study, consume, and value music—from iTunes and Spotify to university degree programs in, say, classical versus jazz piano. But what is it, really? For many music historians and classically trained performers, "classical music" refers to the music of late eighteenth- to early nineteenth-century Vienna, a repertoire centered around the composers Franz Joseph Haydn, Wolfgang Amadeus Mozart, and Ludwig van Beethoven. But of course this very narrow definition is by no means the standard use of the term in mainstream culture. If we trust iTunes, for example, just about all music composed from the Middle Ages to about 1900 in Western nations is classical—except, of course, for the music that gets placed in the equally broad categories of folk music or world music. Classical also includes a fair amount of music composed after 1900, except what we'd consider popular music or jazz. In that view, classical music is essentially defined negatively: it's classical because it's not something else. But that approach ignores the most important, if often unspoken, criterion that many people believe makes music classical: art.

In fact, this identity as art—whatever that means—is so fundamental to classical music as a concept that we can substitute the term "art music" in nearly any situation. This understanding of classical or art music emerged near the beginning of the nineteenth century, mostly as a way to grant certain musical repertoires, especially European instrumental music from the mid-eighteenth century onward—Bach, Mozart, Beethoven, etc.—a preferred cultural status. Gradually the works protected under this "classical" aegis expanded significantly, on the one hand reaching back further and further into history to incorporate repertoires like Gregorian chant and Renaissance choral music, and on the other hand looking forward into the twentieth century to accommodate new musical developments. Yet even as the definition expanded to accommodate an ever-larger body of works, the core concept remained the same: it was "good music" (itself a label that persisted well into the twentieth century), a civilizing influence that uplifted the spirit and ennobled the listener.[1] As musicologists Denise Von Glahn and Michael Broyles explain in their entry "Art Music" in the *Grove Dictionary of American Music*, throughout the nineteenth and early twentieth centuries, art music was understood to be "composed by specially trained musicians," "universal because of its transcendence," and "unparalleled in its complexity, expressivity, originality, and thus meaning."[2]

In academic circles, these attitudes have largely—though by no means universally—given way to a more inclusive understanding of music. Resisting the idea that classical music is somehow superior to other musical traditions, this broader perspective holds that all musical traditions offer value, and that art (if that concept still means anything) is not restricted to certain musical styles. Furthermore, this position acknowledges that drawing stark distinctions between "classical" and "not classical" music runs the risk of reinforcing classist, racist, sexist, and otherwise undesirable narratives. Even among music scholars, however, more traditional views on the subject have not entirely dissipated. In his book *Who Needs Classical Music? Cultural Choice and Musical Value* (2002), the musicologist and composer Julian Johnson succinctly, if polemically, describes "classical music" as "music that functions *as art*, as opposed to entertainment or some other ancillary or background function."[3]

In fairness, Johnson does allow that classical music can, in fact, be entertaining—but entertainment cannot be its sole (or primary) function. "Art," he says,

> is frequently contrasted with entertainment, an opposition that immediately invokes a series of binary divisions (e.g., high and low, serious and light,

---

[1] On "good music" in early twentieth-century America, see Mark Katz, *Capturing Sound: How Technology Has Changed Music*, rev. ed. (Berkeley: University of California Press, 2010), chap. 2.

[2] Denise Von Glahn and Michael Broyles, "Art Music," in *The Grove Dictionary of American Music*, 2nd ed., available online at oxfordmusiconline.com.

[3] Julian Johnson, *Who Needs Classical Music? Cultural Choice and Musical Value* (Oxford: Oxford University Press, 2002), 6. The musicologist Richard Taruskin took particular umbrage at Johnson's pat definition. Not one to mince words, Taruskin summarizes Johnson's entire book as "an elaboration of this categorical, invidious, didactically italicized, and altogether untenable distinction." Richard Taruskin, "The Musical Mystique," *New Republic* (October 21, 2007), available online at https://newrepublic.com/article/64350/books-the-musical-mystique.

intellectual and sensual) that seem like so many aesthetic versions of opposing class positions. . . . Art and entertainment are perhaps better understood as social functions than as categories that divide cultural products as if they were sheep and goats. Classical music, I have argued, is made as art but frequently serves as entertainment. Even when it serves as art, it doesn't necessarily stop serving as entertainment. But it also exhibits qualities that are neither acknowledged nor accounted for by the category of entertainment, qualities that can be understood only from the expectations of a different function—that of art.[4]

This serpentine argument is difficult to straighten out, but the gist seems to be that classical music is by definition always art, but sometimes also entertainment. The distinction is that it can never *just* be entertainment; there must always be some profundity of artistic expression that surpasses, say, popular music. Ironically, this problematic view seems prevalent—and often unquestioned—in the very popular culture that it seems to denigrate. According to film scholar Dean Duncan, for example, the "popularly accepted sense" of classical music is "art music which has, either in its time of composition or by some evolutionary process, come to be accepted as 'serious.'"[5] This definition is a masterpiece of circular reasoning. The music is art because it is classical, classical because it is art, and serious because it is—both, maybe? Moreover, the music has "come to be accepted" as serious—but accepted by whom? Despite the illogical nature of this definition, however, Duncan isn't wrong. That *is*, quite often, the popularly accepted sense of classical music, which is frequently portrayed in media and in the press as somehow more serious or important than other types of music.[6] That viewpoint is the focus of my interest here not because I agree—I emphatically do not—but because it continues to be so widespread and enduring.

As I write this, for example, the first sentence of Wikipedia's entry on "classical music" identifies it as "art music in the traditions of Western music."[7] Following the hyperlink to "art music" yields a well-balanced (if fairly brief) article on the topic, but one predicated on the circular definition of art music as "music descending from the tradition of Western classical music." Significantly, the article opens

---

[4] Johnson, *Who Needs Classical Music?*, 47.

[5] Dean Duncan, *Charms That Soothe: Classical Music and the Narrative Film* (New York: Fordham University Press, 2003), 8.

[6] On the privileging of art in American culture (as one example), the classic resource is Lawrence W. Levine, *Highbrow, Lowbrow: The Emergence of Cultural Hierarchy in America* (Cambridge, MA: Harvard University Press, 1988).

[7] "Classical Music," *Wikipedia*, available online at http://en.wikipedia.org/wiki/Classical_music (accessed July 17, 2014).

with the informative note the "art music" is "also known as **formal music, serious music, erudite music**, or **legitimate music**," terms that reinscribe an elitist system of value judgments.[8] Who would admit to preferring "illegitimate" or "frivolous" music? Other sources of popular knowledge embrace similarly troubling definitions. Dictionary.com, for example, tells us that "classical music" is "a loose expression for European and American music of the more serious kind, as opposed to popular or folk music."[9] Again, this explanation offers no clear sense of what "serious" means— even should we choose to believe, all evidence to the contrary, that classical music is always serious.

Ultimately, finding a working universal definition of "classical music" that doesn't depend on its artistic superiority to other musical forms is simply impossible. So what do we do? Can "classical music" exist *without* a definition? An explanatory 2013 article from the Minnesota Public Radio website seems to suggest that it can:

> Musicologists can stay up all night talking about the shape and trajectory of classical music, debating questions like the importance of the score, the role of improvisation, and the nature of musical form. Where you come down on these questions determines who precisely you think falls into the broadly defined genre of "classical music." Renaissance troubadours? Frank Zappa? Duke Ellington? Yes, no, maybe?
>
> Everyday enjoyment of classical music doesn't require you to strain your brain with such fine distinctions, but it definitely helps to understand that classical music is a living tradition that's being defined and redefined every day.[10]

Although the article seems to exhort us to simply sit back, relax, and stop worrying so much, this conception is actually fairly complex. We can, it seems to suggest, acknowledge that classical music as an idea is rife with contradictions—if not entirely intellectually bankrupt—yet still understand what the term means in daily usage.

As heretical as it may seem, I am inclined to agree. Musicologists, performers, and critics alike have spilled considerable ink in a quest to define exactly what, if anything, classical music is—all to little avail. I am not interested in following them into

---

[8] "Art Music," *Wikipedia*, available online at http://en.wikipedia.org/wiki/Art_music (accessed July 17, 2014) (bold text in original).

[9] "Classical music," available online at dictionary.com (accessed August 7, 2014). This definition is drawn from *The New Dictionary of Cultural Literacy*, 3rd ed. (Boston: Houghton Mifflin, 2005)

[10] Jay Gabler, "What Is Classical Music?," *Minnesota Public Radio* (October 16, 2013), available online at http://minnesota.publicradio.org/display/web/2013/10/15/what-is-classical-music accessed August 7, 2014).

this linguistic and conceptual quagmire, and neither am I willing to strictly define the boundaries of classical music for this book. I am, however, deeply interested in how the concept of classical music tends to be viewed within the context of popular culture. The terminological and conceptual fluidity that sometimes results throughout *Unlimited Replays* illustrates the contradictions inherent in classical music as a concept—complexities that factor into how this music works in relation to video games. Classical music, then—like art itself—is what culture *perceives* as art, and what it therefore imbues with particular cultural capital.

Despite—or, more likely, because of—its aura of cultural prestige, classical music is often also viewed as antithetical to youth culture. To put it bluntly, classical music is decidedly uncool. Consider, for example, the numerous instances in which businesses and cities have (usually successfully) attempted to prevent unwanted loitering by playing classical music in spaces where teenagers tend to gather. In her intriguing book *Music in American Crime Prevention and Punishment*, the musicologist Lily E. Hirsch notes that since the 1980s (the very period of video games' ascendency)

classical music has been used as a crime deterrent all over the English-speaking world: in Canadian parks, Australian railway stations, London Underground stops, and different cities all over the United States. . . . In these locales, various authorities employ classical music to reduce hooliganism and ward off undesirables.[11]

Some advocates for this use of classical music would argue for its quasi-Orphic powers to ennoble the souls of these troubled youths—no doubt attributing their departure to a collective decision to find gainful employment and/or volunteer at soup kitchens. But the practical underlying assumption at work here is that many members of youth culture detest classical music to the point where they would rather pack up and leave an area than willingly subject themselves to hearing it. The author of a 2005 article in the *Los Angeles Times* notes a "bizarre irony" in the process: "After decades of the classical music establishment's fighting to attract crowds—especially young people and what it calls 'nontraditional audiences'—city councils and government ministers are taking exactly the opposite approach: using high culture as a kind of disinfectant."[12] Thus, we find a wide perception of classical music as being

---

[11] Lily E. Hirsch, *Music in American Crime Prevention and Punishment* (Ann Arbor: University of Michigan Press, 2012), 14. The entirety of Hirsch's chapter 1 is dedicated to classical music's role in deterring crime.

[12] Scott Timberg, "Halt, or I'll Play Vivaldi!," *Los Angeles Times* (February 13, 2005), available online at http://articles.latimes.com/2005/feb/13/entertainment/ca-musichurts13 (accessed August 7, 2014).

fundamentally opposed to the same youth culture that dominates discussions of video games.

Video Games

For the most part, the term "video games" (or "videogames," as some prefer) is interchangeable with "computer games" or "electronic games," indicating a distinction from other types of games, such as sports or tabletop board games.[13] We might reasonably quibble about distinctions between these kinds of labels, and in some circles the connotative differences are significant: the philosopher Grant Tavinor, for example, notes that "*computer game* is sometimes taken to refer to games on a personal computer, but it is also used as the generic term; *electronic game* might also refer to toys as well as video games; while *videogame*, as well as being the generic term, is sometimes used to refer exclusively to console games."[14] Though I acknowledge these distinctions, throughout this book I use "video games" in the broadest and most inclusive sense possible. Although for some readers the term might conjure images of neon-laden 1980s arcades, or teenagers gripping their PlayStation controllers, video games and their players are a rather diverse lot. Aside from the many millions of players across all demographic lines who regularly enjoy video games on their computers or consoles, the ubiquity of smartphones and social media allows casual games to reach astoundingly massive audiences.[15] As we saw with classical music, however, settling on a term doesn't necessarily give us a good sense of what video games actually *are*.

A number of academic game scholars, not surprisingly, have given the topic serious attention. Jesper Juul, for example, spends most of his influential book *Half-Real: Video Games between Real Rules and Fictional Worlds* in search of a clear definition, as a necessary step toward building a unifying theory. Video games, Juul contends, have broken out of the classical game model that describes thousands of years of games, from ancient Egyptian senet to poker. Games are "a combination of rules and fiction," and so any definition or theory must describe "the intersection between games as rules and games as fiction, and the relation between the game, the play, and the world."[16] Yet Juul's definition, while useful, doesn't take into account

---

[13] See, for example, the discussion of the terms in Veli-Matti Karhulahti, "Defining the Videogame," *Game Studies* 15, no. 2 (December 2015), available online at http://gamestudies.org/1502/articles/karhulahti.

[14] Grant Tavinor, *The Art of Videogames* (Malden, MA: Wiley-Blackwell, 2009), 17 (emphasis in original).

[15] On the rise of casual games, see Jesper Juul, *A Casual Revolution: Reinventing Video Games and Their Players* (Cambridge, MA: MIT Press, 2010).

[16] Jesper Juul, *Half-Real: Video Games between Real Rules and Fictional Worlds* (Cambridge, MA: MIT Press, 2005), 197.

the function of video games—it might tell us what they *are*, but it doesn't tell us what they're *for*.

Other theorists, however, have embraced function as a central aspect of games, and such a definition is essential to understanding how games interact with classical music (which, as we have seen, can be defined by its function as "art"). For the purpose of contrasting games and classical music, I borrow Tavinor's frequently quoted definition:

> X is a videogame if it is an artifact in a visual digital medium, is intended as an object of entertainment, and is intended to provide such entertainment through the employment of one or both of the following modes of engagement: rule and objective gameplay or interactive fiction.[17]

Particularly noteworthy here is the idea that a game *must* be "intended as an object of entertainment." While I would join a number of scholars and philosophers in arguing that the intention of the game's creators is less significant than how the audience understands and receives the game, the point is nonetheless intriguing.[18]

The idea that entertainment is video games' core function seems, in fact, to be an unquestioned truth. Take, for example, Gonzalo Frasca's assertion that video games encompass "any forms of computer-based *entertainment software*, either textual or image-based, using any electronic platform such as personal computers or consoles and involving one or multiple players in a physical or networked environment."[19] James Newman adopts this definition in his influential book *Videogames* (2004), noting that he "follow[s] Frasca in using the term videogame *in its broadest possible sense.*"[20] In other words, even the widest conceivable definition of games depends on that entertainment factor; without that, it's just not a video game. Although Tavinor ultimately argues halfheartedly that some (but by no means all) video games qualify as art, he takes note of the intense cultural resistance that idea faces:

> Art involves something more than *mere entertainment or amusement*, and some might think that it is that extra something that videogames lack. It may

---

[17] Tavinor, *Art of Videogames*, 26. For an earlier version of this definition (along with explanation), see Grant Tavinor, "Definition of Videogames," *Contemporary Aesthetics* 6 (2008), available online at http://www.contempaesthetics.org/newvolume/pages/article.php?articleID=492&searchstr=tavinor.

[18] For a discussion of how games fit into this perspective, see John Sharp, *Works of Game: On the Aesthetics of Games and Art* (Cambridge, MA: MIT Press, 2015), chap. 5.

[19] Gonzalo Frasca, "Videogames of the Oppressed: Videogames as a Means for Critical Thinking and Debate" (master's thesis, Georgia Institute of Technology, 2001), 4 (emphasis added).

[20] James Newman, *Videogames* (London: Routledge, 2004), 27 (emphasis added).

also be argued that videogames are immature, derivative, mass produced, distasteful, and do not afford the sorts of perceptual and cognitive pleasure that proper artworks do.[21]

Thus while classical music may belong to the realm of high art, video games are often understood to occupy an altogether less exalted sphere. Created, in most instances, for entertainment value and commercial success, video games form part of the vague but artistically suspect realm of popular culture.

As Tavinor predicted, the very idea that some games *might* be art, in fact, has proved controversial. A major flashpoint in this debate was the film critic Roger Ebert's insistence that games were not, and probably never would be, an art form. Ebert's article "Video Games Can Never Be Art" (2010) offers his most detailed explanation of this point of view, systematically debunking the claims to art of some of the most artistic video games, such as the independent games *Braid* (2008) and *Flower* (2009).[22] *Braid*, he says, "exhibits prose on the level of a wordy fortune cookie," while nothing in *Flower* "seemed above the level of a greeting card." As the critic Harold Goldberg points out in his book *All Your Base Are Belong to Us: How Fifty Years of Videogames Conquered Pop Culture*, games were perceived in the late twentieth and early twenty-first centuries "the way rock 'n' roll was in the fifties: they were dirty, sex-stinking, over-the-top with no redeeming social value, despicably lowbrow."[23]

On the other hand, a number of other critics have recently made compelling arguments for understanding (some) games as art. Goldberg makes such a claim for *BioShock* (2007), and Ebert's 2010 missive was prompted by a TED Talk by the game designer Kellee Santiago, who strongly advocated that games have crossed the boundary into artistic status.[24] Art museums, including the Smithsonian Institution, the San Francisco Museum of Modern Art, and New York's Museum of Modern Art, have staged exhibitions of games, suggesting that games have

---

[21] Tavinor, *Art of Videogames*, 175.

[22] Roger Ebert, "Video Games Can Never Be Art" (April 16, 2010), available online at http://www.rogerebert.com/rogers-journal/video-games-can-never-be-art.

[23] Harold Goldberg, *All Your Base Are Belong to Us: How Fifty Years of Videogames Conquered Pop Culture* (New York: Three Rivers Press, 2011), 185.

[24] See Goldberg, *All Your Base Are Belong to Us*, chap. 12, "*BioShock*: Art for Game's Sake." The game, according to Goldberg, "made people who eschewed videogames see the art in an entertainment that dealt with profound ideas and twisted emotions . . . . *BioShock* expressed its ideas clearly and deftly, like the best movies, music, and books. It was art for game's sake . . . proof of the concept that art and commerce could successfully and happily coexist in the world of videogames" (207). Kellee Santiago, "Stop the Debate! Video Games Are Art, So What's Next?," TED Talk (March 23, 2009), available online at https://www.youtube.com/watch?feature=player_embedded&v=K9y6MYDSAww.

attained at least a certain level of artistic distinction. Game scholars, not surprisingly, have also jumped into the fray, falling generally on the side of games as art.[25] In the book *Works of Game*, for example, John Sharp has explored in some detail the development of artgames—video games intended (that dangerous term again!) to have artistic aspirations beyond entertainment—as well as game art, in which artists manipulate or alter games to create new works.[26] Despite these efforts, however, it seems clear that video games do not yet claim the same amount of artistic cultural capital that classical music does. They remain, in Juul's words, "notoriously considered lowbrow catalogues of geek and adolescent male culture."[27]

As was the case with the specific boundaries of classical music, when it is taken by itself, I don't find the question of whether games are art particularly meaningful.[28] What does interest me, however, is how games navigate these uncharted artistic waters by steering toward less contested art forms. Classical music frequently offers a convenient point of reference for scholars and critics seeking to legitimize games at artworks, for example. Tavinor suggests as much when he ponders "whether videogames are art in something like the way that the exemplars of a more traditional conception of art—Shakespeare's *Hamlet*, Mahler's Ninth Symphony, Van Eyck's *The Arnolfini Marriage*, Joyce's *Ulysses*—are art."[29] He wonders, in other words, whether games can compare to what he labels "uncontested artworks."[30] Other critics have drawn similar connections between classical music and games: in an article on games as art, for example, James Paul Gee associates the video game *Castlevania: Symphony of the Night* (1997) with an actual classical symphony:

> Moving through this game is like moving through a symphony where every "tone" (image) and combination of "tones" (images) creates moods, feelings, and ambiance, not primarily information (as in movies and books). The experience of playing the game is closer to living inside a symphony than to living inside a book. And the symphony is not just visual, but it is composed as well

---

[25] For example, see Aaron Smuts, "Are Video Games Art?," *Contemporary Aesthetics* 3 (2005), available online at http://hdl.handle.net/2027/spo.7523862.0003.006; and James Paul Gee, "Why Game Studies Now? Video Games: A New Art Form," *Games and Culture* 1 (2006): 58–61.

[26] Sharp, *Works of Game*, especially chap. 3.

[27] Juul, *Half-Real*, 20. Juul goes on to note that "while games are regularly considered lowbrow, this is often due to some very naïve notions of what is highbrow or what is *art*. In a very simple view of art, art is what is ambiguous, whereas most games tend to have clear rules and goals."

[28] For another perspective on the irrelevance of the question, see Ian Bogost, *How to Do Things with Videogames* (Minneapolis: University of Minnesota Press, 2011), chap. 1.

[29] Tavinor, *Videogames as Art*, 174.

[30] Tavinor, *Videogames as Art*, 175.

of sounds, music, actions, decisions, and bodily feelings that flow along as the player and virtual character . . . act together in the game world.[31]

The musical language Gee intriguingly employs as a metaphor for the gameplay experience—tones creating ambience, and so on—shouldn't be inherently limited to classical music. He could, in other words, just as easily have suggested that the game was akin to "living inside" the Beatles' song "Hey Jude" or the Broadway musical *West Side Story*. True, the choice of a symphonic metaphor here ties in neatly with the game's title. But his specific choice of a symphony goes beyond mere rhetorical expediency. The symphony remains (in the popular mindset, at least) a pinnacle of musical artistry—classical music at its purest and most artistic. Connecting a video game to this tradition reinforces its claim to artistic merit by association. Like Tavinor's Mahler symphony, here we see the "uncontested" value of classical music linked to the comparably contested, artistically ambiguous space games occupy.

The Art of Classical Music in Video Games

At this point, you can no doubt spot the problem. If we accept the proposition that games must inherently be first and foremost entertainment products, *and* we accept Johnson's assessment that classical music must function "*as art*, as opposed to entertainment or some other ancillary or background function," the paradox becomes clear. Mixing classical music and video games thus always transgresses boundaries—in one way or another, it issues an existential challenge. Let me return briefly to Johnson's conception of classical music—"music that functions *as art*, as opposed to entertainment or some other ancillary or background function." What this definition seems to suggest is that the music must be the fundamental focus: it must be listened to and embraced as art to fully function. The musicologist Lawrence Kramer has espoused a similar focus on intent listening as the primary focus of classical music, which, he writes, "developed with a single aim: to be listened to. Listened to, that is, rather than heard as part of some other activity, usually a social or religious ritual."[32] Playing video games would certainly count as another activity, and one in which listening is most often relegated to a secondary role. From the perspective of games, on the other hand, recall Tavinor's requirement that games be "intended primarily as an object of entertainment." Though he in no way precludes the possibility that games could be art, they nonetheless *must* primarily be vehicles for

---

[31] Gee, "Why Game Studies Now?," 59.
[32] Lawrence Kramer, *Why Classical Music Still Matters* (Berkeley: University of California Press, 2007), 18.

entertainment. Most commonly they are commercial products aimed at the broadest possible audience—anathema, many would argue, to artistic expression.

These definitions are unmistakably mutually exclusive. Classical music shouldn't exist in video games, for instance—and yet it does. This seeming impossibility raises a number of complex philosophical questions. What happens to classical music when it becomes part of a commercial product, and as background music, no less? Does it—in function if not in content—cease to be classical at all when appearing in an entertainment-based medium? And can music be classical at all if it's working in the background rather than at the forefront of conscious attention? Some would say no—the musicologist James Parakilas suggested as much in an 1984 article in which he declared that "classical music is no longer itself when it is used as background music."[33] If we're not regarding it as art, in other words, it ceases to function artistically. But if we *do* feel that classical music in games is still art, then what about the games themselves? Do they cease to be primarily entertainment vehicles when classical music enters the mix? Are they, in other words, elevated to artistic status by the presence of art within them, and if so, are they at that point even video games? In short: What happens when the irresistible force of entertainment meets the immovable object of art? The chapters that follow are dedicated to addressing, if not necessarily answering, these and other questions that arise from the seemingly unlikely combination of these two media.

---

[33] James Parakilas, "Classical Music as Popular Music," *Journal of Musicology* 3 (1984): 15.

2   Playing with Music History

TUTORIALS USUALLY AREN'T the most exciting parts of video games. These introductory segments are responsible for giving players the necessary tools to play the game, but from a design perspective, they can be tricky to balance. Too much, or too little, direct guidance can result in players getting confused, frustrated, or bored—not an ideal first impression of a game. To overcome these hurdles, game developers use a variety of techniques to impart large amounts of information quickly, and occasionally even enjoyably. Many of these techniques rely on a shared set of experiences—players get some basic instructions from the game and fill in the rest using their existing frame of reference. If you've played one first-person shooter, for instance, you probably have at least some idea of how the next one is going to work. Music often works in a similar way in games and other media: certain styles, genres, or even particular works convey meanings to players based on their previous experiences. Players experiencing a horror game might feel a wave of anxiety when they hear dissonant string music because their prior musical knowledge tells them something scary is about to happen. These powerful intertextual references work as another type of tutorial in games, providing valuable information without resorting to spelling it out directly.

To see how these types of musical choices convey information to players, let's consider the actual tutorial mission from *Assassin's Creed III* (2012). In a major departure from the European Renaissance setting of several previous games in the series, the majority of *Assassin's Creed III* takes place in North America, around the time of the American Revolution. In advertisements and previews, the game promised players a

FIGURE 2.1 The Theatre Royal, as featured in *Assassin's Creed III* (2012).

glimpse of colonial life, complete with burgeoning cities, Native American villages, and lush, pristine wilderness. Yet the tutorial for *Assassin's Creed III* finds players skulking around the backstage of the Theatre Royal in 1750s London in search of an assassination target (Figure 2.1). As they go about their task—all the while learning the basics of gameplay—players hear snippets of music and dialogue, and occasionally even catch a glimpse of the stage. The evening's performance happens to be of *The Beggar's Opera* (1728), an English ballad opera by John Gay that featured music borrowed from popular tunes and opera arias of the time. Thanks to its scandalous plot and well-known melodies, *The Beggar's Opera* was one of the most enduringly popular works of eighteenth-century English theater—but its presence in a video game is surprising, to say the least.

A bit of historical digging, however, offers up several possible explanations for this perplexing choice of music. Because Italian opera dominated the stages of eighteenth-century London, *The Beggar's Opera* was a fairly radical departure. One critic of the time, for example, described it as "Gay's new English Opera, written in a Manner wholly new, and very entertaining, there being introduced, instead of Italian Airs, above 60 of the most celebrated old English and Scotch tunes."[1] Audiences members accustomed to Italian operas, in other words, were instead introduced to a new, English variety. Given that background, players with sufficient historical background might choose to understand *The Beggar's Opera* as a sly nod to the *Assassin's*

---

[1] *Daily Journal* (February 1, 1728), quoted in Calhoun Winton, *John Gay and the London Theatre* (Lexington: University Press of Kentucky, 1993), 99.

Creed games themselves. The previous three *Assassin's Creed* games featured Italian protagonist Ezio Auditore.[2] Perhaps the subtext here is that players used to an Italian *Assassin's Creed*—and skeptical of this new setting—might similarly embrace an English (or colonial) setting. It's also worth considering how the broad social commentary of Gay's work resonates with the main themes of *Assassin's Creed*: both narratives are steeped in class struggles and the justification (or lack thereof) for violence. In fact, as a result of its rough, low-class characters, some eighteenth-century listeners declared *The Beggar's Opera* a bad influence on England's youth—an entertainment liable to corrupt their character and lead them to violence.[3] The parallels to the enduring criticisms of violent video games like the *Assassin's Creed* series are obvious, and perhaps *The Beggar's Opera* works as a kind of subtle cultural counterattack. All of these are valid—if maybe a little far-fetched—interpretations, yet this subtext would likely be completely lost on all but the most historically informed players.

In that case, it might seem arbitrary to choose *The Beggar's Opera* instead of any other eighteenth-century opera popular in London at the time.[4] I would argue, however, that *The Beggar's Opera* is particularly effective in this scene because it helps players quickly situate the game—and themselves—in a specific place and time. The *Assassin's Creed* series, which touches on both near-future science fiction and historical adventure, is an unusual generic hybrid. Its central conceit—an advanced technology that allows users to relive their ancestors' lives—allows designers to set the various games in widely divergent settings while still creating a (semi-)coherent overarching narrative.[5] This variety offers players an essentially unlimited set of exciting new places and times to explore, but it also runs the risk of disorienting them while they adjust to their new environments. This disorientation feels particularly evident in the tutorial for *Assassin's Creed III*. Players familiar with the game's premise, whether from advertising or simply from reading the back of the game box, would likely expect an American Revolutionary setting. Finding themselves in 1750s

---

[2] The so-called *Ezio Triology* of *Assassin's Creed II* (2009), *Assassin's Creed: Brotherhood* (2010), and *Assassin's Creed: Revelations* (2011) takes place primarily in Italy, although *Revelations* abandons that setting for Constantinople.

[3] Winton notes, for example, that well into the nineteenth century critics continued to weigh in on the *The Beggar's Opera*'s "tendency to deprave." Winton, *John Gay and the London Theatre*, 107.

[4] Interestingly—though almost certainly coincidentally—*Polly* (1729), Gay's less popular sequel to *The Beggar's Opera*, sees the characters escape from London to become pirates in the West Indies, which is essentially the plot of *Assassin's Creed IV: Black Flag*.

[5] On this historicity of the *Assassin's Creed* games, see Douglas N. Dow, "Historical Veneers: Anachronism, Simulation and History in *Assassin's Creed II*," in *Playing with the Past: Digital Games and the Simulation of History*, ed. Matthew Wilhelm Kapell and Andrew B. R. Elliott (New York: Bloomsbury, 2013), 215–232.

England instead might cause some initial confusion while players are already struggling to familiarize themselves with the game.

So, how does *The Beggar's Opera* help us understand this scene better? Most obviously, it reinforces the game's shift from the future (where it begins) into the past. Before the opera begins, the player—acting as Haytham Kenway, a major character—hears the overture to *The Beggar's Opera* while directing Haytham to his seat. The music has all the trappings of English baroque theater music: a small orchestra with harpsichord, baroque dance rhythms, and so on. Historically savvy players might be able to use this aural evidence to date the action, but—much more important—even players unfamiliar with music history would almost certainly be able to identify the music as classical. And even if the "when" is not entirely obvious based on the music, the "where" is fairly straightforward. The spoken and sung text is in English, an impression supported by the actors' British accents. By immersing players in this "civilized" European environment and then quickly transitioning to a colonial Boston setting, the game highlights the comparatively uncivilized (or unpretentious) New World.

This short scene from *Assassin's Creed III* illustrates how music in media provides listeners with a wealth of information—often much more than is immediately apparent. Like a good tutorial mission, the music teaches us without being overtly didactic; it shows rather than tells. Because it already has a "life" outside the film, show, or game, preexisting music is particularly effective at conveying a great deal of information efficiently. Listeners have a set of ready-made perceptions and associations already tied to the music—either particular pieces or more general styles—that help them instantly make connections that might take much longer with newly composed music.

Games aren't alone in using these codes, of course. Film, followed later by television and other media, has made use of our prior musical knowledge for more than a century. For that reason, I frequently draw on examples from those media to illustrate how games use players' perceptions of classical music to provide them with essential information.[6] As Peter Larsen notes in his overview *Film Music*, "All music conveys culturally established connotations. By virtue of style, musical idiom, instrumentation, etc. music refers to music of the same type and thereby to particular historical periods, particular countries, particular cultural environments."[7] The same, I believe, is true of music in games, but despite these similarities, games' uniqueness as a medium creates some important differences in how music works,

---

[6] For an overview of the relationship between game music and its cinematic models, see Tim Summers, *Understanding Game Music* (Cambridge: Cambridge University Press, 2016), chap. 6.

[7] Peter Larsen, *Film Music* (London: Reaktion, 2005), 68.

even at a basic level. For the remainder of this chapter, I will focus on one seemingly straightforward use of classical music in games: establishing geographical and chronological setting. Music's potential for indicating these basic elements is, at least at first glance, almost too obvious to be noteworthy. In practice, however, things get substantially more complicated, and what interests me in particular is how games play with our understanding of music history. Much like the *Assassin's Creed* games treat history—sticking *just* close enough to historical fact to fit in with our prior knowledge, yet changing details to create more engaging stories—games often rely simultaneously on our knowledge and our ignorance of music history.

Exploring the World Map

Using classical music to suggest particular countries, regions, or cultures is a time-honored practice in media. In the case of early film, for instance, often the entire soundtrack was compiled from well-known classical works, alongside folk tunes and popular songs.[8] In that setting, musicians might use their own musical knowledge to choose pieces that conveyed the appropriate information to audience members, or they might rely on books of musical examples to help them find appropriate music. The Hungarian-American film musician Ernö Rapée included a number of classical examples in his widely circulated *Encyclopedia of Music for Motion Pictures* (1925), as did other cinema musicians of the era. Lacey Baker's *Picture Music: A Collection of Classic and Modern Compositions for the Organ Adapted for Moving Pictures* (1919), for example, noted that the "Arabian Dance" from Tchaikovsky's *Nutcracker* was "admirable for an Oriental picture," and so on. In that way, the easily identifiable—and often entirely made-up—ethnic flavor of these classical works served as useful shorthand for particular cultures or locations.[9] Particularly in the first decade or so of their history, video games drew heavily on the visual and musical language of early film, including a reliance on this kind of musical cue.

The Nintendo Entertainment System boxing game *Punch-Out!!* (1987, originally titled *Mike Tyson's Punch-Out!!*) offers a clear example of how these kinds of codes can work. Each of the opponents the player faces during the game originates from a different country, which is represented in the game in several ways. The boxers embody often uncomfortable stereotypes of their homeland both visually—through

---

[8] See, for example, the discussion of compilation scores in Rick Altman, *Silent Film Sound* (New York: Columbia University Press, 2004).

[9] Games have occasionally made use of folk musics for the same purposes, as in the 1996 version of the popular edutainment game *Where in the World Is Carmen Sandiego?*, which licensed a large number of global folk musics from the Smithsonian Institution's Folkways music collection.

the boxer's name and appearance—and aurally, by way of a short introductory musical cue played before each match. These themes can relate to the character's nationality in a few different ways, but one straightforward technique is to use a familiar musical work from that country.[10] The German boxer Von Kaiser, for instance, is introduced via a brief quotation from the "Ride of the Valkyries" portion of Richard Wagner's opera *Die Walküre* (1870). This cue works identically to early film compilation books—by relying on players' prior knowledge to fill in missing background information. For this choice to make sense, in other words, players have to already associate the tune with Germany. They might make that association by recognizing it from its original source or from its previous appearances in media to represent the idea of "Germany." For example, Wagner's music appeared frequently World War II era cartoons as a means of identifying Germans through musical stereotyping, just as Von Kaiser himself is a stereotype of early twentieth-century Germans.[11] Rather than anything immanent in the music itself, it is Wagner's reputation as the archetypical German composer, combined with the work's reception history, that allows the "Ride of the Valkyries" to work so effectively in *Punch-Out!!*.[12]

Using a composer's music to signify their country of origin is one of the most common ways of using classical music to indicate setting in games. We find a similar use of classical music in the NES version of the popular puzzle game *Tetris*.[13] In this particular version, players begin by choosing one of three options for background music. The first choice—though never identified in the game as anything other than "Type A"—is the "Dance of the Sugar Plum Fairy," from the Russian composer Pyotr Tchaikovsky's ballet *The Nutcracker* (1892). As with Wagner's music in *Punch-Out!!*, Tchaikovsky's music brings to mind what players already know about

---

[10] Dana Plank briefly examines *Punch-Out!* in her article "'From Russia with Fun!': *Tetris*, 'Korobeiniki,' and the Ludic Soviet," *Soundtrack* 8 (2015): 7–24.

[11] On the use of Wagner's music in cartoons to represent Germanic opera and culture, see Daniel Goldmark, *Tunes for Toons: Music and the Hollywood Cartoon* (Berkeley: University of California Press, 2005), chap. 5; and Neil Lerner, "Reading Wagner in *Bugs Bunny Nips the Nips* (1944)," in *Wagner and Cinema*, ed. Jeongwon Joe and Sander L. Gilman (Bloomington: Indiana University Press, 2010), 210–224. On Wagner's music in video games, see Tim Summers, "From *Parsifal* to the PlayStation: Wagner and Video Game Music," in *Music in Video Games: Studying Play*, ed. K. J. Donnelly, William Gibbons, and Neil Lerner (New York: Routledge, 2014), 199–216.

[12] Roger Hillman has suggested a similar role for late nineteenth-century Italian opera in historical films from that country, noting that "the gap between the composition of a piece of music that pre-exists the film and its use on that film's soundtrack at a distance corresponding to the work's reception history can in turn suggest—or even provide—historical interpretation." Roger Hillman, "Sounding the Depths of History: Opera and National Identity in Italian Film," in *A Companion to the Historical Film*, ed. Robert A. Rosenstone and Constantin Parvulescu (Chichester, UK: Wiley Blackwell, 2013), 328.

[13] In fact, two versions of *Tetris* were released on the NES, one produced by Nintendo (which is the one I discuss) and a rival version produced by Tengen.

FIGURE 2.2 The title screen from the Nintendo NES version of *Tetris* (1989).

the composer. Without that aspect, in fact, the "Dance of the Sugar Plum Fairies" is an odd choice for background music. For one thing, at least in the United States, *The Nutcracker* is typically associated with the holiday season. Moreover, there is nothing particularly "Russian" about its music, at least to my ear—there are certainly works by Tchaikovsky and others composed in a much more overtly national style. But what the "Dance of the Sugar Plum Fairies" lacks in "Russianness" it more than makes up for in familiarity; even players unfamiliar with sounds of the Russian classical repertoire would likely be able to name its source, and perhaps its composer.[14] Tchaikovsky's music gains particular salience here as a result of *Tetris*'s marketing in the United States as an explicitly Soviet product (Figure 2.2). The Nintendo box art, for example, proclaims "From Russia with Fun!," and if players earn a high enough score, they are treated to an image of the Kremlin—complete, ominously, with some kind of missile being launched. Nearly every aspect of the NES release, in short, was calculated to remind players of the game's Soviet origins, and Tchaikovsky's music went a long way toward creating a sense of national identity in a game entirely devoid of plot.[15]

Other games have made use of similar techniques. For example, several games in the *Civilization* series of strategy games use classical works to indicate the nationality

---

[14] We might find a cinematic parallel here in the extensive use of Sergei Prokofiev's music in Woody Allen's film *Love and Death* (1975), a parody of Russian literature.

[15] For a fuller look at classical music in the NES *Tetris*, see my article "Blip, Bloop, Bach? Some Uses of Classical Music on the Nintendo Entertainment System," *Music and the Moving Image* 2, no. 1 (2009): 40–52. Plank's "From Russia with Fun!" also explores in some detail the uses of the folk song "Korobeiniki," in various versions of *Tetris*, and her insightful work has informed my discussion of *Tetris* here.

of world leaders. In *Civilization V* (2010), for instance, the music for Catherine the Great's Russia is an arrangement of a movement from the Russian composer Sergei Prokofiev's ballet *Romeo and Juliet* (1935), and the "Ode to Joy" from Beethoven's Ninth Symphony (1824) represents Otto von Bismarck's Germany. Understanding these musical choices rests on the player's awareness of the composer's nationality— quite an assumption, given the relative obscurity of some of the selections. In some cases, games ask even more of players, depending on a familiarity with the musical work itself. *Punch-Out!!* offers another clear example: the Spaniard Don Flamenco enters the ring accompanied by the opening strains of Georges Bizet's opera *Carmen* (1875). Here the player infers "Spanishness" not by knowing the nationality of the composer—Bizet was French—but by knowing that *Carmen* takes place in Spain. This kind of reference asks a bit more of players: they must be familiar either with the story of an opera or with its use in other media to signify Spain.

On the whole, the use of classical music to signify nationality or geography seems to have declined in games since the 1990s. There are a number of possible reasons for that change, but I suspect that just as films moved beyond the musical codes of compilation scores, game composers may have become more adept at using original music to give players a sense of place. Their task was undoubtedly made easier by the technological innovations in game audio that emerged in the 1990s, such as CD audio. The use of prerecorded acoustic instruments, for instance, allowed composers to use indigenous instruments to suggest geographical locations. A bit of flamenco guitar might suggest "Spain" just as quickly as, and likely more effectively than, a reference to a nineteenth-century operatic plot, which is precisely what happens in the update/sequel/reboot of *Punch-Out!!* released for the Nintendo Wii in 2009. In this newer version, Don Flamenco's intro music is still from *Carmen*, but now it features guitar—an instrument nowhere to be found in Bizet's original music—to reinforce his nationality.

Time Management

Even if classical music has been outpaced as a technique for game designers to indicate geographical location, however, it remains an extremely useful and effective way of providing players with a sense of the historical era The *Assassin's Creed* example at the beginning of this chapter illustrated how a piece of music can evoke a particular historical moment, a technique that appears in most of the games in the series. Once again, there are ample parallels to how classical music works in film and television. The music of Henry Purcell (1659–1695) helps situate the film *Restoration* (1995) in seventeenth-century England, just as that of George Frederic Handel (1685–1759) does for the next century in *The Madness of King George* (1994). In contrast to films, however, relatively few games are set in a realistic (or even quasi-realistic) historical past, with a particular dearth of games taking place before the twentieth century. Consequently, instances of game designers using preexisting music in precisely this way are relatively uncommon.[16] Classical music requires, for the most part, some pretense of historical reality; it might be jarring to hear "real-world" works in the context of a pseudo-medieval fantasy world, for example. On the other hand, classical works can play a vital role in games that do aspire to a certain degree of historical authenticity.

Consider, for example, the point-and-click adventure game *Versailles 1685* (1996) and its sequel, *Versailles II: Testament of the King* (2001). As their titles suggest, both games take place in the monumental palace of Louis XIV, where the player solves mysteries to unravel far-reaching conspiracies against the throne. These games came about through a somewhat unlikely collaboration between the Réunion des Musées Nationaux in France (Association of National Museums) and Cyan Entertainment— the developer behind the 1990s game phenomenon *Myst* (1993). The goal was to wed the enjoyable puzzle-solving mechanics of adventure games with educational background on French history and culture, meaning that historical accuracy was of paramount importance. Indeed, the art historian Béatrix Saule—a leading expert on Versailles and the reign of Louis XIV—oversaw nearly every aspect of both games' development. Music is front and center in this quest for authenticity; the games exclusively contain music drawn from the French baroque period, coinciding with the period in which they take place (Table 2.1). *Versailles 1685* included excerpts of three religious choral works by Jean-Baptiste Lully (1632–1687) and François Couperin (1668–1733)—two of the most notable composers of the period—along with a single instrumental work by the lesser-known Étienne Lemoyne (d. 1715).

These choices, already carefully selected for their period, were chosen with equal consideration of location. Not only were all three composers French, but each of them also had close ties to the palace of Versailles: Lully and Couperin were court composers and musicians under the employ of Louis XIV (though at different times), while Lemoyne was one of the king's chamber musicians. In fact, the recordings themselves were connected with Versailles as well, emerging from projects undertaken under the auspices of the Centre de Musique Baroque (Baroque Music Center) at Versailles in the early 1990s.[17] Although the works by

---

[16] On historical games, see many of the essays in Matthew Wilhelm Kapell and Andrew B. R. Elliott, eds., *Playing with the Past: Digital Games and the Simulation of History* (New York: Bloomsbury, 2013).

[17] All examples are from the same *Musique à Versailles* series of recordings. The Lully works are taken from the 1994 recording *Lully: Grand Motets Vol. 1*, by Le Concert Spirituel, directed by Hervé Niquet (originally released by FNAC Music, later later released under the Naxos label); the Couperin motets are taken from a

TABLE 2.1

Preexisting French baroque music in *Versailles 1685* (1997)

Composer	Work	Date of composition
Jean-Baptiste Lully (1632–1687)	*Miserere*, LWV 25 (excerpts)	1664
Lully	*Plaude Laetare Gallia*, LWV 37 (excerpts)	1668
Lully	*Te Deum*, LWV 55 (excerpts)	1677
Lully	*Dies Irae*, LWV 64 (excerpts)	1684
François Couperin (1668–1733)	*Ignitum eloquim tuum*, from *Quatre versets d'un motet composé de l'ordre du roy*	1703
Couperin	*Tabescere me fecit*, from *Quatre versets d'un motet composé de l'ordre du roy*	1703
Couperin	*Etenim Dominus*, from *Sept versets du motet composé de l'ordre du roy*	1704
Étienne Lemoyne (d. 1715)	Courante, from *Pièces de théorbe en sol majeur*	Date uncertain

Couperin do stretch the date slightly (having been published almost two decades after the events of *Versailles 1685*), the game's emphasis on authenticity is nonetheless remarkable and underscores the importance of sound to establishing a sense of historical immersion.

Versailles II takes the same approach but considerably broadens its range. In addition to more of Lully's and Couperin's works, its soundtrack also includes music by a laundry list of influential but less celebrated French baroque composers, each related in some way to Versailles and the royalty who lived there.[18] In contrast with predominant religious choral works of the first game, here the selections lean toward instrumental music, running the gamut from solo harpsichord pieces to opera overtures. More significantly, the emphasis on music as an important way of understanding cultural history is even more apparent. Rather than using existing albums, as the first game had done, *Versailles II* featured a large number of new recordings to create the perfect historical compilation. As the back of the English-language game box

---

1993 recording by Les Talens Lyriques, directed by Christophe Rousset, later released on the Virgin Veritas label; and the Lemoyne work began as an interlude on the 1994 recording *Sébastien Le Camus: Airs de Cours*, also available on Virgin Veritas.

[18] Aside from Lully and Couperin, *Versailles II* contains music by Jean-Henri D'Anglebert (1629–1691), Michel Lambert (1610–1696), Jacques Champion de Chambonnières (1601–1672), Gaspard Le Roux (ca. 1660–1707), Louis Couperin (1626–1661), André Campra (1660–1744), and Marin Marais (1656–1728).

proudly explains, the soundtrack consists of "an orchestra of 25 musicians directed by the harpsichordist Skip Sempé, who has specially recorded more than an hour of music for the game."

Music was a clear priority in both *Versailles* games, a crucial part of creating an authentic, educational, and immersive gaming experience. It is, to say the least, an impressive effort. Between the two games, players are exposed to a wide and representative variety of French music of the seventeenth and eighteenth centuries—far more, in fact, than a typical music student might encounter in the course of an obtaining an undergraduate degree. Because most players will be unfamiliar with French baroque music, the process of musical signification works a bit differently than in the preceding examples. Instead of depending on players' prior knowledge, the music and gameplay work together to create a kind of feedback loop: the games teach players to associate the sound of the music with the era of the game, while the overtly historical (that is, "old") sound of the music encourages a sense of immersion.

The *Versailles* games were reasonably successful critically and financially, particularly in France, where they were often used in educational settings. Yet these kinds of historical games remain scarce, and the ways in which they can fruitfully include classical music are often less effective in other games. The role of music in *Versailles* has more in common with traditional cinematic uses of classical music than it does with other games. The use of historically accurate music in the French period films *Tous les matins du monde* (1991) and *Le roi danse* (2000), for instance—the latter of which also centers on Louis XIV—provides obvious parallels. The music works in those films, as in *Versailles*, because it grounds the viewer in a unique historical moment. At most, these kinds of games and films typically address only relatively short spans of time—a lifetime, perhaps. Television tends to work similarly; even the shows with the longest timelines usually focus on a few decades, as, for example, in *Downton Abbey* (2010–2015).

A number of games, on the other hand, contain narratives that stretch over much longer spans of time—centuries, or even millennia—and in which time itself becomes a central main gameplay element. For the most part these are games in the strategy genre, popular mostly on computers from the 1990s to the present. These games are defined primarily by the player's need to effectively manage time and resources. In historically based strategy games (however loosely defined), players often guide the development of a real-world civilization, fighting wars, advancing technology, and so on. A sense of immersion in historical periods—whether a particular era or the gradual march of progress—is a highly enjoyable part of the game for many players. To that end, a number of strategy games employ classical music from one or more periods to establish a sense of chronological setting.

Civilization IV (2005), for example, uses classical music from multiple periods to help guide the player through centuries of in-game time. Players assume one of multiple world cultures and guide that culture from its infancy to modern times by making military and diplomatic choices. Each playthrough is different in terms of how exactly the culture develops, but the same emphasis on forward motion—cultural progress—underlies each attempt. As the player develops his or her chosen culture, the time advances through several eras ("Medieval," "Industrial," "Modern," etc.), each featuring corresponding musical choices, ranging from antiquity to the contemporary composer John Adams (b. 1947).[19] The gradual evolution of the music conveys a sense of forward momentum, culminating in the minimal musical styles often associated with advanced technology and modern life.[20] As Karen Cook has pointed out in a study of the game, the musical selections reinforce and reflect "the sense of chronological motion and technological progress on which *Civ IV* is based."[21] In other words, the classical music of *Civ IV* creates a narrative of music history that runs parallel to the historical narrative created in each playthrough.

This music-historical narrative conveys the progression of time in a way that the user interface, graphics, and even gameplay might not. Someone might reasonably argue that because each era is clearly identified as it arrives, *Civ IV* encourages us to correlate the music and the era, much like the *Versailles* games. But here, I think, the process works in a different way. I would hazard a guess that most players have at least a general sense of the progression of music history, whether they know it or not. Chant might make us think of medieval monks, harpsichords of nobility in powdered wigs, minimalism of busy modern cities, and so on. In *Civ IV*, the player's sense of musical progress affects how they perceive the rest of the game. My in-game version of America suddenly feels much more advanced because the music has progressed, even though in gameplay terms it hasn't changed significantly from two minutes ago. Players understand that Adams is more advanced than Bach in the same way they understand that nuclear power is more advanced than steam. That perception of progress isn't without problems, however. For one thing, it (perhaps unintentionally) asserts that older styles of music are inherently less advanced or—less charitably—perhaps even primitive. Furthermore, as Cook suggests, it encourages a fundamentally Western understanding of all of world history, even though many cultures have an equally rich (and often much longer) tradition of music making.

---

[19] Karen M. Cook, "Music, History, and Progress in Sid Meier's *Civilization IV*," in *Music in Video Games: Studying Play*, ed. K. J. Donnelly, William Gibbons, and Neil Lerner (New York: Routledge, 2014), 166–182.

[20] Robert Fink, for example, has argued compellingly for an interpretation of American minimalist music as in part "a sonorous constituent of a characteristic repetitive existence of self in mass-media consumer society." Robert Fink, *Repeating Ourselves: American Minimal Music as Cultural Practice* (Berkeley: University of California Press, 2005), 4.

[21] Cook, "Music, History, and Progress in Sid Meier's *Civilization IV*," 168.

Yet as much as *Civ IV*'s musical narrative building relies on players having a basic knowledge of Western classical music history, it also counts on them misreading that same history. Listeners with *too much* awareness of music history will undoubtedly notice jarring anachronisms and significant liberties taken by the game designers. Beethoven (1770–1827)—whose music and life bridged the gap between the eighteenth and nineteenth centuries—shows up in the Renaissance. The actual Renaissance composer Giovanni Pierluigi da Palestrina (1525–1594), however, is part of the the medieval era of the game. And so on. This creative historical reimagining might seem just a quirk of *Civ IV*'s already loose take on historical progress, but it actually highlights a recurring use of classical music in games. Rather than conforming to historical fact (as in the *Versailles* games), designers often will appeal to what players *think* they know about music history. In other words, they find a sweet spot between, on the one hand, conforming slavishly to historical fact and, on the other, alienating players by stretching reality too far—an intriguing interplay to which I turn in the next section.

Wrong Place, Wrong Time

The previous sections explored several ways in which carefully selected classical music helps establish a game's geographical and chronological setting—or both, as in the *Versailles* games. For the most part, this process works by drawing music directly from the place or time that the game is attempting to evoke. That approach seems obvious: German music equals Germany, sixteenth-century music indicates the Renaissance, and so on. But can music suggest the "right" setting by using the "wrong" music? In other words, can games tap into players' musical experiences and expectations to indicate one setting by using music from somewhere or sometime *different*? The short answer is yes, and it happens more often than many players may realize. Take, for example, the case of the point-and-click adventure game *Quest for Glory: Shadows of Darkness* (1993; also known as *Quest for Glory IV*). Each of the games in this computer game series takes place in a fantasy realm based loosely on a culture or location in the real world. The first game, *Quest for Glory: So You Want to Be a Hero* (1989), takes place in and around the vaguely Bavarian town of Spielburg, while subsequent games adapt other cultures—*Quest for Glory II: Trial by Fire* (1990) takes place in the quasi-Persian Shapeir, and *Quest for Glory III: Wages of War* (1992) in the Central African–inspired savannas of Fricana. In each case, the music composed for the game draws on musical signifiers of these respective cultures to help ground players in each new location.

Quest for Glory: Shadows of Darkness brings the player to Mordavia, a pastiche of Slavic cultures featuring characters and monsters drawn from Eastern

FIGURE 2.3 The interior of the Hotel Mordavia, *Quest for Glory IV* (1994).

European folklore. The only instance of borrowed classical music in the game appears as the background music in the Hotel Mordavia, a cozy lodge that players visit on several occasions (Figure 2.3). The music is an arrangement of "Anitra's Dance," from the incidental music to the play *Peer Gynt* (music composed in 1875) by Edvard Grieg (1847–1907)—music that features in a number of games throughout this book.[22] When I played *Quest for Glory* for the first time in 1994, I didn't recognize this music. Its inviting but somewhat melancholy quality seemed to fit the hotel (and Mordavia itself) perfectly, and I assumed it was composed for the game, like the rest of the score. Knowing what I know now about music history, however, this musical selection feels fascinatingly "wrong." In contrast with the musical choices mentioned in the previous sections of this chapter—those for *Assassin's Creed*, *Versailles 1685*, or *Tetris*, for example—the game seems to deliberately avoid obvious ways of suggesting its setting. For example, there are plenty of Eastern European composers whose music might have served the same purpose, but Grieg was Norwegian— and an ardent nationalist at that. By the same token, the play *Peer Gynt*, written by Grieg's compatriot Henrik Ibsen, has nothing to do with the Slavic legends found in *Quest for Glory IV*. While the play does contain some supernatural elements, they emerge from Scandinavian folklore, not Slavic. For that matter, the section of the play in which "Anitra's Dance" appears takes place in North Africa. In other words,

---

[22] Grieg's well-known "In the Hall of the Mountain King," also from *Peer Gynt*, is particularly prevalent in early games, appearing, for example, in *Mountain King* (1983), *Maniac Miner* (1983), and *Jet Set Willy* 2 (1985).

it's difficult to imagine a piece of classical music that has *less* to do with Eastern Europe. Yet its effectiveness in the game is hard to dispute.

To be sure, the way Grieg's composition was adapted from its original version to fit the game does help players make a connection between sound and in-game location. The pitches were altered to include a repeating bassline reminiscent of folk music, and the added emphasis on the bass (particularly beginning about halfway through the loop) gives the piece a ponderous feel suitable for its rustic setting. But these alterations alone are not enough to justify the music's success here, or its presence at all. A more likely possibility is that, despite all the geographical distance between Norway (or North Africa) and Eastern Europe, Grieg's music fits with what many listeners expect from Slavic music. As a number of film-music scholars have pointed out, the kinds of shorthand codes that composers use to indicate nationality or ethnicity need not necessarily conform to *actual* musical practices—they just have to be close enough to meet audience expectations. K.J. Donnelly, for instance, notes the extent to which the music often used to indicate "Indians" in Hollywood Westerns became a "fake sonic . . . film prop that could easily be unrecognizable to Native Americans."[23] This same "wrongness" is frequently found on television, where strict time constraints often make musical shorthand even more crucial than in film. Ron Rodman, for example, points to the rampant ethnic cues in the "Shore Leave" episode of *Star Trek* from 1966, which contains Irish and Japanese characters drawn from the imaginations of the *Enterprise* crew. Rather than being "authentic," the episode's composer (Gerald Fried) relied on "the intersubjective semantic field" of the audiences—in other words, their frame of reference. "This is the musical verisimilitude of film and television, where meaning relies on the negotiated meanings of previous texts more than on the authentic texts that may or may not be known to the viewer."[24]

The same concepts apply in terms of representing chronological setting. *Civilization IV* already illustrated this kind of musical anachronism, yet because history doesn't necessarily progress realistically in that game, the player isn't precisely "misled" into believing the music is from another place or time.[25] In some

---

[23] K. J. Donnelly, *The Spectre of Sound: Music in Film and Television* (London: BFI, 2005), 56.

[24] Ron Rodman, *Tuning In: American Narrative Television Music* (Oxford: Oxford University Press, 2010), 124.

[25] On the historical simulation of *Civilization* and similar games, see, for example, Rolfe Daus Peterson, Andrew Justin Miller, and Sean Joseph Fedorko, "The Same River Twice: Exploring Historical Representation and the Value of Simulation in the *Total War, Civilization*, and *Patrician* Franchises," in *Playing with the Past: Digital Games and the Simulation of History*, ed. Matthew Wilhelm Kapell and Andrew B. R. Elliott (New York: Bloomsbury, 2013), 33–48; and Tom Apperly, "Modding the Historians' Code: Historical Verisimilitude and the Counterfactual Imagination," in *Playing with the Past: Digital Games and the Simulation of History*, ed. Matthew Wilhelm Kapell and Andrew B. R. Elliott (New York: Bloomsbury, 2013), 185–198.

cases, however, music *can* be deceiving, signifying a particular time through music of an entirely different era. That is certainly the case in *Pirates!* (1987), a much-loved simulation game in which players guide their avatars through a Caribbean career in swashbuckling. Originally released on the Commodore 64, *Pirates!* was popular enough to warrant versions on a number of other computers and consoles in the late 1980s, as well as remakes in the 1990s (*Pirates! Gold*), again in 2004, and most recently in mobile form in the early 2010s. For the sake of convenience, I will discuss the 1991 release on the Nintendo Entertainment System, although the same general points apply to most of the other versions, as well. Immediately after starting a new game of *Pirates!*, players choose a time for their adventures, with options ranging from 1560 to 1680. After another few questions, they're then treated to a brief introduction, featuring an excerpt from a minuet by Handel, from his *Water Music* suite No. 1, HWV 348 (1717). After a few moments of gameplay, players see another screen of text, this time underscored by a portion of the bourée (another type of dance) from the same suite.

Players' choice of period has a significant impact on several aspects of gameplay, yet no matter what, the music is always the same. This choice is both a pun and a historical allusion: the title *Water Music* suggests the game's focus on ships and the sea, and Handel's suite was composed for performance on a barge, during a trip down the Thames. But *Water Music* isn't the only baroque music to appear in *Pirates!*: a visit to any of the governors' mansions is accompanied by J. S. Bach's Two-Part Invention in G Major, BWV 781 (ca. 1720), a keyboard work. From a historical perspective, these pieces are intriguing. Bach's invention and Handel's *Water Music* were composed in almost the same period, which suggests that the designers intended to create a uniform musical environment—somewhat akin to that in the *Versailles* games. Yet while those titles took great pains to ensure historical accuracy, here players are faced with "impossible" music, composed well after even the latest time players can choose. Even given that the NES might not have had enough memory—or the developers might not have had the patience—to include music from each of the possible periods, they could have at least chosen music from *one* of the possibilities. Instead, something else is at play. Although the works by Bach and Handel don't correspond to any of the eras available in *Pirates!*, they nonetheless evoke them *all*. Untethered from a single period, the music instead creates a broad sense of a historical past. Historical accuracy is less important, in other words, than conforming to players' expectations of what old music sounds like.

The soundtrack to *Pirates!* assumes that players either don't know or don't care that the music is, from a purely historical perspective, "wrong." At the same time, however, players still have to possess enough of an understanding of music history to recognize that the music sounds sufficiently old. These choices of classical pieces play with music history, building on general expectations while exploiting the hazier details in the name of creating an enjoyable gaming experience. In the next chapter, I continue to explore this fascinating contradiction, turning to a specific example of just how complicated these types of associations can become.

3 A Requiem for Schrödinger's Cat

EARLY ON IN *BioShock Infinite* (2013), protagonist Booker DeWitt arrives in the city of Columbia—which, despite the game's setting in 1912, happens to be floating in the sky. Still adjusting to his impossible surroundings, Booker tries to blend in at a carnival, surrounded by excited residents milling through impeccably tidy streets. As players explore, they might notice an airship pull up alongside the city, a stage prominently featured on its deck. Improbably, the deck of this ship hosts a dapper barbershop quartet, complete with red-and-white-striped coats, bow ties, and top hats (Figure 3.1). The first time I played the game, the barbershop quartet seemed like a nice historical touch—a clever but not particularly innovative way of keeping players grounded (so to speak) in the Gilded Age. I almost continued on my way, but at the last minute, I decided to stop and listen. As I did, it dawned on me that I *knew* the song the quartet was singing, but I couldn't quite place it. A few moments later, however, I realized both why I knew the song and why I didn't: the music was an arrangement of "God Only Knows," from the Beach Boys' album *Pet Sounds* (1966). For first-time players who know the original version of the song, this moment might be *BioShock Infinite*'s earliest instance of foreshadowing—a warning to players that not all is as it seems in this idyllic city in the clouds. Indeed, before long, everything goes horribly awry, and Columbia's utopian veneer is violently and irrevocably stripped away.

The previous chapter explored how classical music in games builds on players' prior musical knowledge and experiences to create setting. In this chapter I'm interested in how *BioShock Infinite* uses the same tools for the opposite purpose: rather

FIGURE 3.1 Columbia's barbershop quartet performs "God Only Knows" in *BioShock Infinite* (2013).

than anchoring the game in a particular time and place, the music keeps players temporally and geographically unmoored. Because *Infinite* builds its complex web of references by using several different musical styles, I broaden the scope of this chapter beyond music we might typically think of as classical. The game's diverse soundtrack includes American popular music of multiple eras, jazz standards, blues, Protestant hymnody, and classical music—all in addition to the newly created score by series composer Garry Schyman. The mélange comes as no surprise to those familiar with the previous *BioShock* games. Since the series began in 2007, it has garnered attention from players, critics, and scholars alike for its intellectual depth and attention to detail, including in its music selection.[1] In fact, much of the music in *BioShock Infinite* works in the same ways as the music in the previous two games, reinforcing the historical position while also offering commentary (often ironic) on the actions of the game.

Yet *Infinite* also differs in significant ways from its predecessors and, on a grander scale, from how preexisting music usually works in media.[2] It does so, I argue, in

---

[1] On the scholarly attraction to the *BioShock* series, see, for example, Ryan Lizardi, "*Bioshock*: Complex and Alternate Histories," *Games Studies* 14, no. 1 (August 2014), available online at http://gamestudies.org/1401/articles/lizardi.

[2] Scholars have begun to consider *Infinite*'s rich soundscape from a variety of fruitful perspectives—and there is indeed much to say on the topic. The music of *BioShock Infinite* has been a prominent topic at music conferences since its release—the only game to receive such individual attention. See Enoch Jacobus, "Lighter Than Air: A Return to Columbia" (paper presented at the North American Conference on Video Game Music, Texas Christian University, January 17–18, 2015); Enoch Jacobus, "There's Always a Lighthouse: Commentary and Foreshadowing in the Diegetic Music of *BioShock: Infinite*" (paper presented at the North American

service of a specific goal. These musical selections and arrangements echo the game's philosophical reflections on certain aspects of quantum mechanics and, in particular, on the simultaneous coexistence of mutually exclusive realities. By dwelling on that topic, *BioShock Infinite* invokes the specter of Schrödinger's cat, the 1935 thought experiment from which I draw this chapter's title. Though of course the field of quantum mechanics is complex and at times esoteric, this experiment illustrates one of its better-known principles. In the words of astrophysicist John Gribbin:

> It is possible to set up an experiment in such a way that there is a precise fifty-fifty chance that one of the atoms in a lump of radioactive material will decay in a certain time and that a detector will register the decay if it does happen. Schrödinger . . . tried to show the absurdity of those implications by imagining such an experiment set up in a closed room, or box, which also contains a live cat and a phial of poison, so arranged that if the radioactive decay does occur then the poison container is broken and the cat dies. In the everyday world, there is a fifty-fifty chance that the cat will be killed, and without looking inside the box we can say, quite happily, that the cat inside is either dead or alive. But now we encounter the strangeness of the quantum world. According to the theory, *neither* of the two possibilities open to the radioactive material, and therefore to the cat, has any reality unless it is observed. The atomic decay has neither happened nor not happened, the cat has neither been killed nor not killed, until we look inside the box to see what has happened. Theorists who accept the pure version of quantum mechanics say that the cat exists in some indeterminate state, neither dead nor alive, until an observer looks into the box to see how things are getting on. Nothing is real unless it is observed.[3]

One solution to this apparent paradox was the many-worlds theory of quantum mechanics, which suggests that a virtually infinite series of parallel universes exists alongside our own, differing from one another in large or small ways based on the

---

Conference on Video Game Music, Youngstown State University, January 18–19, 2014); Matt Thomas, "Give Me That Old-Time Religion: American Folk Music in the Video Game *BioShock: Infinite*" (paper presented at the annual meeting of the Society for American Music, Sacramento, CA, March 4–8, 2015); and Sarah Pozderac-Chenevey, "Breaking the Circle: Analyzing the Narrative Function of Music Manipulation in *BioShock Infinite*" (paper presented at the North American Conference on Video Game Music, Youngstown State University, January 18–19, 2014). Both of Jacobus's presentations are available online at the author's personal website: http://thetheoretician.weebly.com/presentations.html. Pozderac-Chenevey's presentation is available online at https://www.academia.edu/5740701/Breaking_the_Circle_Analyzing_the_Narrative_Function_of_Music_Manipulation_in_Bioshock_Infinite.

[3] John Gribbin, *In Search of Schrödinger's Cat: Quantum Physics and Reality* (New York: Bantam, 1984), 2–3.

choices of their inhabitants and the random effects of probability. Originally developed in the late 1950s, this idea gained more attention in the following two decades, thanks in part to the work of physicist Bryce DeWitt—the inspiration for *Infinite* protagonist Booker DeWitt's name.

Succinctly summarizing the plot of *BioShock Infinite* is challenging (I say, having just attempted to succinctly summarize a branch of theoretical physics), but the many-worlds idea is central to its narrative. In the game's universe, scientists have discovered how to create "Tears" in the fabric of space and time—ruptures that allow travel between alternate realities. Elizabeth, one of the game's main characters, can open these Tears at will, allowing her and Booker to travel into alternate universes or to bring objects and people from one universe into another—typically with unforeseen, and occasionally disastrous, consequences. Elizabeth gained this power by virtue of a mistake: while she was being transported from one universe to another as an infant, the tip of her finger was caught in a Tear, severing it and leaving it behind in her original universe of origin. Because each new universe is created because of a difference in choice or chance, each one is mutually exclusive. Like Schrödinger's cat, then, Elizabeth thus inhabits two contradictory realities simultaneously. *Infinite* subtextually (if not directly) delves deeply into this conflict, repeatedly calling attention to the impossible coexistence of things that both *are* and *are not*. This central dichotomy features into the game's musical choices in ways that are both obvious and subtle.

Space, Time, Music

As I've already discussed, it's virtually impossible to detach music we already know from our prior experiences with it. Sound design in games often depends on those associations, which allow the music to work as a kind of shorthand—a code designed to trigger certain associations in the viewer or player. Popular music (broadly speaking) can be especially helpful in this regard. While many players might not be able to distinguish between, say, music of the fifteenth and seventeenth centuries, they probably have a decade-by-decade understanding of historical trends in popular music styles. Take the *Grand Theft Auto* games, for example, which rely on in-game radio stations to help create the setting. *Grand Theft Auto: Vice City* (2002) sonically immerses the player in a fictionalized version of 1980s Miami, *Grand Theft Auto: San Andreas* (2004) does the same for 1990s Southern California, and so on.[4] I have argued elsewhere that mid-twentieth-century popular music plays this role in

---

[4] On the uses of music for setting in the *Grand Theft Auto* games (particularly *San Andreas*), see Kiri Miller, *Playing Along: Digital Games, YouTube, and Virtual Performance* (Oxford: Oxford University Press, 2012), chaps. 1 and 2.

multiple ways in the original *BioShock*: the style of the music itself reminds players of the game's chronological setting despite the futuristic technology surrounding them, while the song lyrics frequently comment on the action at hand.[5]

That multilevel functionality persists in *BioShock Infinite*, although there the choices of period music are a bit looser in their chronological grounding. Because it was difficult to find "music from that era that sounds great to a modern ear," as *BioShock* series designer Ken Levine explained in an interview, the popular music in *Infinite* encompasses a longer time frame (in some cases a decade or more after 1912) and a wider variety of musical styles than its predecessors.[6] Yet the function of these songs remains the same. The 1907 gospel hymn "Will the Circle Be Unbroken," for example—heard multiple times throughout the game—contributes to the chronological setting and reinforces Columbia's Protestant cultural foundation. More significantly, the song also gradually transforms into a commentary on the game's central metaphysical concern: breaking the cycle of historical repetition in alternate universes.

But if songs like "Will the Circle Be Unbroken" work in much the same way that popular music did in the first two *BioShock* games, the anachronistic music is something new to *Infinite*—and vitally important to its soundscape.[7] Let's consider an example. Booker travels to Columbia with a singular goal: liberating Elizabeth from the prison where she has been kept for most of her life. Accomplishing that feat occupies the first several hours of the game, but after a harrowing escape, the duo find themselves on a picturesque beach, where they (and the player) get some much-needed respite. As Booker contemplates their next move, Elizabeth meanders along the beach, enjoying her newfound freedom and taking in the sights. Eventually the pair head toward an arcade, following a lighthearted tune from a calliope (a steam-powered organ popular at fairs and carnival settings in the late nineteenth and early twentieth centuries).

The calliope's unique old-timey sound suggests its historical period, as does the distinctive oom-pah-pah of the arrangement. Upon close listening, however, players may recognize "Girls Just Want to Have Fun," a song originally written in 1979 but popularized by Cyndi Lauper four years later and covered by a number

---

[5] William Gibbons, "'Wrap Your Troubles in Dreams': Popular Music, Narrative, and Dystopia in *BioShock*," *Game Studies* 11, no. 3 (2011), available online at http://gamestudies.org/1103/articles/gibbons.

[6] John Mix Meyer, "Q&A: Ken Levine's Brave New World of *BioShock Infinite*," *Wired* (April 26, 2012), available online at http://www.wired.com/2012/04/ken-levine-interview/all/ (accessed November 11, 2014).

[7] These arrangements were created by Scott Bradlee, founder of the music ensemble Postmodern Jukebox, which specializes in these kinds of antihistorical arrangements. On the arrangements and their narrative significance, see also Pozderac-Chenevey, "Breaking the Circle," who discusses the commentary functions of several of the anachronistic songs found in the game.

TABLE 3.1

Anachronistic popular music in *BioShock Infinite* (2013)

Title	Artist	Date
"Everybody Wants to Rule the World"	Tears for Fears	1985
"Fortunate Son"	Creedence Clearwater Revival	1969
"Girls Just Want to Have Fun"	Cyndi Lauper	1983
"God Only Knows"	Beach Boys	1966
"Shiny Happy People"	R.E.M.	1991
"Tainted Love"	Gloria Jones; Soft Cell	1964; 1981

of artists in the years since. Although the calliope arrangement is strictly instru-mental, players who know the song will no doubt consider the text—or at least the title, which seems to comment on Elizabeth's childlike exuberance. Delving deeper into the lyrics suggests other connections. "Some boys take a beautiful girl," the song tells us, "And hide her away from the rest of the world / I want to be the one to walk in the sun / Oh girls they want to have fun." Clearly, these lines reflect the situation at hand: Elizabeth was hidden away from the world, yet now she is literally both walking in the sun and having fun. These anachronistic arrange-ments (Table 3.1 for a complete list) still perform the historicizing and commen-tary functions players have come to expect from *BioShock* games, but their unusual chronological position complicates things, adding another layer onto an already multilayered allusion.

Anachronistic popular music in media (particularly games) is relatively un-common, but there are nonetheless numerous antecedents going back to early cinema. The influential Western *Stagecoach* (1939), for instance, included several songs that would be written only decades after its story takes place.[8] More recently, the director Quentin Tarantino uses this technique in many of his films; the soundtrack of *Pulp Fiction* (1994), for example, includes popular music from multiple decades, obscur-ing when precisely the film takes place. In other films, directors use anachronistic music in historical settings to help audiences find an equivalent contemporary ex-perience. Both Sofia Coppola's *Marie Antoinette* (2006) and Baz Luhrmann's *The Great Gatsby* (2013) feature music of the "wrong" period—1980s pop and 2010s hip-hop, respectively. In both cases, the music is intended to capture a feeling of opu-lence and excess that historically accurate music might not convey to listeners who

---

[8] On popular music in *Stagecoach*, see Kathryn Kalinak, *How the West Was Sung: Music in the Westerns of John Ford* (Berkeley: University of California Press, 2007), chap. 3.

FIGURE 3.2 The penalty for interracial relationships in Columbia, accompanied by Wagner's "Wedding Chorus."

were less familiar with those styles. These films come into closer dialogue with the present by encouraging audience members to draw connections between the unfamiliar and the familiar (the 1780s and the 1980s, for example).

Games offer an analogue in the post-apocalyptic *Fallout* series of role-playing games. Although these games take place in the distant future, they extensively feature midcentury American popular music. The dystopian environments in which players find themselves are rendered even more jarring by the optimism of the chronologically misplaced midcentury music.[9] In other words, preexisting music in games typically either (1) evokes a particular period and/or geographical setting, as in the first two *BioShock* games; or (2) actively works against those settings (whether to disorient players or to create meaningful transhistorical connections for them). By definition, these functions are mutually exclusive—each is useful, but game designers must make a choice.

What makes *BioShock Infinite* particularly innovative in this regard is that the game designers opt for both: songs like "God Only Knows" and "Girls Just Want to Have Fun" are simultaneously historically/contextually appropriate *and* noticeably anachronistic. The resulting cognitive dissonance has the unusual effect of both reinforcing and destabilizing the player's sense of time and place. Players (distinct from the characters in the game) thus know two things about the chronological setting of

---

[9] *Fallout* conveniently justifies these musical selections by suggesting that the atomic blasts destroyed all post-vinyl recording technology, but that tortured logic seems both unconvincing and unnecessary.

BioShock Infinite: it's 1912, and it cannot possibly be 1912. The songs we hear are both new and old—and, moreover, "new" again in their "old" arrangements.[10]

The game eventually offers players a logical explanation (relatively speaking) for the temporal confusion these songs incite. Unbeknownst to his devoted Columbia audience, the songwriter Albert Fink has been opening Tears to alternate dimensions and plagiarizing the melodies of songs that shouldn't exist in 1912. As in the case of "God Only Knows" and "Girls Just Want to Have Fun," the historical juxtapositions can initially confuse players, becoming understandable only during replays. (Indeed, many design aspects of *BioShock Infinite* seem calculated to encourage players to experience the game multiple times—resonating with the game's cyclical theme, and perhaps offering a kind of metacommentary on video games as a medium.) Even more important, however, these songs reinforce *Infinite*'s focus on the cognitive dissonance of mutually exclusive realities. In the following section, I examine this aspect more fully by exploring *Infinite*'s use of classical music.

Tears and Mourning

Back at the carnival, just after the encounter with the barbershop quartet, Booker receives a raffle ticket (a baseball)—a chance at the grand prize at the carnival's main event. Upon joining a large crowd to witness this spectacle, Booker has the unexpected (and undesired) good luck to win the raffle. The prize is then revealed to be somewhat less than grand: an opportunity to be the first to throw his baseball (America's pastime!) at an interracial couple imprisoned onstage in a grotesquely racist tableau of a wedding (Figure 3.2). (Player can opt to maintain their cover by throwing the ball at the couple, or instead choose the immensely satisfying route of hitting the carnival barker instead.) The couple comes onstage to some familiar music: the raucous crowd, out for blood, joins together in singing the bridal chorus from Richard Wagner's 1850 opera *Lohengrin* (the tune is often called "Here Comes the Bride"). The music is ironic—a twisted parody of its appearance at countless joyous weddings.[11] Yet like the musical commentary

---

[10] Moreover, because players are likely to know at least some of this music in its form, identifying the arrangements can even become a kind of metagame, existing outside the narrative framework. Andra Ivănescu astutely notes that "the player becomes the tourist through time and space, noticing anachronisms that the characters in the game, even the playable character, would not be able to identify. The game and its music show the player the cracks forming in the fourth wall, reminding them that they are just a player." Andra Ivănescu, "The Music of Tomorrow, Yesterday! Music, Time and Technology in *BioShock Infinite*," *Networking Knowledge* 7, no. 2 (2014). Available online at http://ojs.meccsa.org.uk/index.php/netknow/article/view/337/168.

[11] Tim Summers also points out some uses of Wagner's music in video games to indicate similar ideas, as in the use of the "Bridal Chorus" during a wedding in *King's Quest VI: Heir Today, Gone Tomorrow* (1992). Tim Summers,

in "Girls Just Want to Have Fun" (and numerous songs throughout the *BioShock* series), there is another level to the bridal chorus—and one that is both strikingly apt and deadly serious.

Wagner was a well-known and vociferous anti-Semite, a firm believer in the purity of the German people and the inferiority of other races—a legacy that has cast a dark shadow over his music for generations. Exacerbating the problem is the knowledge that Wagner's music was much beloved of Adolf Hitler, inextricably linking the composer and his works to the Nazi Party and its deeply racist ideology. The appearance of the bridal chorus in *BioShock Infinite* thus casts the shadow of white supremacist thought and forebodingly suggests the tragic endpoint of the route on which Columbia's citizens find themselves.[12] As with the popular-music covers I have already examined, understanding Wagner's music in this way takes some anachronistic thought on the player's part. World War II was decades away in 1912, and of course it might never occur at all in the alternate universe that contains Columbia. Nevertheless, Wagner's music still carries the weight of this baggage, suggesting to historically minded players the true depravity of Columbia's social injustice. This fairly brief scene illustrates how classical music functions as commentary in *BioShock Infinite*, and several other instances in the game work in a similar way. Rather than trace all those examples, however, the rest of this chapter explores one particularly extended, prominent, and multilayered example: the game's use of Mozart's Requiem in D Minor, K. 626 (1791) as a sonic manifestation of the larger issues of quantum mechanics and uncertainty at play in *BioShock Infinite*.

At one point in the game, Booker and Elizabeth travel to the memorial and mausoleum of Lady Annabelle Comstock, the murdered wife of Columbia's "Prophet" and leader, Zachary Comstock—and ostensibly Elizabeth's mother. The beloved Lady Comstock initially supported her husband's vision for Columbia but later came to question his extreme measures. Elizabeth was the final straw: rendered sterile from the overuse of Tears, the Prophet sought out an heir by abducting a child from an alternate universe version of himself. Unable to accept this turn of events, Lady Comstock threatens to reveal the truth to Columbia's citizens, at which point her husband has her assassinated and blames her murder on anarchists. The martyred Lady Comstock now lies entombed in a mausoleum, where her body and belongings are venerated like holy relics by the Prophet's cultish followers. By way of plaques

---

"From *Parsifal* to the PlayStation: Wagner and Video Game Music," in *Music in Video Games: Studying Play*, ed. K. J. Donnelly, William Gibbons, and Neil Lerner (New York: Routledge, 2014), 199–216.

[12] Pozderac-Chenevey suggests a similar aspect of race conflict in her reading of the use of Frédéric Chopin's Nocturne in E-flat Major, Op. 9, No. 2. Pozderac-Chenevey, "Breaking the Circle."

and sculptures scattered throughout the mausoleum, players learn the (fictionalized) narrative of Elizabeth's birth and Lady Comstock's assassination, each room revealing a bit more of the tale. As my preceding explanation likely makes clear, this narrative is overtly religious, drawing parallels to the Christian Holy Family. Elizabeth is depicted as Columbia's messiah, "the Lamb"; Comstock as its great Prophet and Saint Joseph; and Lady Comstock as the Virgin Mary.

Mozart's Requiem can be heard throughout the mausoleum, the hiss and pops of a phonograph record making clear that the music emanates from some kind of hidden speaker system. The choice of music is appropriate, given the memorial and religious functions of the space. A requiem is a Catholic mass for the dead, a multipart liturgy frequently set to music by composers from the Middle Ages to the present. Beyond its overall significance, however, different movements (that is, discrete sections) of Mozart's work also cleverly reflect the subject of each room (Table 3.2). Despite being sung in Latin, the texts work much like the popular songs in the *BioShock* series: they contribute to the overall tone, while their texts provide additional commentary.

Sometimes that commentary is on a fairly basic level. Consider, for example, the final room of the memorial, "The Vengeance of the Prophet," which tells the story of Zachary Comstock's retribution on his wife's supposed murderers. The fiery Confutatis movement provides musical accompaniment to this scene, with text describing the damnation of the guilty:

Confutatis maledictis,	When the wicked are confounded,
Flammis acribus addictis,	Doomed to flames of woe unbounded,
Voca me cum benedictus.	Call me with thy saints surrounded.
Oro supplex et acclinis,	Low, I kneel, with heart-submission;
Cor contritum quasi cinis:	See, like ashes, my contrition;
Gere curam mei finis.	Help me in my last condition.

TABLE 3.2

Mozart's Requiem in *BioShock Infinite*

Location	Movement of Requiem
"The Memorial to Our Lady"	Lacrimosa
"The Transport of the Child"	Agnus Dei (opening only)
"The Murder of Our Lady"	Rex tremendae
"The Vengeance of the Prophet"	Confutatis
Lady Comstock's Tomb	Lacrimosa

Here the music and text work largely unironically, unless the player chooses to consider the irony of Comstock claiming to smite the wicked when he himself was (by proxy) the murderer.

Similarly, in the room labeled "The Murder of Our Lady," we hear the Rex tremendae movement—a text pleading for mercy set to a loud and oddly accusatory bit of music from Mozart:

Rex tremendae majestatis,	King of majesty tremendous,
Qui salvandos savas gratis,	Who dost free salvation send us,
Salve me, fons pietatis.	Fount of pity, then befriend us.

On a musical level, the excerpt functions unironically, conveying the sense of righteous fury the scene would suggest. Yet the text seems out of place—why reference a king except to suggest Zachary Comstock? The game designers could easily have chosen the much more suitable text of, say, the Dies irae (Day of Wrath) portion of the Requiem. On the other hand, perhaps we can read the text as a subconscious acknowledgment of Comstock's guilt, the choir's loudly repeated cries of "Rex!" casting subtle judgment on Comstock as much as they do on his enemies.

In other rooms, however, the textual commentary is even more subtle. "The Transport of the Child," for instance, depends more on what *isn't* said than what is. That room depicts Elizabeth's relocation to the secluded tower where Booker finds her in the game's first hours. Because Elizabeth has been raised almost entirely in seclusion, it's only in this room that she realizes—much to her chagrin—that Comstock is her father, and Lady Comstock her mother. Because Elizabeth's epiphany takes center stage, there is very little music here. As the pair first enter the room, however, we hear the opening of the Agnus Dei (Lamb of God) portion of the Requiem. Although on first visiting the room we do not hear the text, the title of the movement in particular is highly significant. Throughout the game, Elizabeth is portrayed as "The Lamb of Columbia." Just after Booker arrives, for instance, a stained-glass window shows a haloed baby Elizabeth surrounded by her parents, featuring the caption "The Lamb: The Future of Our City" (Figure 3.3). Again and again, *Infinite* positions Elizabeth in a messianic role, Columbia's counterpart to Jesus (the "Lamb of God") in the Christian faith. Mozart's music introduces the movement instrumentally but cuts off just before the voices actually sing the text "Agnus Dei." Yet at that very instant Elizabeth grasps that *she* is the Lamb of Columbia, and her startled outburst takes the choir's place. Likewise, Booker is referred to repeatedly throughout the game as the "False Shepherd," brought to Columbia to "lead the Lamb astray." By connecting with these titles ("False Shepherd" and "Lamb of

FIGURE 3.3 Stained-glass window depicting Elizabeth as "The Lamb."

Columbia"), the Agnus Dei subtly connects Booker and Elizabeth with the narrative Comstock's memorial seeks to create, raising questions of how precisely they fit into Columbia's story.

Beyond this type of commentary, though, Mozart's Requiem and its careful manipulation in the game allow the work to comment not just on the action at hand but also on the larger metaphysical questions surrounding *BioShock Infinite*. The entrance to the memorial ("The Memorial to Our Lady") features what is probably the best-known portion of the Requiem: the Lacrimosa, with melancholic music accompanied by a text that focuses on lamentation, conjuring images of weeping mourners:

Lacrimosa dies illa,	Ah! that day of tears and mourning!
Qua resurget ex favilla	From the dust of earth returning
Judicandus homo reus;	Man for judgment must prepare him.
Huic ergo parce, Deus.	Spare, O God, in mercy spare him.
Pie Jesu Domine,	Lord all pitying, Jesu blest,
dona eis requiem.	Grant them thine eternal rest
Amen.	Amen.[13]

---

[13] The texts and poetic translations for the Requiem are taken from Simon P. Keefe, *Mozart's Requiem: Reception, Work, Completion* (Cambridge: Cambridge University Press, 2012), which also provides valuable historical and cultural background on Mozart's work.

Booker and Elizabeth encounter the Lacrimosa again shortly after passing through the memorial, at Lady Comstock's actual tomb. As with the entryway, inside the tomb the Lacrimosa replays constantly—an eternal, unremitting sonic reminder of the tragedy of her loss.

When the pair arrive at the tomb, Elizabeth unwittingly creates a Tear in reality, opening a window into a universe where Lady Comstock was never murdered. The results are ghastly. Lady Comstock is only partially "resurrected," at least one living version from an alternate universe merged with the dead version from the tomb. Like Schrödinger's cat, Lady Comstock exists in an impossibly liminal space, at once alive and dead—her rage at her murderer and the cognitive dissonance of her horrific state drive her instantly insane. Unable to latch onto a single reality, she manifests as the Siren, a rampaging specter. The soundscape surrounding the Siren is a distortion of the same Lacrimosa movement players have now heard on several occasions. Its familiar musical elements are twisted and manipulated, combined with static, as if heard underwater and from a great distance. Even more disturbingly, the Siren occasionally seems to hum along, suggesting that somehow Lady Comstock absorbed the music that has been her constant companion for years. The persistence of Mozart's music suggests that some part of the Siren remains trapped in her glass coffin in Lady Comstock's tomb, listening all the while.

The Siren is certainly a dramatic representation of quantum uncertainty, but at this point in the game, that same idea is also playing out on several other levels—not all of which are musical. For instance, Elizabeth's existence in mutually exclusive realities isn't entirely unlike Lady Comstock's own situation. As I have already mentioned, her powers stem from her simultaneous existence in two realities. Her parentage is similarly complicated: Zachary and Annabelle Comstock both *are* and *are not* her parents. This already complex situation is further complicated by the fact that the alternate Comstock from whom Elizabeth was taken is, in fact, Booker DeWitt, who in some realities experiences a religious conversion and becomes the Prophet of Columbia. Thus—like Lady Comstock's manifestation as the Siren—all the main characters (and several supporting characters) in *BioShock Infinite* are both who they are and *not* who they are, as mutually exclusive realities converge in unexpected ways.

First-time players won't be equipped with all the information necessary to understand the interplay of these alternate realities, which only become clear after multiple playthroughs. The distorted version of the Lacrimosa, however, is an eerie sonic representation of precisely this uncertainty. Neither music nor sound effect, neither in the tomb nor out of it, the Lacrimosa inhabits the same impossible space as Lady Comstock. Moreover, unlike essentially every other example of popular or classical music in Columbia, there's no clear source for the sound (aside from possibly Lady

Comstock herself). Its lack of a visible origin—often called acousmatic sound in film studies—may be unsettling to the player, at least subconsciously. Is the music/ sound that we hear near Lady Comstock audible to the characters, as her humming would seem to imply? If so, what could be producing it? On the other hand, Booker and Elizabeth don't comment on the sound—but then they seldom draw attention to music. There is no clear answer, and thus players may interpret the music either way. It may emerge from the combination of any number of realities—including our own.

The history of the Requiem itself offers one final example of how the work becomes a sonic symbol of quantum uncertainty. It occupies a unique position in Mozart's life: he died of illness midway through its composition, leaving sections unfinished; the version we typically hear today was completed by his student Franz Xaver Süssmayr. The Requiem is thus a work that is simultaneously *by* Mozart and *not by* Mozart. But because typically Mozart is identified as the sole composer (I suspect tickets for the Süssmayr Requiem would not sell quite so well), it is also a work written both while its composer was alive and after he had died. This macabre and pseudo-paradoxical history echoes its use in *BioShock Infinite*, corresponding to Lady Comstock's commingling of life and death and creating parallels with the game's numerous other mutually exclusive realities.

BioShock Infinite focuses on creating a complex and compelling narrative centered on the relationship between Elizabeth and Booker. Yet it also touches on a wide range of social and philosophical issues, from class and race relations to the fundamental nature of our universe. As with previous *BioShock* games, carefully selected and placed music plays several important roles, but whereas this music in the first two games served largely to establish setting and comment on the on-screen action, in *Infinite* it takes on additional—and occasionally contradictory—functions as well. In addition to its sly commentary on the game's narrative, here music also ties into the metaphysical concerns of quantum mechanics in various ways. Anachronistic popular music creates cognitive dissonance for the player by simultaneously reinforcing and destabilizing the game's Gilded Age setting, while the repeated use of Mozart's Requiem at key points subtly raises existential concerns of life and (un)death. In doing so, *BioShock Infinite* further expands the musical trends established in the first two games and continues to explore how music can contribute to the artistic development of video games.

4　Allusions of Grandeur

IN DISCUSSION OF video games and art, one question is virtually guaranteed to trigger eye rolls from game critics and scholars: "When will video games have their *Citizen Kane*?" Ad nauseam repetition has long ago relegated the issue to cliché and parody, but it illustrates a set of stubbornly persistent artistic values.[1] For one thing, the question reinforces the position of Orson Welles's 1941 film as the apex of cinematic "great art"—the masterpiece that indisputably proved the artistic bona fides of the medium. Claiming games haven't found their *Citizen Kane* is a way of suggesting that they aren't yet worthy of being considered art, which is of course a central concern of this book. Specifically for this chapter, however, the *Citizen Kane* trope exposes the balance of artistic power in the relationship between film and games.

Even outside the realm of so-called art films, cinema enjoys a kind of cultural capital that games currently don't possess—and certainly didn't in prior decades. Films, and to a lesser degree television, are understood to be serious business; for the most part, games just aren't. And so, to bridge this value gap, games routinely borrow from film in a variety of ways. Most obviously, for decades there have

---

[1] For a representative, if unusually well-thought-out, example of the "*Citizen Kane* trope," see Mikel Reparaz, "The Citizen Kanes of Videogames," *GamesRadar* (July 24, 2009), available online at http://www.gamesradar.com/the-citizen-kanes-of-videogames/ (accessed August 1, 2016). As of my writing, there is a very amusing Tumblr account entitled "The Citizen Kane of Video Games," which aggregates the many times game critics (and similar authors) fall back on the cliché. Available online at http://thecitizenkaneofvideogames.tumblr.com/ (accessed August 1, 2016).

been games based on well-known film franchises, as a way of allowing players to experience their favorite movies interactively.[2] Many other games seek to capture this same feel for players by tapping into cinematic styles. As game designer Cliff Bleszinski wrote in the introduction to the instruction manual for *Gears of War 2* (2008): "This video game . . . was designed around the idea of cinematic action. We wanted the gameplay experience to feel like a summer blockbuster where you, the gamer, are the star."

Many different audiovisual elements can contribute to creating a cinematic feeling for players, as designers emulate how movies look and sound. The laserdisc-based arcade classic *Dragon's Lair* (1983), for example, was notable mostly because its advanced graphics looked like an animated film. The introduction of CD gaming in the 1990s prompted a brief era of games that heavily employed full-motion video (FMV) sequences complete with live actors. Among the most successful of those were the space dogfighting games *Wing Commander III: Heart of the Tiger* (1994) and *Wing Commander IV: The Price of Freedom* (1996), which lured sci-fi fans by casting well-known genre actors like Mark Hamill and Malcolm McDowell.[3]

Even in games not featuring live actors, however, developers often take great pains to recreate cinematic experiences. That simulation takes a variety of forms. Some games, such as the *Mass Effect* series, offer players the option to turn on a film grain filter to make the experience feel more like watching a movie. Others employ more specific types of borrowing to emulate certain film genres, such as the Western-influenced camera angles and shots in *Red Dead Redemption* (2010), or the option to play the noir-styled game *L.A. Noire* (2011) in black and white. Cutscenes—noninteractive scripted moments in games—are even frequently referred to as cinematics, in reference to their filmlike qualities. Sound also plays a major role in how games reference film. Developers pay well-known film and television actors to lend their voices (and sometimes their likenesses) to games, for example. Geek icons Patrick Stewart and Sean Bean both voiced characters in *The Elder Scrolls IV: Oblivion* (2006), while Seth Green, Martin Sheen, and Carrie-Anne Moss lent voices to the original *Mass Effect* trilogy (2007–2012). Music plays a large role, as well. Hollywood film composers such as Hans Zimmer, Harry Gregson-Williams, and Danny Elfman, to name a few, have each contributed to video game soundtracks.

---

[2] On the relationship between films and licensed game spin-offs, see, for example, Robert Alan Brookey's study *Hollywood Gamers: Digital Convergence in the Film and Video Game Industries* (Bloomington: Indiana University Press, 2010).

[3] FMV games have made something of a recent resurgence, with the most notable example being the critically lauded independent title *Her Story* (2015).

These are ways in which games refer back to film in general. On occasion, however, game designers may use these techniques to allude to a specific film—whether as a form of homage or parody, or just to draw connections between the two products. Casting the lead actor from the original *Star Wars* trilogy in the space opera *Wing Commander* series, for instance, was no accident—the games' creators hoped to capitalize on the nostalgia and positive associations players felt toward the films. Music can serve much the same function. Alluding to music from a specific film or television program in the context of a game can easily call that source to mind, even when the music originated someplace else. For example, I can't hear the overture to Gioachino Rossini's opera *Guillaume Tell* (1829) without thinking of the television program *The Lone Ranger* (1949–1957), even though I've never seen a single episode of the show. Mozart's Piano Concerto No. 21 in C Major, K. 467 (1785) is now commonly called the *Elvira Madigan* concerto because it was used prominently in the 1967 Swedish film of that name. "Ride of the Valkyries" from Richard Wagner's opera *Die Walküre* (1856) is virtually inextricable from the chilling helicopter scene from *Apocalypse Now* (1979). And so on.

When a game uses a musical work that's closely associated with a different media product—most commonly a film or film series—players receive multiple levels of signification. The original and new sources engage in a kind of dialogue—what the musicologist Melanie Lowe describes as "the additive process of signification and resignification."[4] Much like hiring famous voice actors or replicating cinematic special effects, the point here is to capitalize on players' positive experiences with valued entertainment forms that are meaningful to them.[5] In other words, some of the cultural capital of the film transfers over to the game. Classical music does double duty in this case, because it also transfers some of *its* prestige. Thus, by using classical music associated with particular films, games can get a double boost, plus the game designers stand a better chance of connecting with the player's own experiences by appealing to players' musical and cinematic knowledge frames of reference.

---

[4] Melanie Lowe, "Claiming Amadeus: Classical Feedback in American Media," *American Music* 20 (2002): 104.

[5] Ironically, of course, classical music has been a way of imbuing film with cultural value at a time when that genre was generally regarded in a less exalted light. I am not the first to identify the combination of the "low art" of media with classical music as a point of tension. In his discussion of the uses of pre-existing classical music in Stanley Kubrick's classic horror film *The Shining* (1980), film music scholar K. J. Donnelly notes the contrast between the perceived cultural values of the music and the film. Donnelly explains that some might understand its musical choices as "subordinating what some may see as 'great art' to the leviathan of popular culture." Furthermore, he continues, "There is an apparent contradiction between the low status that traditionally has been accorded to film music and the status of sublime high art, as the apogee of western culture." K. J. Donnelly, *The Spectre of Sound: Music in Film and Television* (London: BFI, 2005), 41, 42.

An example might be helpful to explain precisely what I mean. As mentioned earlier, one of the best-known instances of classical music in film is Wagner's "Ride of the Valkyries" during a helicopter strike in Francis Ford Coppola's film *Apocalypse Now*.[6] This remarkable scene has inspired a number of video game allusions, most frequently in games associated with helicopters. The trend seems to have begun a mere seven years after the film, with the helicopter-combat simulator *Gunship* (1986). "Ride of the Valkyries" features prominently as the game's title screen music—and, in fact, as the only music in the game. This placement reappeared almost a decade later in the Super Nintendo helicopter-combat game *Air Cavalry* (1995), which also used "Ride of the Valkyries" for its title screen music. The same year saw the release of the 3DO game *Return Fire* (later rereleased on the Sony PlayStation), which allowed players to choose whether to control a helicopter, a jeep, or a tank. Depending on that choice, the soundtrack would be a CD-quality recording of a classical work—and, of course, the choice for the helicopter is "Ride of the Valkyries."

More recent games have taken a slightly subtler approach, but they still connect the helicopter action to Coppola's film. In *Far Cry 3* (2012), the "Ride" plays during a helicopter escape; in *Battlefield 4* (2013) during a portion where the player (in a helicopter) attacks targets in the jungle; and in *Metal Gear Solid V: Ground Zeroes* (2014), players hear the "Ride" on the main character's Walkman while he sneaks around a helicopter. This list is far from complete, but hopefully it conveys some sense of how frequently games make these types of musical references to *Apocalypse Now*. At a certain point, however, the allusion becomes recursive. Were the makers of *Air Cavalry* alluding to Wagner's opera, to *Apocalypse Now*, or to *Gunship* (or none of them, or all of them)? What about *Metal Gear Solid V*? That reference could be to any or all of the preceding examples, and individual players could make entirely different sets of connections than the designers intended.

The rest of this chapter explores a few instances of these complex intertextual webs that form between games and other media. In the first instance, I look at how the classical compilation score—a musical soundtrack made up entirely of classical works—made the transition from early cinema to video games. I then turn to two examples of games that draw upon music and imagery from specific films, with remarkably different results.

---

[6] *Apocalypse Now* is of course not the only film to employ "Ride of the Valkyries." As Lowe points out, for example, this music also features prominently in sources as diverse as D. W. Griffith's *Birth of a Nation* (1915) and the Bugs Bunny animated short *What's Opera, Doc?* (1957). Lowe, "Claiming Amadeus," 103–104.

Compiling Codes

Compilation scores have been part of cinema from its earliest days and have persisted into the present in a variety of forms.[7] On an aesthetic level, using familiar music allowed early film musicians to quickly and effectively communicate essential information to the audience. Practically speaking, compilation soundtracks were necessary when time and finances precluded other options. For instance, films were often produced quite rapidly, and composers had insufficient time (or financial incentive) to create hours of original music. Using classical music skirted these issues while lending an "artistic" element to the cinema experience; by the 1920s, many theaters featured full orchestras, and showings often began with classical overtures.[8]

The musicologist Neil Lerner has convincingly demonstrated connections between early cinema practices and early video games with compilation scores—in this case soundtracks composed of snippets drawn from a variety of sources, including classical music and folk songs. This technique was common in the late 1970s and early 1980s, with compilation scores found in arcade games like *Crazy Climber* (1980), *Kangaroo* (1982), and *Crystal Castles* (1983).[9] From an economic standpoint, this choice makes perfect sense. Using music from the public domain allowed game designers to avoid either paying composers to create new works or paying the hefty fees required to license contemporary popular music.[10]

Maniac Miner (1983), initially released on the ZX Spectrum (a UK-based home computer), offers an early example of this classical compilation approach on a home computer. Or rather, it does so if the incessant repetition of the eight-measure melody of Edvard Grieg's "In the Hall of the Mountain King" (1876) counts as a compilation. As mind-numbing as it might be to hear the tune stuck on replay, the choice makes sense given the game's setting in an underground cavern, evoking

---

[7] On compilation practices in early film, see, for example, Rick Altman, *Silent Film Sound* (New York: Columbia University Press, 2004); Martin Miller Marks, *Music in Silent Film: Contexts and Case Studies, 1895–1924* (Oxford: Oxford University Press, 1997); and Michael Slowik, *After the Silents: Hollywood Film Music in the Early Sound Era, 1926–1934* (New York: Columbia University Press, 2014).

[8] For an enlightening contemporary description of these practices, see, for example, Erno Rapée's *Encyclopedia of Music for Pictures* (1925), the relevant portions of which are reproduced with helpful contextual information in Julie Hubbert, ed., *Celluloid Symphonies: Texts and Contexts in Film Music History* (Berkeley: University of California Press, 2011), 84–96.

[9] See Neil Lerner, "The Origins of Musical Style in Video Games, 1977–1983," in *The Oxford Handbook of Film Music Studies*, ed. David Neumeyer (Oxford: Oxford University Press, 2014), 319–347; and Lerner, "Mario's Dynamic Leaps: Musical Innovations (and the Specter of Early Cinema) in *Donkey Kong* and *Super Mario Bros.*," in *Music in Video Games: Studying Play*, ed. K. J. Donnelly, William Gibbons, and Neil Lerner (New York: Routledge, 2014), 1–29.

[10] On the other hand, a number of early games simply ignored copyright rules and recreated popular music anyway, likely assuming (for the most part correctly) that the music industry would remain unaware.

the cavern-dwelling trolls depicted in the music.[11] In *Jet Set Willy* (1984), *Maniac Miner*'s sequel, players explore Willy's new mansion, purchased with the proceeds of the previous game's mining adventures. I'm aware of two version of the game: the original release on the ZX Spectrum and a later release for the Commodore 64. In both cases *Jet Set Willy* follows *Maniac Miner*'s model in using classical music, though mercifully the game includes more than one piece. Both versions feature the opening measures of Beethoven's "Moonlight" piano sonata on the title screen, but they differ significantly once the game begins. The Spectrum release features both "In the Hall of the Mountain King" and the song "If I Were a Rich Man," from the Broadway musical *Fiddler on the Roof* (1964)—an obvious allusion to Willy's newfound wealth. Perhaps fearing copyright issues with "If I Were a Rich Man," the Commodore 64 version instead features J. S. Bach's Invention in C Major, BWV 772 (1720–1723), likely a last-minute substitution, given that the piece has no apparent relevance.

This lack of connection between music and images occurs in several low-budget games of the late 1980s and early 1990s. The NES version of the action game *Captain Comic* (1989, original released in 1988) is a case in point. Its soundtrack consists entirely of classical tunes, shortened into thirty-second loops and repeated over each level, with seemingly little consideration of aligning music to image.[12] (One possible exception would be the use of Johann Strauss Jr.'s *Blue Danube Waltz* in an outer-space level, which suggests the film *2001: A Space Odyssey* (1968)—more on which in the next chapter.) The music in *Captain Comic* runs the gamut from well-known works like Mozart's "Ronda alla Turca" (ca. 1783) or Nikolai Rimsky-Korsakov's "Flight of the Bumblebee" (1900) to obscure keyboard works by Handel or W. F. Bach (which, it turns out, were probably chosen by virtue of being in the same collection of easy piano music).[13] Even worse than the seeming randomness, however, are the wrong notes. In multiple cases the programmer made errors or misread the music, with occasionally cringe-worthy results. Here the soundtrack indicates a familiarity with the *concept* of the compilation score as a way of saving time and money but not with its cinematic functions as signifier of emotion or narrative reference point.[14]

---

[11] Interestingly, Grieg's *Peer Gynt* music—in this case multiple movements—also provides the soundtrack for the game *Mountain King* (1983), another straightforward allusion to the title. It seems unlikely that the similarity of *Mountain King* and *Maniac Miner* is totally coincidental, but may be an intertextual reference or attempt to copy a successful model.

[12] On music in *Captain Comic*, see my article "Blip, Bloop, Bach? Some Uses of Classical Music on the Nintendo Entertainment System," *Music and the Moving Image* 2, no. 1 (2009): 40–52.

[13] See Gibbons, "Blip, Bloop, Bach?"

[14] The 1993 MS-DOS platformer *Heroes: The Sanguine Seven*, created entirely by Jeffrey Fullerton, employed a compilation score in much the same way, though with perhaps a bit more finesse in the execution (fewer

TABLE 4.1

Selected classical compilation scores in games, 1983–2011 (asterisks indicate that the game also includes a small number of original cues)

Title	Date of Release
Maniac Miner	1983
Jet Set Willy (*Maniac Miner 2*)	1984
Mountain King	1984
Captain Comic (NES version)	1988
Fantasia	1991
Heroes: The Sanguine Seven	1993
Return Fire	1995
Asterix and the Power of the Gods	1995
Versailles 1685	1997
Wargasm	1998
Versailles II: Testament of the King	2001
Civilization IV *	2005
Little King's Story	2009
Stacking *	2011

Though less common after the 1980s, entirely classical compilation scores continue to appear in games for a variety of reasons (see Table 4.1 for a partial list). Recall, for example, the extensive use of French baroque music in *Versailles 1685* and its sequel (see chapter 2) to create a sense of time and place. In other circumstances, recent games have turned to classical compilation scores for intriguing artistic reasons. Allow me to offer two fairly contrasting examples. The 2009 Wii game *Little King's Story* is a cartoonish strategy game aimed mostly at younger players. As with many strategy games, which lend themselves to repeated playthroughs, the amount of music in the game is extensive, consisting of more than sixty (!) lighthearted arrangements of classical works.[15] Some pieces suggest their role in the game by their titles: the Dies Irae from Mozart's Requiem (1791) triggers at the king's death; Chopin's "Military" Polonaise, Op. 40, No. 1, as an enemy in the game plots world domination; and the drinking song from Verdi's opera *La Traviata* during a festival, to name three examples. More often, however, the tracks seem to be chosen for

---

wrong notes, for example). More interestingly, Fullerton lists the composers in the game's opening credits—a choice that was at the time unusual.

[15] A more-or-less complete listing of the works arranged in *Little King's Story* is available online at http://littlekingsstory.wikia.com/wiki/Music (accessed July 29, 2016).

their musical qualities, tapping into shared musical codes developed in the concert hall, opera house, and, later, the movie theater—much the same way that silent-film musicians learned to do.

If connecting *Little King Story* to early cinema practices feels a bit tenuous, it's indisputable in the playful adventure game *Stacking* (2011), which takes place in a whimsical, vaguely turn-of-the-century fantasy world populated by living matryoshka dolls (Russian stacking dolls). Its aesthetic borrows heavily from the musical and visual language of early film; conversations take place on title cards rather than through spoken dialogue, and the game's cutscenes are conveyed through what appear to be staged dioramas, or perhaps sets. (A particularly self-aware part of the game involves navigating a silent-film set.) Some of the sepia-toned cutscenes even feature the clicking sounds of a film camera—a tongue-in-cheek way of transforming cinematics into cinema. The game's soundtrack is crafted in much the same way. The vast majority of musical selections in the game are nineteenth-century classical works, in live recordings rather than synthesized performances. Frédéric Chopin's music dominates—the Mazurka in B-flat Major, Op. 7, No. 1 (1830–1832) serves as a kind of theme for the main character—but there are also significant works by Niccolò Paganini, Johannes Brahms, Felix Mendelssohn, Pyotr Tchaikovsky, and others. Intriguingly, the Chopin piano works are often rearranged in some way—shortened, lengthened, or recomposed to fit the needs of the scene. While relatively uncommon in games since the introduction of CD audio in the 1990s, adapting classical works is highly reminiscent of early film practices, where major alterations were the norm.[16]

Among the most interesting musical moments in *Stacking* is the introductory cutscene. Composed by Peter McConnell for piano and cello, the cleverly written score evokes a sense of improvising silent-film musicians. Rapid-fire allusions to classical works fly by almost too quickly to identify, as the music shifts in response to the melodramatic narrative unfolding on-screen. The result is a score that foreshadows the classical compilation soundtrack, while also reinforcing that game's relationship to musical traditions of early cinema. Like most of the examples in this section, *Stacking* aligns itself with cinema in search of a real or imagined shared heritage, imbuing games with a sense of history and gravitas that they might not possess on their own. This trend continues in the games described in the following sections, but in far narrower fashion. Instead of using classical works to

[16] William Ayers has explored this aspect of *Stacking* in his "Recomposition of Chopin and Narrative Design in Double Fine's *Stacking*" (paper presented at the North American Conference on Video Game Music, Youngstown State University, January 17–18, 2014). I am grateful to Ayers for sharing this unpublished research with me.

connect to a general cinematic style, these games use music to allude to a specific high-profile film.

Classical Mouse-terworks

Few films are more closely associated with classical music than Disney's *Fantasia* (1940). As Daniel Goldmark suggests in his book *Tunes for Toons: Music and the Hollywood Cartoon*, *Fantasia* remains both "probably the most ambitious attempt in the history of film (animated or otherwise) to integrate classical music into the medium" and an example of "how one studio used animation to glorify classical music, instead of seeking to tear it down."[17] Each of the film's scenes merged a classical orchestral work—recorded in new performances by conductor Leopold Stokowski, a household name at the time—with new animated interpretations. Aside from its pure entertainment value, the film had two goals: educating young audiences about classical music, and using these works' cultural cachet to elevate animation to a loftier artistic level. Disney's experiment in blending symphonic music with animation initially met with a mixed reception. Many critics of the time found it simply inappropriate to cheapen great classical music by association with lowly cartoons. To quote Goldmark again, Disney's "aim proved difficult to achieve, as animation, no matter how lofty its high-art aesthetic aspirations, was never seen by the public as anything but pop culture."[18] It fared little better with fans of cartoons, many of whom were put off by *Fantasia*'s length and overtly artistic tone. Yet somehow, in the decades since its theatrical release, Disney's experiment in music appreciation has become a cultural touchstone, a source of enduring enjoyment and education for generations.

Video games based on Disney films have been common since the early 1980s, but considering its unique format, *Fantasia* seems an unlikely choice for that kind of multimedia collaboration. Thanks to its cultural ubiquity, however, some or all of it has been recreated in at least eight games since 1983—possibly more than any other Disney film (Table 4.2). To a greater or lesser extent, each of those games depends on players' existing knowledge of *Fantasia*. And since the visual and musical aspects of the film are virtually inseparable, effectively incorporating classical music usually becomes an essential part of the games. In most video games featuring classical music, the designers had at least some choice as to which works to include. In the

---

[17] Daniel Goldmark, *Tunes for Toons: Music and the Hollywood Cartoon* (Berkeley: University of California Press, 2005), 127–128.

[18] Goldmark, *Tunes for Toons*, 130.

TABLE 4.2

Disney's *Fantasia* in video games, 1983–present

Title	Date of Release
Sorcerer's Apprentice	1983
Fantasia	1991
Kingdom Hearts	2002
Epic Mickey	2010
Kingdom Hearts 3D: Dream Drop Distance	2012
Epic Mickey 2: The Power of Two	2012
Disney Infinity	2013–2016 (online game)
Fantasia: Music Evolved	2014

case of *Fantasia* games, however, many of those decisions are made already, meaning that designers' choices instead become more about *how* to include the music. Most of the more recent games in this list—those in the *Kingdom Hearts* and *Epic Mickey* franchises—treat *Fantasia* as one of a number of Disney worlds to which the player travels. In those cases, the classical music serves as a sonic reminder of the film, the same way the games include music from other Disney properties (*Snow White*, *Sleeping Beauty*, etc.). More interesting for my purposes are two relatively early games that attempted to adapt *Fantasia* into a traditional narrative game: the Atari 2600 title *Sorcerer's Apprentice* (1983) and the Sega Genesis platformer *Fantasia* (1991).

Both games are loosely based on what is perhaps *Fantasia*'s best-known segment: "The Sorcerer's Apprentice." Or, to be precise, they are games based on an animated film that was based on a symphonic work that was based on a poem. In the film, Mickey Mouse—bedecked in wizard's cap and robes—enacts a version of Johann Wolfgang von Goethe's eighteenth-century poem *Der Zauberlehrling*, the same poem the French composer Paul Dukas depicted in his tone poem *L'apprenti sorcier* (1896–1897). The story is a familiar one: left alone by his master, an apprentice magician gets bored with his assigned chores. Shirking his duties, he instead uses his powers to animate his broom, with predictably catastrophic results. Although things initially seem to be going well, the apprentice soon realizes he doesn't know the magic word to make the broom stop. Panicked, he chops the broom into ever-smaller pieces with an ax, only to find that each fragment creates a new broom. Just as disaster looms, the master sorcerer fortuitously reappears, returning things to normal and chastising his overly ambitious apprentice.

The first game interpretation of this *Fantasia* scene, *Sorcerer's Apprentice* (Figure 4.1), was the only title to emerge from a partnership between Disney and Atari. That sort-lived deal aimed at creating a series of children's games that would be both

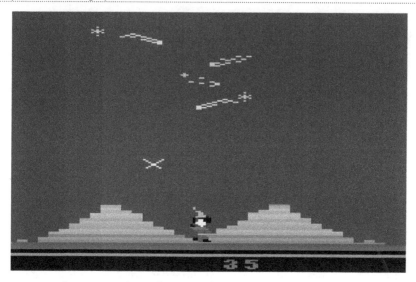

FIGURE 4.1 Mickey Mouse in *Sorcerer's Apprentice* (1983).

entertaining and in some way educational. Yet in *Sorcerer's Apprentice* the central focus was apparently capitalizing on young players'—and their parents'—nostalgic fondness for *Fantasia*. In keeping with trends in early film-to-game adaptations, the original story is almost unrecognizable. Apprentice Mickey shoots fireballs into the sky to prevent stars and meteors from reaching the ground, at which point they transform, for some reason, into water-carrying brooms. If enough of them get past his defenses, the brooms flood the sorcerer's basement, ending the game. From a game-design perspective, the goal here was replicating memorable symbols from the film—Apprentice Mickey and his living brooms—rather than narrative fidelity. In the words of game scholar Jessica Aldred, "Well-known, iconographic characters that could be readily translated from film to game were crucial to [the] early period of movie-game convergence, since, in theory at least, these figures were typically the easiest way to tap into preexisting brand awareness and set new titles apart."[19] In other words, *Sorcerer's Apprentice* attempts to create a quasi-cinematic experience by encouraging players to project their knowledge of *Fantasia* onto the game.

Music performs a similar role in *Sorcerer's Apprentice*. Because the game's narrative differs so greatly from the original story—and because it lacks the lavish visuals

---

[19] Jessica Aldred, "A Question of Character: Transmediation, Abstraction, and Identification in Early Games Licensed from Movies," in *Before the Crash: Early Video Game History*, ed. Mark J. P. Wolf (Detroit: Wayne State University Press, 2012), 94. This effect was not, of course, limited to early games. See, for example, Mark Rowell Wallin, "Myths, Monsters and Markets: Ethos, Identification, and the Video Game Adaptations of *The Lord of the Rings*," *Game Studies* 7, no. 1 (2007), available online at http://gamestudies.org/0701070l/articles/wallin/.

of Disney's animation—sound is central to bridging the gap between *Fantasia* and *Sorcerer's Apprentice*. To do so, the Atari game needed to evoke the soundscape of the 1940 film, which meant somehow recreating a nine-minute work for a large orchestra. At the risk of understatement, the Atari 2600 was not well-suited to that task. Its audio hardware was capable of playing only one sound at a time, including sound effects. Not only could there be no harmony at all—and the rich harmonies of Dukas's music are central to its appeal—but the music had to drop out whenever a sound effect played. As if that wasn't enough obstacles, the memory available for music on the 2600 was so limited that only a short snippet would be possible. All these limitations meant that a lengthy and complex orchestral work had to be distilled into a few seconds of melody.

Somewhat like *Maniac Miner*'s unfortunate use of "In the Hall of the Mountain King," the solution was to focus exclusively on the central melody of Dukas's piece—an orchestral earworm if ever there was one. In both the orchestral work and Disney's film, that main theme symbolizes the brooms; it first appears (in the bassoons) when the apprentice brings the broom to life, and gradually increases in volume and urgency throughout the piece. *Sorcerer's Apprentice* begins with a shortened, four-second statement of the theme, after which it appears in short one- or two-second bursts to let players know a broom has delivered a bucket of water.[20] Dukas's music thus serves two important functions. On the one hand, it arms the connection between the musical theme and the brooms, connecting *Sorcerer's Apprentice* to *Fantasia* (and the original tone poem, for that matter). On the other hand, the music also becomes part of the gameplay, letting players know where they need to direct their attention.

Despite the music's importance to both *Fantasia* and *Sorcerer's Apprentice*, however, nothing in the game or its manual gives any information about Dukas or his music. The theme is described only as the "Sorcerer's Apprentice tune," which suggests that players were meant to associate the music with Disney's film rather than with classical music—some might even argue that the music in *Sorcerer's Apprentice* isn't classical at all. In fact, so far removed is the music from its original orchestral form and function, we might even understand this cue as a sound effect rather than as music. More fruitfully, perhaps, we might consider the tune's role in *Sorcerer's Apprentice* not as music per se but as an abstracted symbol—a memory trigger that invokes *L'apprenti sorcier* without trying to replicate it. Players' experiences fill in the gaps, they same way players understand the abstracted collection of pixels as a symbol

---

[20] The game manual even includes a "Sound Guide" to make sure players know the meanings of the various sounds, including what it labels the "Sorcerer's Apprentice tune."

of Apprentice Mickey from the film.[21] Not surprisingly, *Sorcerer's Apprentice* failed to live up to expectations. This kind of musical abstraction asks a lot of players—perhaps too much, in this case. It would be almost a decade before game technology and culture advanced to the point where developers felt comfortable attempting a *Fantasia* video game.

Fantasia's fiftieth anniversary in 1991 saw a massive celebration of the film, a marketing push that included a major theatrical rerelease with restored audio and visual elements. The Sega Genesis game *Fantasia* was an important part of that celebration—another effort at bringing the title to a younger, game-obsessed demographic. Although the Genesis *Fantasia* game shares with its predecessor a new plot that focuses on the adventures of Apprentice Mickey, here classical music plays a much greater role. In fact, the music is the whole point. The game's backstory is revealed by an introductory poem (a nod, perhaps, to Goethe's original text), accompanied by the ominous opening notes of J. S. Bach's Toccata and Fugue in D Minor. "While the Apprentice Sorcerer slept," the game tells players, "his master's music was stolen away. / Now his dreams must restore the notes / so the music again can play." This focus on music was made possible by the relatively advanced sound hardware of the Genesis, which Sega often touted as superior to that of its primary competitor, the Super Nintendo Entertainment System. I suspect the choice to make a Genesis *Fantasia* game was in part a way to highlight the system's audio capabilities.[22] One advertisement for the game, for example, opened with "No wonder Mickey Mouse has such big eyes and ears. Considering the vivid 16-bit graphics and crisp stereo sound of his Sega Genesis video games, Mickey is built just right" (Figure 4.2).

Evoking the original film, the silhouette of an orchestra, accompanied by a digital emulation of the sound of tuning instruments, introduces each of the game's four main worlds.[23] Those choices immediately draw the player's attention to the music, and with good reason. Far from the short melodic outbursts of *Sorcerer's Apprentice*, the Genesis's hardware allowed for synthesized digital instruments that by and large stay reasonably close to the original orchestration—an impressive technological achievement for the time. And while the 1983 game had featured only one musical selection, most of the music from the film appears in the 1991 *Fantasia* in one form or another. Each hub world recreates one of the segments from the original film, as well as several side levels that offer briefer glimpses into additional scenes. Each of

---

[21] On this kind of visual abstraction in early transmedia games, see Aldred, "A Question of Character."

[22] In chapter 6, I make a similar argument regarding the use of Bach's Toccata and Fugue in D Minor in the 1980s arcade shooter *Gyruss*, which similarly featured advanced hardware for the time.

[23] The four "hub worlds" are based (in order) on *The Sorcerer's Apprentice*, Igor Stravinsky's *Rite of Spring* (1913), Beethoven's "Pastoral" Symphony (1808), and Mussorgsky's *Night on Bald Mountain* (1867).

No wonder Mickey Mouse has such big eyes and ears.

Considering the vivid 16-bit graphics and crisp stereo sound of his Sega™ Genesis™ video games, Mickey is built just right.

Journey with him to magnificent lands as he tries frantically to save Minnie from the evil Witch Mizrabel in The Castle of Illusion.

Or venture into Sega's newest Disney adventure, Fantasia. Based on the actual movie, this game follows Mickey on his quest to become an almighty sorcerer.

So if you really like Mickey Mouse, and who doesn't, check out the Disney products for Sega Genesis. You won't believe your eyes. Or your ears.

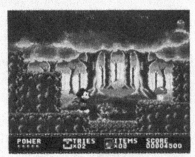
Castle Of Illusion

Fantasia

WARNING:
Genesis is far too graphic for tender young minds.

Sega and Genesis are trademarks of Sega of America Inc. The Castle of Illusion Starring Mickey Mouse and Fantasia are copyrights of The Walt Disney Company. ©1991 Sega of America, Inc. P.O. Box 2167, South San Francisco, CA 94060

FIGURE 4.2 Advertisement for *Fantasia* (1991).

these levels features the associated music from the Disney film. In all cases, the music is arranged into long repeating loops—often in excess of one minute. That length was uncommon for the time and would undoubtedly have required a substantial amount of dedicated memory and programming effort. And because the fast-paced action means players switch rapidly between levels, many players might never stay in one place long enough to reach the end of the loop—creating the illusion that the game contains even more music than it actually does.[24]

The Atari 2600 *Sorcerer's Apprentice* and the Genesis *Fantasia* share a number of similarities. Both focus on allowing players to interactively engage with the Disney film, and both feature classical music to help create that transmedia experience. Yet the two titles illustrate strikingly divergent approaches to incorporating music into the gameplay experience. The earlier game employs a heavily abstracted model, using the bare bones of a classical work as a sonic signifier of the original source. Sega's version, however, focuses on representing as much of the music as possible, in as much detail as possible. Neither attempt at translating *Fantasia* into a game was particularly successful.

In subsequent years, Disney and game developers alike seem to have realized that replicating the musical and cinematic experience of *Fantasia* in a narrative game is a difficult, if not impossible, task.[25] The success of any *Fantasia* game is dependent on its use of music, but unlike film, games as a medium are generally ill-suited to replicating lengthy classical works. In their eagerness to tap into the universal familiarity of Disney's beloved film, these early game developers underestimated the challenges of using classical music in a way that players find meaningful. Imitating the film, in other words, is not necessarily the same thing as capturing its essence. Like the sorcerer's apprentice, these games bring *Fantasia* to life but without truly understanding the limits of their own power to recreate what animates (pardon the pun) the original. My next example, by contrast, explores a much subtler, and more ambiguous, use of cinematic classical music.

Lives Out of Balance

Despite its impressive attention to detail and clever uses of music, the violent sandbox world of the *Grand Theft Auto* series has just never clicked with me. But the first

---

[24] To my knowledge, the Genesis *Fantasia* game does, in fact, contain more music from the original film than any other game to date, despite the vastly increased capabilities of more recent consoles and computers.

[25] Notably, the most recent *Fantasia*-based game, the Xbox 360 Kinect game *Fantasia: Music Evolved* (2014), eschews narrative almost entirely—save for setting up the premise that the player is the sorcerer's new apprentice.

trailer for *GTA IV* (2008), "Things Will Be Different," caught my attention immediately. Its voice-over seemed to speak for my experiences with previous games: "I killed people, smuggled people, sold people. Perhaps here, things will be different." What I found even more intriguing, however, were the music and visuals of the trailer, which were at once brand new and strikingly familiar. What I saw and heard on the screen was in a sense several decades old, drawn from the 1982 art film *Koyaanisqatsi*. In this case, at least, advertising works: I bought *GTA IV* specifically with that trailer in mind, eager to discover what connections might exist between a critically lauded avant-garde film and a video game series known for its juvenile humor, violence, and misogyny.

Koyaanisqatsi might be a relatively unfamiliar film to general audiences, but in the years since its release it has greatly influenced filmmakers and popular culture alike.[26] The title of the film, which comes from the Hopi language, translates loosely as "life out of balance." That concept is translated on-screen by a series of wordless scenes exploring the uneasy relationship between the natural world, on the one hand, and civilization and its technology, on the other. Because *Koyaanisqatsi* has no dialogue, music assumes an unusually conspicuous role in creating the experience—a bit like *Fantasia*, in fact. In this case, however, rather than turning to preexisting works, filmmaker Godfrey Reggio collaborated with the American minimalist composer Philip Glass to produce an original score. Glass's music has continued to develop in the years following the film's initial release. In 1998, the Philip Glass Ensemble rerecorded the score with updated instrumentation and some new music, releasing the result as a stand-alone album rather than a score designed to accompany the film. In more recent years, music from *Koyaanisqatsi* has made its way onto a number of classical concerts, and the ensemble frequently performs the music in live screenings of the film (as it does with several of Glass's other film scores).

Koyaanisqatsi unfolds as a series of long scenes, each with its own pace and tone. I'm particularly interested here in two well-known scenes—"Pruit Igoe" and "The Grid"—which have gradually become reference points for a variety of media. "Pruit Igoe" refers to the Pruitt-Igoe housing projects in St. Louis, an ill-planned and poorly executed 1950s complex that became infamous for its crime and urban decay before its demolition two decades later. The "Pruit Igoe" scene in *Koyaanisqatsi* lasts about seven and a half minutes. A long tracking shot along the skyline of what appears to be a thriving city transitions to close shots of the Pruitt-Igoe projects—abandoned, dilapidated buildings surrounded by piles of garbage. The scene climaxes in the

---

[26] *Koyaanisqatsi* is the first of the so-called Qatsi trilogy, which also includes *Powaqqatsi* (1988) and the much later *Naqoyqatsi* (2002).

projects' demolition, after which the scene ends with an iconic time-lapse shot of clouds peacefully passing over the distant downtown. Although the scene resists simple interpretations, for me the implication is that close scrutiny reveals the filth and decay beneath the surface of even the most civilized spaces.

Glass's score for "Pruit Igoe" echoes the tempo of the visuals—or perhaps vice versa, since many of the film's scenes were actually cut to fit the music. It begins quietly, with simple repeating patterns over a bass drone and occasional interjections when all the strings play a unison melody. In typical Glass fashion, however, about two and a half minutes in (based on the original film recording), the music becomes much more bombastic. Repeated dissonant chords in the brass coupled with an increasingly insistent wordless (or unintelligible) choir, lead to a sense of forward momentum spiraling out of control—a trajectory that culminates with the destruction of the buildings. As the last of the buildings is destroyed in slow motion, the music resumes its initial, more contemplative tone, reflecting the final shots of the time-lapse cityscape. The musicologist Mitchell Morris has noted this time-lapse function of Glass's music throughout much of the film:

> The score . . . contributes to the film's overall sense of large temporal spans within which smaller motion that seems at once particular and de-individualized takes place. Instead of a human-sized world in which protagonists and antagonists move, or in which the documentarian presents a particular point of view, there is an impersonalized space in which aggregates of things come into being, undergo transformations, and pass out of being.[27]

The music gives viewers a sense of time on a monumental scale, illustrating the inevitability of rising and collapsing civilizations. The city itself, a stand-in for the flaws and beauty of human culture as a whole, becomes in effect the scene's only character.

"The Grid," *Koyaanisqatsi*'s longest scene and the source of its most lasting visual impact, also puts the city front and center. But in place of the monumental time from "Pruit Igoe," here the film presents modern life as frantic, monotonous, and thoroughly mechanized. Viewers are subjected to endless scenes of banal daily life, sped up into a blur—parades of cars on city streets and highways, factory machines producing Twinkies, subway escalators ferrying commuters, and so on. As Morris says, "This scene evokes the phenomenology of the assembly line, and our attendant

---

[27] Mitchell Morris, "Sight, Sound, and the Temporality of Myth Making in *Koyaanisqatsi*," in *Beyond the Soundtrack: Representing Music in Cinema*, ed. Daniel Goldmark, Lawrence Kramer, and Richard Leppert (Berkeley: University of California Press, 2007), 121.

sense of overprocessing."[28] "The Grid" links this same overprocessing with media consumption. Images of people watching television or playing video games gradually fragment into faster and faster cuts, bombarding the viewer with almost unrecognizable clips of news, commercials, sports, and more. As Rebecca M. Doran Eaton has persuasively argued, the time-lapse effect, combined with Glass's incessant and indifferent music, renders even the film's human beings into machines. "The Grid" in effect "suggests a loss of subjective experience and the dehumanization and mechanization of mankind."[29]

Yet while *Koyaanisqatsi's* cinematic and musical style has proved quite influential since the film's initial release, its anti-mechanization message has often been lost in translation. Several scholars, for example, have noted the 2006 BMW commercial "It's Only a Car," which combines Glass's "Pruit Igoe" with time-lapse highway driving footage reminiscent of "The Grid."[30] In fact, Eaton argues compellingly that Glass's music and even minimalism more broadly have become associated with machines, including automobiles. But the association is anything but negative; if the prevalence of Glass's music (or its knockoffs) in car commercials from the 1990s to the present is any indication, the clockwork-like precision of the music suggests a refined, high-quality driving experience.

The 2009 film *Watchmen* finds the same music from "Pruit Igoe" (along with "Prophecies," also from *Koyaanisqatsi*) performing a much different function. Based on the well-known 1986–1987 comic book/graphic novel, *Watchmen* is a dark superhero film. In a sense, Glass's music works here as a kind of chronological indicator—like *Koyaanisqatsi, Watchmen* depicts the ills of 1980s urban life. But it also recalls other uses of minimalism to evoke *Koyaanisqatsi's* dire warnings, represented as "madness, economic collapse, exploitation, and sci-fi disaster."[31] In *Watchmen,* Glass's music is tied to the hero, Doctor Manhattan, a nearly omnipotent being created from atomic energy. The connections between minimalism and machinery are again readily apparent. The film shows the character assembling a clock as a child, for instance, and later his Martian home resembles a clock mechanism. Yet the music also conveys the grime and decay of 1980s urban culture—a connection made most

---

[28] Morris, "Sight, Sound and the Temporality of Myth Making in *Koyaanisqatsi*," 125.

[29] Rebecca M. Doran Eaton, "Marking Minimalism: Minimal Music as a Sign of Machines and Mathematics in Multimedia," *Music and the Moving Image* 7 (2014): 7.

[30] On the similarities, including comparative images, see Eaton, "Marking Minimalism," 10–12. Eaton includes a useful table of Glass's and similar music in media on p. 13. See also Pwyll ap Siôn and Tristan Evans, "Parallel Symmetries? Exploring Relationships between Minimalist Music and Multimedia Forms," in *Sound and Music in Film and Visual Media*, ed. Graeme Harper, Ruth Doughty, and Jochen Eisentraut (New York: Continuum, 2009), 671–691.

[31] Eaton, "Marking Minimalism," 18.

manifest in the use of "Pruit Igoe" during gritty street scenes in one of the film's trailers, musically recalling the desolation from that scene in *Koyaanisqatsi*. On a larger scale, the music foreshadows *Watchmen*'s grim conclusions regarding the nature of social and cultural unrest. So, to recap: on the one hand, we have Glass's music from *Koyaanisqatsi* associated with technology, and frequently the complex machinery of automobiles. On the other, we have it associated with urban decay, a sense of failed civilization.

Grand Theft Auto IV sits at the nexus of these two competing associations. The story follows Niko Bellic, a new Eastern European immigrant to Liberty City (*GTA*'s version of New York). In search of a better life, Niko instead becomes embroiled in the underworld politics of the Russian mob. Despite his intentions to leave his past misdeeds behind him, he lies, cheats, steals, and murders his way through Liberty City's various crime families and beyond. But perhaps even more than Niko himself, Liberty City is *GTA IV*'s protagonist, as a number of critics noted upon the game's release. The *New York Times* review was typical: "The real star of the game is the city itself. It looks like New York. It sounds like New York. It feels like New York. Liberty City has been so meticulously created it almost even smells like New York. . . . [T]he game's streets and alleys ooze a stylized yet unmistakable authenticity."[32] The game's designers went to great lengths to capture that authenticity—down to meticulously recording the ethnic makeup and traffic patterns of individual neighborhoods—with the end result being a vibrant virtual city.

Music plays a major role in the *Grand Theft Auto* games, mostly by way of in-game radio stations. Those expertly curated stations help maximize players' enjoyment and immersion—always with an eye toward authenticity. Indeed, as ethnomusicologist Kiri Miller has noted with regard to *Grand Theft Auto: San Andreas* (2004), developers and players alike are keenly aware that the music plays a crucial role in creating a sense of place in these games.[33] That sense is clearly in evidence in *GTA IV*. To quote again from the *New York Times* review, the music supervisors "demonstrate a musical erudition beyond anything heard before in a video game. . . . It is not faint praise to point out that at times, simply driving around the city listening to the radio . . . can be as enjoyable as anything the game has to offer."[34] For the most part, the game's music comes from a range of popular styles, from metal to jazz to hip-hop and everything in between. But there's one glaring exception: the radio station

---

[32] Seth Schiesel, "*Grand Theft Auto* Takes On New York," *New York Times* (April 28, 2008), available online at http://www.nytimes.com/2008/04/28/arts/28auto.html (accessed July 28, 2016).

[33] Kiri Miller, *Playing Along: Digital Games, YouTube, and Virtual Performance* (Oxford: Oxford University Press, 2012).

[34] Schiesel, "*Grand Theft Auto* Takes On New York."

"The Journey." This eclectic station includes "Pruit Igoe" from *Koyaanisqatsi* alongside a portion of the landmark electronic work *A Rainbow in Curved Air* (1969) by minimalist composer Terry Riley—a major stylistic influence on Glass—as well as minimalist-influenced ambient electronic music from composers such as Jean-Michel Jarre and Steve Roach.[35]

"Pruit Igoe" also appears during *GTA IV*'s bittersweet epilogue. After the final missions, we overhear a phone call between Niko and the people close to him, depending on the player's choices in the game. This conversation reflects on the game's events and the tragedy that seems to inevitably follow in Niko's violent path. Rather than depicting Niko, these final visuals are of Liberty City itself. And like the game's first trailer, these lengthy time-lapse images of the city strongly evoke *Koyaanisqatsi*. In particular, the visuals suggest the closing of the "Pruit-Igoe" scene—the precise moments in the film where we would hear the same music—creating an unmistakable, almost ostentatious, parallel.

So what are we to make of these connections between *GTA IV* and *Koyaanisqatsi*? Although it might not be immediately obvious, the two share some thematic similarities, which are reinforced by allusions to *Koyaanisqatsi* (and minimalism more generally) in other media. I noted earlier, for example, how the film's focus on technology led to an ironic association with precision machinery, particularly automobiles. As the title suggests, cars play a significant role in *Grand Theft Auto*. Much of the player's time is spent behind the wheel of purloined vehicles, and for the most part, players have to be in a car to hear Glass's music. Players who tune in to "The Journey" can in essence live out the fantasies peddled by those car commercials, driving at will through the streets of Liberty City.

Beyond this fairly straightforward association with the fine-tuned machinery of cars, however, I also understand this music as a kind of commentary on the technology of the game itself. The radio stations of *GTA IV* each have a scripted DJ, often a kind of celebrity cameo. "Liberty Rock Radio" is hosted by Iggy Pop, the alt/indie station "Radio Broker" is hosted by Juliette Lewis, and so on. "The Journey," by contrast, is hosted by "a computer"; the script is read aloud by the AppleTalk speech synthesis voice "Vicki." The predominantly electronic, minimalist music station is presented *by* electronics—technology embodied. Notably, players also hear "The Journey" whenever they visit Internet cafes in the game, reinforcing its association with computers. On a self-referential level, the host of "The Journey" seems to understand its own fictional status, evidenced in the tongue-in-cheek breaking of the fourth wall that occurs through its narration. "Do you ever wonder who created

---

[35] A full listing of all the radio stations in *GTA IV* is available online at http://gta.wikia.com/wiki/Radio_Stations_in_GTA_IV (accessed July 24, 2016).

your character," the computer asks at one point, "and why your life is a computer simulation? Do you ever wonder who decided the rules of the game? We can only guess at the longing of the creator." The station reminds us of its own unreality—of, in fact, the unreality of everything we see and do in *GTA IV*. By doing so, it also calls to mind the advanced hardware and feats of programming underpinning this incredibly detailed virtual world, again linking minimalism with the idea of complex technology.

And yet at the game's end, these technological associations are left by the wayside. Instead, we return to the association with urban decay and rampant crime—something much closer to the actual "Pruit Igoe" scene in *Koyaanisqatsi* (or, for that matter, its use in the trailer for *Watchmen*) than it is to luxury car commercials. As in the *Koyaanisqatsi* "Pruit Igoe," here we are left to ponder the fundamental nature of the city. Despite Niko's hope that "maybe this time will be different," ultimately Liberty City's decadence and corruption shatter his illusions, calling into question whether civilization is truly civilized at all. By evoking the specter of *Koyaanisqatsi* repeatedly throughout the game, Glass's music operates on multiple levels in *GTA IV*, and much more deeply than tapping into "the joy of driving." In "The Journey," it reminds players of the game's fundamental unreality, and of the almost unfathomably complex technology that creates and animates Liberty City and its denizens. And in the epilogue, it evokes the unreality of our own world, the equally complex fantasies we collectively construct about the nature of civilization.

One final point: it is remarkable that the makers of *GTA IV* selected an avant-garde film like *Koyaanisqatsi* rather than a more mainstream choice. Previous games in the series had been deeply influenced by existing media, of course: *GTA: Vice City* was inspired by the neon lights and pastel colors scheme of 1980s Miami as depicted in the TV show *Miami Vice* (1984–1989) and the Brian De Palma film *Scarface* (1983). Likewise, *GTA: San Andreas* brought its 1990s Los Angeles analogue to life by emulating films such as *Boyz N the Hood* (1991), *Menace II Society* (1993), and *Friday* (1995).[36] While not all those films were blockbusters, they were certainly closer than Reggio and Glass's arthouse favorite, which grossed only $1.7 million at the box office. It's not even immediately clear how many of *GTA IV*'s players caught the *Koyaanisqatsi* references, as obvious as they were. But perhaps the appeal of the allusions lay at least in part with *Koyaanisqatsi*'s status as an art film. As with a number of other examples in this book, these references were one path toward capturing the

---

[36] In fact, DJ Pooh, who wrote the screenplay for *Friday*, was a co-writer for *GTA: San Andreas*. See Soraya Murray, "High Art/Low Life: The Art of Playing *Grand Theft Auto*," *PAJ: A Journal of Performance and Art* 27 (2005): 92.

cultural capital that goes hand in hand with art cinema. If games haven't yet found their *Citizen Kane*, *GTA IV* seems to say, then at least they have found their *Koyaanisqatsi*. In the next chapter, I trace this artistic borrowing further, exploring several games that pay homage to the films of a single well-known director: Stanley Kubrick.

5   A Clockwork Homage

THE *SAINT'S ROW* series of open-world crime games is built on a foundation of sheer audacity, juvenile humor, and over-the-top antics—in other words, not really my kind of video game. But when I got a free download of *Saint's Row: The Third* (2011) a few years ago, curiosity compelled me to give it a chance. In the ten or so hours I spent with it, my avatar destroyed an army of tanks with a grenade launcher while riding on the roof of a car, fraudulently collected insurance money by throwing himself into traffic, and attacked a group of gang members with a giant purple sex toy. Pretty standard for the *Saint's Row* universe, all things considered. In fact, what surprised me the most was the opening sequence. Against the backdrop of a scrolling introductory text (à la *Star Wars*), I heard some familiar music: Richard Strauss's tone poem *Also sprach Zarathustra* (1896). As a lengthy orchestral piece based on Friedrich Nietzsche's complex philosophical novel of the same title, Strauss's music seemed very much at odds with what I knew about *Saint's Row*. But, then, I imagine this musical choice probably had very little to do with Strauss *or* Nietzsche. Instead, it has more to do with *Also sprach Zarathustra*'s appearance at the opening of director Stanley Kubrick's sci-fi classic *2001: A Space Odyssey* (1968).

The pioneering and provocative director of films including *Lolita* (1962), *A Clockwork Orange* (1971), and *The Shining* (1980), Kubrick remains among the most influential and highly respected filmmakers in cinema history—and one of the most frequently imitated. For instance, films as diverse as *History of the World, Part I* (1981), *Charlie and the Chocolate Factory* (2005), and *WALL-E* (2008) have used Strauss's music to parody the opening of *2001* just as we find in *Saint's Row*. These references take on particular importance in video games, I think. Many of Kubrick's films are viewed as artistic masterpieces that elevated cult genres like sci-fi and horror to a loftier cultural status. References to his films in games often seem to take that possibility into account, perhaps as a way of elevating their own status.

Like *Saint's Row*, each of the games I examine in this chapter targets the so-called core gaming audience—players who gravitate toward big-budget action, sports, and shooter games. Despite welcome shifts in recent years, that demographic still tends to skew heavily in favor of young men.[1] Art films generally target small groups of connoisseurs, and even many classic films have limited audiences, despite their cultural capital. On the other hand, the Hollywood blockbusters that tend to appeal to the core gaming demographic often lack cultural cachet. Allusions are only as useful as they are recognizable, so this divide between audience and aspiration poses a challenge to game developers who hope to raise games' artistic status. As one of a small group of directors whose films are both critically lauded *and* popular with a core gaming audience, Kubrick presents an ideal solution.

Few, if any, directors are as closely associated with their musical choices as Kubrick. As the musicologist Kate McQuiston notes, music is "a consistent, vital force in Kubrick's imagination and an aesthetic foundation for the creation and reception of music of Kubrick's films—and famous moments within them."[2] Kubrick was among the type of director that Claudia Gorbman describes as "*Mélomanes*"—directors, such as Quentin Tarantino or Wes Anderson, who "treat music not as something to farm out to the composer or even to the music supervisor, but rather as a key thematic element and marker of authorial style."[3] Classical music in particular plays an enormous role in most of Kubrick's films, in many cases assuming as much prominence as the characters themselves. "Kubrick's deployments of pre-existing music exert a particular force," Gorbman tells us—"a tendency to assume an iconic status. . . . Welding themselves to the visual rhythms onscreen, they become the music of the specific movie scene rather than the piece one may have known before."[4] Here

---

[1] "Hardcore" gamers, the top 10 percent of the core group, skew even younger and more male-dominated. Data are somewhat difficult to come by—and definitions for terms like "core gamers" are often nebulous—but a 2015 study from the Pew Research Center is instructive in this regard. See Maeve Duggan, "Gaming and Gamers," *Pew Research Center: Internet, Science & Tech* (December 15, 2015), available online at http://www.pewinternet.org/2015/12/15/gaming-and-gamers/.

[2] Kate McQuiston, *We'll Meet Again: Musical Design in the Films of Stanley Kubrick* (Oxford: Oxford University Press, 2013), 1. For an overview of Kubrick's musical uses, see also Christine Lee Gengaro, *Listening to Stanley Kubrick: The Music in His Films* (London: Rowman and Littlefield, 2014).

[3] Claudia Gorbman, "Auteur Music," in *Beyond the Soundtrack: Representing Music in Cinema*, ed. Daniel Goldmark, Lawrence Kramer, and Richard Leppert (Berkeley: University of California Press, 2007), 149.

[4] Claudia Gorbman, "Ears Wide Open: Kubrick's Music," in *Changing Tunes: The Use of Pre-existing Music in Film*, ed. Phil Powrie and Robynn Stilwell (Burlington, VT: Ashgate, 2006), 4.

classical music loses its concert hall associations and transforms into film music—or perhaps it becomes a kind of hybrid, existing as both simultaneously. Players who find musical references to Kubrick's films are thus likely to understand them first as cinematic allusions and only secondarily as references to classical music. This close connection between particular classical works and specific film scenes allows video games (or any media) to easily call those scenes to mind—an invaluable asset, as we will see.

Classical music in Kubrick's films also often symbolizes high culture. Many of his works address art (and indeed civilization itself) as an illusory concept, or at the least one under constant attack. In a way that echoes this book's central concern with perceptions of classical music as culturally valuable and video games as trivial, Kubrick often positions "the classically refined against modern vulgarity and brutality, the ideal of order against the reality of the beast."[5] For the rest of this chapter, I explore three games in which classical music engages with this aspect of Kubrick's films, the conflict of classical music and "modern vulgarity." To greater or lesser extents, each of the three games also employs these allusions to legitimize themselves artistically by piggybacking on Kubrick's artistic legacy.

Elite Company

If the opening credits are the best-known part of *2001*, the space station docking sequence is a close second. Near the beginning of the film, a spacefaring plane arrives at a space station, famously accompanied by the sounds of Johann Strauss Jr.'s *An der schönen blauen Donau*, Op. 314 (1866)—commonly known as the *Blue Danube Waltz* (Figure 5.1). The striking ambiguity of Kubrick's musical selection has led to a wide range of critical and scholarly interpretations. Some recurring themes are the perceived irony of the music, and, relatedly, how familiarity renders even the most wondrous technologies banal. Others suggest the scene's use of music is sincere rather than ironic. These interpretations note the balletic quality of the scene's choreography, and the music's lightness (perhaps weightlessness) as reflective of the environment and on-screen action.[6] For my part, I take an all-of-the-above approach; the brilliance of Kubrick's musical selection is that it works on multiple levels simultaneously.

---

[5] Robert Philip Kolker, "Oranges, Dogs, and Ultra-violence," *Journal of Popular Film* 1 (1972): 167, 169.

[6] See, for example, McQuiston, *We'll Meet Again*, chap. 6; as well as David W. Patterson, "Music, Structure and Metaphor in Stanley Kubrick's *2001: A Space Odyssey*," *American Music* 22 (2004): 444–471.

FIGURE 5.1 The arrival at the space station in *2001: A Space Odyssey* (1968).

From a special-effects standpoint, the docking sequence astounded audiences in 1968 and remains impressive today. The science historian and journalist Piers Bizony, for instance, recalled in his book on *2001*, "I thought the orbiting station and the other ships looked so real, I could never quite believe they didn't exist."[7] Despite the lack of gravity, the scene's remarkable realism weighed heavily on the minds of Ian Bell and David Braben, the Cambridge undergraduates who created the video game *Elite* (1984). Bell and Braben set out to create a game that featured 3D space combat, a seemingly impossible goal given the limited technology available at the time. Against all odds, they succeeded. Yet the pair quickly realized that despite their technological achievements, the game quickly got old. They began adding new features, including space station docking explicitly modeled on *2001*, in which players align their ships to the station's rotation (Figure 5.2).[8] These new elements helped make *Elite* a massive success. After its humble beginnings on the BBC Micro computer system, the game was released on virtually every existing computing platform over the following seven years.

Like many BBC Micro games of the early 1980s, *Elite* originally had no music—the technology and memory restrictions simply wouldn't allow for it. Subsequent versions, however, began to include more and more sound. The 1985 Commodore 64 version of the game was, to my knowledge, the first to include a significant amount of music. There was an apparently original composition for the title sequence, and

---

[7] Piers Bizony, *2001: Filming the Future* (London: Aurum, 1994), 8. McQuiston discusses this passage with relation to the docking sequence in *We'll Meet Again*, chap. 6.

[8] Tristan Donovan, *Replay: The History of Video Games* (East Sussex, UK: Yellow Ant, 2010), 118.

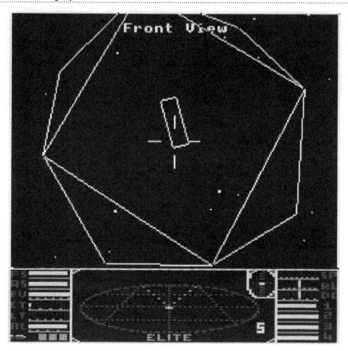

FIGURE 5.2 The space station docking sequence in *Elite* (1985 Commodore 64 version).

a piece reserved for the docking sequences: the *Blue Danube Waltz*. If the homage to *2001* wasn't clear enough previously, the music leaves no doubt whatsoever. Just as in Kubrick's film, the *Blue Danube* begins when players approach a space station and accompanies their efforts to safely dock the ship. Later versions of the game follow the Commodore 64's lead, though sometimes in slightly different ways. The only music in the 1987 IBM-compatible PC version, for example, is the melody of the *Blue Danube*, accompanying a three-dimensional model of a starship during the title screen—an image evoking the rotating station and ship in *2001*. The 1991 PC remake, *Elite Plus*, employs exactly the same technique, albeit with far enhanced sound quality.[9]

The Nintendo Entertainment System version of *Elite* was released in 1991, quite late in the console's life span. Unique among the versions I've encountered, the NES *Elite* includes a large amount of newly composed music, looped to create the wall-to-wall placement common on consoles of the time. This fast-paced, drum-heavy music

---

[9] This placement on the title screen of *Elite* rather than during the docking itself may seem a bit surprising, but the game's processors likely couldn't handle the complex graphics, sound, and music simultaneously in actual gameplay. Additionally, although the *Blue Danube* is most associated with the space station docking scene of *2001*, we may recall that it also accompanies the film's ending credits, so the idea of using the piece as a framing device as we see in the PC version of *Elite* is actually in keeping with Kubrick's own usage.

differs sharply from its predecessors—yet even here, during docking sequences the music shifts to the Strauss waltz. And the length of that loop suggests its importance. Typically, on the NES cues longer than about thirty seconds were looped to conserve resources, but the *Blue Danube* lasts almost two minutes. Evidently, the developers found its presence important enough to merit taking up a fairly large chunk of valuable memory.

There are many other versions of *Elite*, but I hope these examples suffice to illustrate the game's fundamentally allusive quality. Over and over, designers and programmers devoted time and processing power to musically recreating Kubrick's famous scene. But why? What's the purpose of this allusion, aside from a sly nod to a sci-fi classic? A number of possible explanations present themselves. Admittedly, it makes sense from a musical and technological perspective. The melody and accompaniment texture of the *Blue Danube* are well-suited for the limited audio capabilities of 1980s gaming, and the waltz's repetitive structure makes for easy looping. In fact, Kubrick himself repeats a portion of the waltz in the film, presumably for timing purposes, without creating any significant issues.[10] Yet any number of musical works could do that job just as easily, including with newly composed music.

A much grander reason for evoking *2001* was to tap into players' memories of experiencing Kubrick's film. For instance, recalling the technical accomplishments of *2001*'s special effects might be a subtle way of drawing attention to *Elite*'s own impressive graphics. Just as Kubrick's film created a startling level of realism for viewers, *Elite* gave players what was at the time an extraordinarily lifelike spacefaring experience. The game hardly compares to the visual splendor of *2001*, but by triggering players' memories, it encourages them to imagine the cinematic splendor of Kubrick's scene. The musicologist Peter Kupfer has noted how Strauss's waltz works in a slightly similar way in a 2011 Apple iPhone commercial, building on the advanced technology on display in the space station docking sequence to make the smartphone seem even more technologically impressive.[11] In other words, *Elite* enhances players' gaming experience by building on their prior knowledge.

While intertextual homages and parodies are by no means unique to games, certain types of allusion are particularly salient to the interactive nature of games as a medium. Players who project their knowledge of *2001* onto their gameplay may experience *Elite* in dramatically different ways from those who do not, and that distinction might affect how the game proceeds. Players might choose to re-enact *2001*'s docking sequence, for example, or they might simply understand their avatar's

---

[10] For an in-depth analysis of the waltz in *2001*, see McQuiston, *We'll Meet Again*, chap. 6.
[11] Peter Kupfer, "Classical Music in Television Commercials: A Social-Psychological Perspective," *Music and the Moving Image* 10 (2017): 24.

position in the universe differently—either way could radically alter how they choose to play the game. Because their actions may affect how the game unfolds, players themselves become part of the intertextuality. My next two examples both pay homage to Kubrick's *A Clockwork Orange*, a controversial film that addresses the coexistence of sublime artistry and unfathomable violence. One of the reasons Kubrick's film is both so effective and so alienating lies in how it subtly implicates viewers in the horrible acts of violence. In games, however, implication becomes action— players are both affecting and affected by the events occurring on-screen. Evoking Kubrick's film becomes a form of self-critique, encouraging players to reflect on their own actions, and perhaps on the nature and content of games as a whole.

Squirrels, Bats, and Thieving Magpies

In 1997, Rare Entertainment announced the development of a new family-friendly game for the Nintendo 64. Starring an adorable red squirrel named Conker, the game got as far as magazine previews before Rare took it in a dramatically different direction. Changing demographics and market research had made it clear that, as the average player was getting older, there was more demand for an adult-oriented title instead. Understandably hesitant to abandon all the valuable development time spent on Conker, Rare replaced the cutesy squirrel with a hard-drinking, foulmouthed doppelgänger. The resulting game, *Conker's Bad Fur Day*, was released (appropriately for this chapter) in 2001.[12] Its gameplay was highly praised, but the core appeal of *Conker's Bad Fur Day* lay in its humor—it was, especially for the time, a genuinely funny game. Part of the fun stems from watching cartoon characters behaving badly, a bit like the film *Who Framed Roger Rabbit?* (1988), for instance. But *Conker's Bad Fur Day* is also a highly intertextual game, rife with references and parodies of all kinds of popular culture, especially film. No movies were safe from Conker, from classics like *The Exorcist* (1973), *Jaws* (1975), *Raiders of the Lost Ark* (1981), and *Blue Velvet* (1986) to films that would have been new at the time, such as *The Matrix* (1999) and *Gladiator* (2000). Kubrick's films are especially well represented. At various points in the game, *Conker's Bad Fur Day* references *Full Metal Jacket* (1987), *Eyes Wide Shut* (1999), and *A Clockwork Orange*. This last parody is one of the most prominent, taking up the entire opening cutscene and establishing the game's tone.

---

[12] The game was rereleased in 2005 as *Conker: Live and Reloaded* for the Microsoft Xbox. Throughout I am specifically referring to the original 2001 version, as I have not personally investigated any possible difference in music or content between the two versions.

FIGURE 5.3 Opening shot of Alex from *A Clockwork Orange* (1971).

Film audiences first encounter Alex, the sociopathic protagonist of *A Clockwork Orange*, sitting in the Korova Milk Bar. His head tilted down, his blue eyes peer out ominously from under the brim of his bowler hat (Figure 5.3). As a voice-over from Alex provides some exposition, the camera never wavers from Alex's piercing gaze, even as it slowly pulls back to reveal the room and its other occupants. The opening of *Conker's Bad Fur Day* references this memorable scene in several ways. Conker, head tilted down, greets us with a blue-eyed stare from under his crown; he holds and drinks from a glass of milk, as Alex does in the film; he provides an expositional voice-over; and the camera gradually pulls back in precisely the same fashion (Figure 5.4). The visual similarities are obvious enough to make the homage clear—but the music makes it unmistakable. Both scenes feature a synthesized version of *Music for the Funeral of Queen Mary* (1695) by the English baroque composer Henry Purcell. Kubrick's film features Purcell's music in an electronic arrangement by Wendy Carlos, the pioneering musician best known for the album *Switched-On Bach* (1968). *Conker's Bad Fur Day* includes a different adaptation, but one clearly inspired by Carlos—an adapted synthesized version of an adapted synthesized version of the original baroque work. (I assume the choice to commission a new arrangement rather than use Carlos's music stemmed from a desire to avoid paying licensing fees.)

On one level, this parody is just another of many in-jokes scattered throughout the game, a wink at players familiar with Kubrick's film. And as a joke, it works. Conker's impossibly large eyes and cartoonish voice (think Alvin and the Chipmunks) contrast hilariously with the steely gaze and British accent of Malcolm McDowell's Alex. Digging a little deeper, there's also another joke in the choice of music—although

FIGURE 5.4 Screenshot from the opening cutscene of *Conker's Bad Fur Day* (2001).

maybe not a very good one. The opening scene of *Conker's Bad Fur Day* reveals that Conker has become the king, and the game unfolds as a flashback explaining how this remarkable turn of events occurred. Just before his ascendancy to the throne, however, his girlfriend and would-be queen, Berri, is murdered. Thus the music is, in effect, *Funeral Music for Queen Berri*, rather than Queen Mary—a bit of foreshadowing, and one among many groan-worthy puns scattered throughout the game.

Beyond those fairly straightforward associations, this opening scene also reveals the (relatively) serious undertones that lurk beneath the game's superficially comic surface. *Conker's Bad Fur Day* challenged games' reputation as kids' stuff. Despite its colorful, cartoonish appearance, it earned—and indeed reveled in—one of the few "M for Mature" ratings issued for Nintendo 64 games, which it received for "animated violence," "mature sexual themes," and "strong language."[13] Game designers and marketers knew the game would be controversial. Nintendo declined to advertise the game in its *Nintendo Power* magazine, and some toy retailers even refused to carry it, preventing children (or parents) from accidentally purchasing a copy. *Conker's* ad campaign *did*, however, involve a nationwide tour of college campuses with *Playboy* magazine, and it was featured in adult- and male-focused publications like *Maxim* magazine.[14] Everything about how *Conker's Bad Fur Day* was presented

[13] ESRB rating information for *Conker's Bad Fur Day* is available online at http://www.esrb.org/ratings/synopsis.jsp?Certificate=5327&Title=Conker%27s%20Bad%20Fur%20Day (accessed June 3, 2016).

[14] See, for example, "KB Skips *Conker*," *IGN* (March 6, 2001), available online at http://www.ign.com/articles/2001/03/07/kb-skips-conker (accessed September 1, 2016); and "Conker Goes on Tour with *Playboy*," *IGN* (March 28, 2001), available online at http://www.ign.com/articles/2001/03/29/conker-goes-on-tour-with-playboy (accessed September 1, 2016).

to potential players, in short, emphasized its adults-only character. The *Clockwork Orange* reference works in the same way, reinforcing right off the bat that this was a game created with adult players in mind.

At the same time, however, *Conker's Bad Fur Day* was a big risk for its developers. Games were (and remain) under intense scrutiny, constantly battling spurious claims that they contribute to moral decline in the younger generation. But games are certainly not the first media to endure such accusations. Upon its release, in fact, *A Clockwork Orange* was widely condemned for its extreme violence and the amorality of its central character, among other complaints.[15] Perhaps the developers hoped that by invoking *A Clockwork Orange*, they could remind players and critics of other controversial but ultimately successful media products. If *A Clockwork Orange* could do it, why not a video game? Using Purcell's *Funeral March for Queen Mary* played a part in that effort. It not only helped call to mind Kubrick's film but did so with *classical music*—a double dose of sophisticated, high-art allusions. At the same time, there's also an absurdity to juxtaposing cultural touchstones like art film and classical music with the immature antics of a deviant squirrel. In that sense, the allusion to *A Clockwork Orange* in *Conker's Bad Fur Day* is simultaneously both a parody of Kubrick's film and an homage to his clever uses of classical music.

As we've seen many times already in this book, classical music is often perceived as a force of cultural and moral uplift.[16] In *A Clockwork Orange*, however, Alex's amorality and love of classical music present the audience with a seemingly irresolvable contradiction. Kubrick subverts our understanding and appreciation of art, just as in the film Alex's affinity for Beethoven becomes a source of physical and psychological torment. *Conker's Bad Fur Day* defies these same assumptions. By parodying an art film in a video game, and by subjecting supposedly serious art music to use in a video game (and for a joke!), it challenges perceptions of who plays video games, just like *A Clockwork Orange* questions the sophistication of classical music audiences. In other words, the Kubrick reference in *Conker's Bad Fur Day* tells us something about the game, but it tells us just as much about our relationship *to* the game—and particularly about our expectations for what video games can and should be.

Conker addresses these philosophical concerns in an oblique and playfully transgressive way. My final example, however, uses classical music to deal with these

---

[15] McQuiston, *We'll Meet Again*, 163. See also David J. Code, "Don Juan in Nadsat: Kubrick's Music for *A Clockwork Orange*," *Journal of the Royal Musical Association* 139 (2014): 339–340.

[16] Code, for example, notes that this aspect of Alex's personality is central even in the Anthony Burgess novel on which Kubrick's film is based. "In addition to his enthusiasm for sex and violence, Alex maintains a passionate love of classical music, which features prominently at all three stages of his story: violence, cure and retribution." Code, "Don Juan in Nadsat," 341.

FIGURE 5.5 Alex exacts revenge on his droogs in *A Clockwork Orange*.

concerns more directly, aiming less at humorous parody than at invoking the seriousness and aesthetic aspirations of Kubrick's film. The overture to Gioachino Rossini's
opera *La gazza ladra* (*The Thieving Magpie*; 1817) makes two significant appearances in *A Clockwork Orange*. In both cases, the lighthearted standard is ironically
combined with scenes of extreme violence: once when Alex and his gang engage in a
brutal showdown with a rival gang in a derelict theater, and slightly later when Alex
lashes out after his leadership of his gang is challenged (Figure 5.5). The violence in
these scenes assumes a surreal, choreographed quality. In the first scene, the fight
feels obviously staged, befitting its theatrical setting, while the slow-motion cinematography of the second scene lends it an uncannily balletic quality.[17] The resulting
aestheticization of violence—a transformation of violence into a kind of pleasurable
visual experience—is a device found in centuries of visual arts, and more recently in
media products like the hyperviolent films of Quentin Tarantino.

This same kind of aestheticization of violence can be found in many video games,
including *Batman: Arkham Origins* (2013), which also bears several other similarities to *A Clockwork Orange*.[18] The plot of *Origins*, which follows Batman's early

---

[17] On the balletic choreography of violence (and other elements) in Kubrick's films, see, for example, Elisa
Pezzotta, "The Metaphor of Dance in Stanley Kubrick's *2001: A Space Odyssey*, *A Clockwork Orange*, and *Full
Metal Jacket*," *Journal of Adaptation in Film and Performance* 5 (2012): 51–64.

[18] *Arkham Origins* was released on the Xbox 360, PlayStation 3, and Wii U consoles. Several pieces of downloadable content were released after its initial release. Although I do not believe the expanded material altered
the musical examples discussed in this chapter in any way, for clarity's sake, note that I refer throughout this
section to the base game (i.e., without DLC).

adventures, is as complicated as the comics from which it draws inspiration. A cabal of assassins attempts to claim a large bounty on Batman's life offered by the game's initial antagonist, the crime lord Black Mask. Midway through the game, however, a shocking (?) plot twist reveals Black Mask to be another villain in disguise: the Joker. Although in *Origins*'s narrative this is Batman's first encounter with the Joker, the relationship between the two would be old hat for most players. Not even taking into account the various Batman comic books, films, and television shows, *Origins* isn't even the first video game in this series to feature the Joker as the primary antagonist. Both *Batman: Arkham Asylum* (2009) and *Batman: Arkham City* (2011), which feature a more mature Batman, already introduced and developed the Joker's character.[19] *Arkham Origins* is, in other words, tasked with introducing players to a character they almost certainly already know.

Wisely, *Arkham Origins* doesn't spend much time explaining the Joker's backstory. It does, however, take the opportunity to delve more deeply into his psychosis than did previous game—partially through the use of classical music. For the most part, the classical music in *Origins* fits comfortably within the cinematic trope of classical music-loving evil geniuses, as, for example, when classical music plays in the background of a meeting of villains.[20] Fortunately, however, *Origins* also occasionally reaches beyond the conventional. Its most intriguing use of classical music occurs in a surreal sequence that is quite unlike any other portion of the game. After the Joker is apprehended and briefly imprisoned, the focus switches to an extended conversation between the villain and his assigned therapist. Strapped to a gurney, the Joker reveals his supposed motivations, giving players some insight into his twisted psyche. The conversation begins as a noninteractive cutscene, but the analysis soon fades into a voice-over, with players' control restored. During this sequence, players control the Joker as he relives significant past moments from his distorted perspective. The most notable of these is an ultraviolent free-for-all in a comedy club—a scene underscored by Rossini's overture to *La gazza ladra*, the same work featured in those two memorably violent *Clockwork Orange* scenes. Just as in Kubrick's film, Rossini's music runs counter to the action, its joviality clashing with the brutality on screen. This type of musical irony in this scene is at odds with the straight-faced, relatively unsubtle tone of the rest of the *Arkham* series and seems intended to reflect the Joker's highly unbalanced mental state. On the other hand, perhaps there's no irony at all for the Joker. Just as *A Clockwork Orange*'s Alex sees no contradiction

---

[19] Since *Arkham Origins*, the series has returned to its original timeline, wrapping up the story with *Batman: Arkham Knight* (2015).

[20] See, for example, Thomas Fahy, "Killer Culture: Classical Music and the Art of Killing in *Silence of the Lambs* and *Se7en*," *Journal of Popular Culture* 37 (2003): 28–42.

in loving Beethoven and committing acts of wanton violence, the Joker might find Rossini's music to be a perfectly appropriate pairing for his rampage.

In fact, I believe this entire scene can be fruitfully interpreted through the lens of *A Clockwork Orange*. We might point to similarities between the Joker and Alex, for instance. Both are of course murderous, amoral psychopaths—"criminal heroes," in the sense that they are "brutal, individualistic, ambitious, and doomed," and seem to associate violence with pleasure.[21] There are also some plot similarities: both characters are imprisoned for violent crimes; both are strapped to gurneys and subjected to psychological examination; and so on. Indeed, in its overt theatricality and sense of choreography, the comedy club scene in *Arkham Origins* strongly evokes the theater gang fight in Kubrick's movie. The cinematic allusion becomes a valuable form of shorthand characterization, helping players better understand this interpretation of the Joker by associating him with someone familiar: Kubrick's Alex.

But here, crucially, players aren't just passive observers of Alex's misadventures. In *Arkham Origins, they* are the psychopaths. To advance in the game, players must use their controllers to inflict virtual violence over and over, and they presumably enjoy doing so (or else why play?). By the time players step into the Joker's shoes, they have fought their way through countless criminals and been rewarded with slow-motion, cinematic close-ups of particularly violent moments. The precisely timed button presses the game requires for combat even have an almost musical quality to them—a choreographed, rhythmic performance reminiscent of the stylized violence in *A Clockwork Orange*. By connecting with Kubrick's film, then, the Joker's surreal dream offers a kind of metacommentary on players' relationship with the game, and perhaps on the aestheticization of violence in games more broadly speaking. In the opening moments of Kubrick's film, Alex's disturbing gaze seems to make viewers somehow complicit in his deeds. *Arkham Origins* goes a step further, alluding to *A Clockwork Orange* as a way of encouraging players to reflect on their own actions—forcing them to question whether they're really so different from Alex or the Joker, after all.

My interpretations in this chapter are to a large extent dependent on the player's prior knowledge—in this case, a familiarity with Kubrick's films. It is certainly likely, however, that many players enjoy these games while remaining entirely unaware of the references. Or, even if they do catch the allusions, players might differ greatly in what they think those references mean—including the larger questions I believe they pose regarding morality and the cultural value of art. Far from negating the

---

[21] McQuiston, *We'll Meet Again*, 163.

value of these Kubrickian allusions, however, that ambiguity is itself fully in keeping with Kubrick's idiosyncratic style of musical placement in film. As the director opined in a 1971 interview, "I particularly enjoy those subtle discoveries where I wonder whether the filmmaker himself was even aware that they were in the film, or whether they happened by accident. I'm sure that there's something in the human personality which resents things that are clear, and, conversely, something which is attracted to puzzles, enigmas, and allegories."[22]

Indeed, perhaps the most significant aspect of classical music in Kubrick's films is the space it allows for many equally rewarding interpretations.[23] Strauss's *Blue Danube Waltz* and Rossini's Overture to *La gazza ladra* will mean something different to each viewer depending on his or her frame of reference. In games, that kind of ambiguity often becomes a necessity. As enigmatic as *2001* might be, for example, the film remains fundamentally the same no matter how many times you watch it. In *Elite*, on the other hand, every playthrough might be dramatically different. A player might avoid the space station altogether on one playthrough, or crash on trying to dock, or any number of variables. Inspired by Kubrick's ingenious and sometimes inscrutable musical selections, this ambiguity enables a wide variety of equally valid gameplay experiences.

---

[22] Quoted in Alexander Walker, Ulrich Ruchti, and Sybil Taylor, *Stanley Kubrick, Director: A Visual Analysis*, rev. ed. (New York: Norton, 2000), 38. As McQuiston points out, "For Kubrick, a good film leaves blanks for the audience to fill in, and leaves them free to discover the films for themselves." Kate McQuiston, "The Stanley Kubrick Experience: Music, Nuclear Bombs, Disorientation, and You," in *Music, Sound and Filmmakers*, ed. James Wierzbicki (London: Routledge, 2012), 141.

[23] Mike Cormack, for example, goes so far as to suggest that this ambiguity as a central aspect of pre-classical music in film. See Mike Cormack, "The Pleasures of Ambiguity: Using Classical Music in Film," in *Changing Tunes: The Use of Pre-existing Music in Film*, ed. Phil Powrie and Robynn Stilwell (Burlington, VT: Ashgate, 2006), 19–30.

6   Remixed Metaphors

ASIDE FROM POLITE nods, there's one response I get most often when I tell people I'm writing a book on classical music and video games: "Oh, you mean like *Gyruss!*"[1] For players who fondly remember 1980s arcades, it seems the notion of classical music in video games is inextricably tied to Konami's 1983 shoot-'em-up. And for good reason. To quote from the *Gyruss* review on the gaming website *HardcoreGaming101*: "*Gyruss*, one of Konami's more popular games in the early 80s, [is] an impressive bit of technology for 1983. . . . It's also notable for its fast paced arrangement of Bach's Toccata and Fugue in D minor, one of the first—and best—uses of music in an arcade game."[2] The Toccata and Fugue, originally a work for solo organ, occupies a prominent position in *Gyruss*.[3] Its opening notes accompany the game's first stage, initially suggesting that the music will be a straightforward

---

[1] Since its initial arcade release, *Gyruss* has enjoyed a long life on a variety of home consoles, ranging from the Atari 2600 and Nintendo Entertainment System to a rerelease on Xbox Live Arcade in 2007. A full list of ports is available at the Arcade History website, available online at http://www.arcade-history.com/?n=gyruss-model-gx347&page=detail&id=1063 (accessed July 15, 2014).

[2] "Gyruss," *HardcoreGamer.net*, available online at http://www.hardcoregaming101.net/konamishooters/konamishooters2.htm (accessed July 15, 2014).

[3] The Toccata and Fugue, BWV 565, appeared in a number of games during (and after) the 8-bit era. Dana Plank examined a number of instances of its appearance (including in *Gyruss*) in "From the Concert Hall to the Console: The 8-Bit Translation of BWV 565" (paper presented at the North American Conference on Video Game Music, Youngstown State University, January 18, 2014). I am grateful to Plank for providing me with a copy of her research.

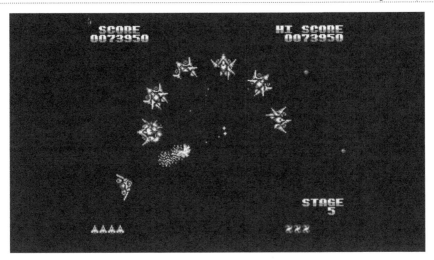

FIGURE 6.1 Gameplay screenshot of *Gyruss* (NES version, 1988).

transcription (Figure 6.1). About five seconds in, however, the music quickly skips to the ending chords of the opening slow section, followed by a jarring drum fill. When the piece picks back up, it's in a much freer—and decidedly popular—form. It's a remix.

By and large, game designers of the late 1970s and 1980s tried to keep classical music as close to its original form as possible, but before the middle to late 1990s *all* classical music in games was in some way remixed. Game technology of that time couldn't replicate the sounds of acoustic instruments or accommodate the number of simultaneous pitches required for most classical music. Though not exactly remixes, these adaptations nevertheless create a similar effect, bringing classical music into closer contact with popular culture. A few early games like *Gyruss*, however, directly and obviously experimented with juxtaposing classical and popular musical styles, a strategy that has persisted into the present day in a variety of forms. Previous chapters have explored some ways in which tension between art and entertainment comes into play in games. In this chapter, I turn to games that engage this perceived conflict directly, in the form of musical remixes. To be clear, by remixes I mean classical music that is significantly altered in style from its original form, usually by incorporating elements of popular music styles—and thus becoming a work of hybrid authorship.

In *Remix Theory: The Aesthetics of Sampling*, cultural critic Eduardo Navas outlines three basic forms of musical remix, all of which apply to some extent in video games: (1) the "extended" remix, in which the length of the work is expanded; (2) the "selective" remix, in which portions of the original are omitted and/or new material is added; and (3) the "reflexive" remix, which "allegorizes and extends the aesthetic of sampling."[4] It's fairly clear how the first two types work in video games: most game remixes of classical music, for example, are designed to be looped infinitely, in effect creating the ultimate "extended" remixes. Likewise, nearly all the examples I've found take only a few elements of the piece being remixed. In most cases, that means only limited melodic and harmonic material, typically fragmented into short, immediately understandable sections—a hook, in other words. I don't know any game remix, for example, that contains an entire movement of a symphony. That would simply be too long—and not nearly repetitive enough—to combine effectively with the pop-remix medium. At the same time, remixes add new musical elements to the original works, most often in the form of drumbeats, but frequently also added harmonies and melodic lines.

Most interesting for my purposes, however, is the reflexive aspect of remixes. There the remix takes on an allegorical meaning, adding new layers of meaning to both the original work and to the added elements.[5] In other words, the work becomes both old and new; it's the original work *and* something entirely different. The works chosen for game remixes tend to be the same few well-known pieces, a practice that we might assume stems from a lack of music-historical knowledge on the part of game designers, composers, and audio directors. That argument does have some merit, especially when considering early games, but it also sells short these often highly educated and knowledgeable professionals. Recognizing the classical music *as* classical is critical to the function of a remix. As Navas tells us, these types of hybrid works "will always rely on the authority of the original composition, whether in forms of actual samples, or in form of reference. . . . The remix is in the end a *remix*—that is, a rearrangement of something already recognizable."[6] In other words, a remix with an unidentified original source ceases to function as a remix at all— and, more important, it loses its ability to harness the cultural value attached to that original. Yet as the musicologist Mark Katz notes regarding digital sampling, "Any sound, placed into a new musical context, will take on some of the character of its new sonic environment," and through this type of manipulation music can be "decontextualized and recontextualized, . . . giving it new sounds, functions, and meanings."[7] To become something new, it must first be recognizable as something old.

[4] Eduardo Navas, *Remix Theory: The Aesthetics of Sampling* (Vienna: Springer, 2012), 65–66.

[5] Here Navas draws heavily on the work of Craig Owens, in particular his two-part article "The Allegorical Impulse: Toward a Theory of Postmodernism," *October* 12 (1980): 67–86; and "The Allegorical Impulse: Toward a Theory of Postmodernism, Part 2," *October* 13 (1980): 58–80.

[6] Navas, *Remix Theory*, 67.

[7] Mark Katz, *Capturing Sound: How Technology Has Changed Music*, rev. ed. (Berkeley: University of California Press, 2010), 174, 154.

This reflexive remixing process has appeared in other media for decades, including with regard to classical music. Popular musicians have long taken advantage of classical tunes, as Michael Broyles and Matthew Brown have recently explored with the music of Beethoven and Debussy, respectively.[8] Consider, for example, Walter Murphy and the Big Apple Band's novelty disco remix "A Fifth of Beethoven" (1976), which takes its inspiration and musical material from the Fifth Symphony (1808).[9] Or the extensive reworking of classical music common in progressive rock of the 1970s, as in the music of the bands Renaissance and Emerson, Lake, and Palmer. On the other hand, although classical music is a common feature in traditional narrative media like film and television, with a few notable exceptions (such as Kubrick's *A Clockwork Orange*), the music usually appears in something like its original form. Remixed classical music in games is thus a melding of these two traditions: popular reinterpretations of classical music, on the one hand, and narrative cinematic uses of classical, on the other.

Given these traditions, why might Masahiro Inoue have chosen Bach's Toccata and Fugue as *Gyruss*'s main theme? Part of the answer may lie with perceptions of Bach's music as the apex of musical complexity—classical music at its most classical. In the early 1980s, arcade cabinets in particular were in a state of constant technological development. Each game was unique, and game developers and programmers were always looking for new ways to attract players. And in the loud, crowded atmosphere of the 1980s arcade, it was often the sound above all that drew players to a particular machine.[10] *Gyruss*'s remixed Toccata and Fugue became a kind of technological benchmark—a dramatic way to illustrate the game's advanced sound capabilities. In contrast with the sporadic musical outbursts of *Galaga* (1981), for example, *Gyruss* simultaneously offered wall-to-wall music and multiple sound effects, no mean task with 1983 game audio technology.[11] The choice of Bach added another dimension—not only could *Gyruss* play music constantly, but it could play *Bach*, the composer of what some regard as the most technically perfect music ever written. The grandiose opening statement of Bach's music echoes

---

[8] Michael Broyles, *Beethoven in America* (Bloomington: Indiana University Press, 2011), chap. 11; Matthew Brown, *Debussy Redux: The Impact of His Music on Popular Culture* (Bloomington: Indiana University Press, 2012).

[9] On the cultural importance of Walter Murphy's transgressive disco reworking, see also Ken McLeod, "'A Fifth of Beethoven': Disco, Classical Music, and the Politics of Inclusion," *American Music* 24 (2006): 347–363.

[10] See, for example, Karen Collins, *Game Sound: An Introduction to the History, Theory, and Practice of Video Game Music and Sound Design* (Cambridge, MA: MIT Press, 2008), 9.

[11] Collins has noted the abnormal amount of sound hardware that went into the making of *Gyruss*, which included "as many as five synthesis chips and a DAC [digital-to-analog converter]." The game seems, she notes, "to use at least two chips for sound effects, one for percussion, and at least one chip to create a rendition of Bach's *Toccata and Fugue in D minor*." Collins, *Game Sound*, 19.

similarly bold promises that *Gyruss*'s creators were making about the game's technical achievements.

The *Gryuss* Bach remix has enjoyed a long afterlife well into the twenty-first century and has itself been remixed on several occasions. The original arcade version was updated and altered for the Nintendo Famicom and NES ports (1987 and 1988, respectively), the DJ/composer JT. 1Up's electronic remix "*Gyruss*—Full Tilt" appeared in the game *Dance Dance Revolution Ultramix 2* (2004), and the Xbox Live Arcade re-release of *Gyruss* (2007) featured yet another meta-remix. At what point, then, is Bach's music less the subject of the remix than Inoue's *Gyruss* music? Clearly, it's nostalgia for *Gyruss* rather than for the original organ work that motivates these new versions. This distinction highlights another, and I think beneficial, consequence of removing a classical work from its privileged status: music becomes inherently more fluid as outmoded concepts of faithfulness to the work give way to a sense of musical play.[12] As Vanessa Chang points out in a study of musical sampling, "Rather than clinging to the myth of the composer savant, sampling maintains an ethics of inclusion that is social as well as musical, creating a tradition that involves the past without submitting to its structures and limitations."[13] *Gyruss* illustrates how remixing allows for kinds of artistic freedom and play that are usually off limits with classical music.

In more recent years, remixed classical music has become the domain of independent games rather than major studio releases. Perhaps that change results from the perceived intellectual rigor of classical music, but it could also be nostalgia for the 1980s, when classical music was more prominent in games. The indie game *FEZ* (2012), a product of game designer Phil Fish, illustrates both categories. An homage to platformer games of the 8-bit era, *FEZ* features deliberately crude graphics designed to appear as two-dimensional pixels, despite actually being three-dimensional polygons (Figure 6.2). As Chris Suellentrop writes in the *New York Times*:

> Mr. Fish is a Quentin Tarantino of 8-bit gaming, prodigiously quoting from the pop culture of his childhood (in this case, the Nintendo Entertainment System, rather than blaxploitation films). The oddly shaped blocks from *Tetris* can be seen everywhere in *Fez*: on the walls, on the ground, on signposts, scrawled on chalkboards, even in the constellations in the sky. Gomez, *Fez*'s protagonist, beams with joy, adorably, when he finds an important item in a

---

[12] For an insightful study of musical play versus fidelity to a work concept, see Roger Moseley, *Keys to Play: Music as a Ludic Medium from Apollo to Nintendo* (Berkeley: University of California Press, 2016), Key 4, 178–235.

[13] Vanessa Chang, "Records That Play: The Present Past in Sampling Practice," *Popular Music* 28 (2009): 156.

FIGURE 6.2 Gameplay screenshot of *FEZ* (2012).

treasure chest, much like Link, the hero of *Zelda*. But it is to *Super Mario Bros.* that *Fez* owes its greatest debts.[14]

The game's soundtrack, by composer Richard "Disasterpeace" Vreeland, matches the gameplay's retrospective quality—as critic Matt Miller pointed out in *Game Informer*, the music "drives home the '80s nostalgia vibe."[15] Buried innocuously on *FEZ*'s soundtrack is one piece of remixed classical music: "Continuum," a remix of Frédéric Chopin's Prelude in E Minor, Op. 28, No. 4 (1839). A highly distorted opening—I initially thought something was wrong with my speakers—evolves into a Vangelis-style synth arrangement before slowly reintroducing the distortion, ultimately transforming from music into pure static.

This remixed work sonically illustrates *FEZ*'s efforts to transcend mere entertainment. As Suellentrop's comparison of Fish to Tarantino illustrates, *FEZ* is often portrayed as an artgame—the critic also refers to it as "a *Finnegans Wake* of video games," for its impenetrable narrative and lack of clear direction. As in *Gyruss*, remixing the Chopin prelude in *FEZ* is a kind of play, but here including classical music is also a subtle way of elevating the game artistically. Notably, the review of *FEZ* in game magazine *Edge Online* observes that "Disasterpeace's mesmerising

---

[14] Chris Suellentrop, "A New Game Delights in Difficulty," *New York Times* (May 16, 2012), available online at http://www.nytimes.com/2012/05/17/arts/video-games/the-video-game-fez-is-complex-by-design.html (accessed July 17, 2014).

[15] Matt Miller, "Fez: Change Your Perspective," *GameInformer.com* (April 11, 2012), available online at http://www.gameinformer.com/games/fez/b/xbox360/archive/2012/04/11/change-your-perspective.aspx (accessed July 18, 2014).

quasi-chiptune soundtrack suggests [Gustav] Holst's back catalogue put through a Mega Drive [Sega Genesis]."[16] The same techniques *Gyruss* used in 1983 to showcase the game's cutting-edge sound hardware ironically exude a retro nostalgia in *FEZ*. Yet both games appeal to classical music's artistic authority, whether to demonstrate technological or artistic achievement. In *Gyruss* and *FEZ*, the remixed classical music remains in the background, separate from both gameplay and narrative. In the following section, however, I explore games in which remixes either form a core component of the game or become an important expression of its central themes.

Carnival Games

Boom Boom Rocket (2007) is simplistic by design. Players rhythmically push buttons on their controllers in response to on-screen indicators—like *Dance Dance Revolution*, say, without the dance mat—and that's all. The reward for doing well, aside from earning points, is visual. Correctly timed button presses trigger colorful fireworks displays against the backdrop of a nighttime cityscape (Figure 6.3). The required inputs correspond to elements of the music, but *Boom Boom Rocket* is less a music game than a music visualizer game. That is, players add a visual accompaniment rather than contributing to the music itself, as they would in a game like *Guitar Hero*. In fact, *Boom Boom Rocket* even contains a music visualizer mode, which creates a noninteractive fireworks display based on any music files players stored on their Xbox 360 hard drives.

The connection between music visualizers and video games can be traced back as far as the Atari Video Music (AVM) system (1976), which connected to a stereo system and provided an abstract graphical accompaniment.[17] Though the AVM system was not a game per se—there were no rules, or ways to score points—its knobs and buttons nonetheless created a kind of interactivity. As game scholar Ian Bogost suggests, "While primitive, Atari Video Music offers a sign of what would become the unique contribution videogames offer to music. Instead of listening, watching, dancing, or otherwise taking in music, videogames offer a way

---

[16] *"Fez* Review," *Edge Online* (April 11, 2012), available online at http://www.edge-online.com/review/fez-review/ (accessed July 18, 2014).

[17] In more recent years, electronic music visualizers like the AVM have given way to software versions, most commonly on personal computers. Many media player programs (iTunes and Windows Media Player, for example) include built-in visualization modes, and there are a number of freestanding programs devoted to music-generated visual displays. Some game consoles have also included built-in (or downloadable) music visualizer programs, including the Atari Jaguar's *Virtual Light Machine* and the Xbox 360's *Neon*, both built into the consoles' media player functions.

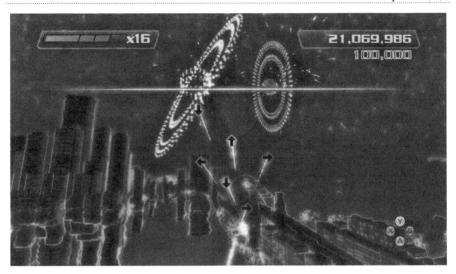

FIGURE 6.3 Gameplay screenshot of *Boom Boom Rocket* (2007).

to *perform* it."[18] Bogost's observation that there is a kinship between the AVM system and games is an astute one, but I disagree that it allowed players to perform music in any meaningful way. I would argue instead that it afforded listeners an opportunity to visually *interpret* music—an important distinction. *Boom Boom Rocket* is thus in some respects closer in design to the AVM system than it is to most music games. Players are not active participants in music making; the audio track is coldly indifferent to all their frantic button mashing. Not surprisingly, the game also lacks what Jesper Juul would call a "mimetic interface"—some kind of object-shaped controller that "allows players to play from the perspective of their physical presence in the real world."[19] As Kiri Miller, Karen Collins, and others have illustrated, in music games this type of mimetic interface—the plastic instruments of *Rock Band*, for example—allows players to assume some agency in the music's creation.[20]

Like the AVM system, *Boom Boom Rocket* is a visual interpretation of music—albeit in a gamified and altogether less abstract fashion. Although the self-directed play of

---

[18] Ian Bogost, *How to Do Things with Videogames* (Minneapolis: University of Minnesota Press, 2011), 32.

[19] Alternative inputs were allowed in *Boom Boom Rocket*, though that was not the default method of play. It was possible, for example, to play *Boom Boom Rocket* with *Rock Band* or *Guitar Hero* instruments, or with the dance mat from *Dance Dance Revolution* games. Jesper Juul, *A Casual Revolution: Reinventing Video Games and Their Players* (Cambridge, MA: MIT Press, 2010), 107.

[20] On the player-participant aspect of mimetic interface music games, see Kiri Miller, *Playing Along: Digital Games, YouTube, and Virtual Performance* (Oxford: Oxford University Press, 2012), chaps. 3 and 4; and Karen Collins, *Playing with Sound: A Theory of Interacting with Sound and Music in Video Games* (Cambridge, MA: MIT Press, 2013), chap. 3.

the AVM system's buttons and knobs gives way to the structure of preassigned button presses, *Boom Boom Rocket* is as close to a pure listening experience as one could expect to find in a video game. It's essentially a gamified AVM system, with fireworks as an updating of the original abstract light show. And as with Atari's early experiment, the music remains the focus of the player's attention. *Boom Boom Rocket*'s soundtrack is heavily influenced by electronic music styles, perhaps not a surprising choice, given the long-standing relationship between electronica and the technological visualization of music. The AVM system, for example, was featured prominently as the backdrop of the synth-pop band Devo's video for "The Day My Baby Gave Me a Surprise" (1979), as well as the background of the video for electronica duo Daft Punk's "Robot Rock" (2005). In video games, the same kinds of connections between electronic music and music visualization crop up in titles like *Rez* (2001), *Child of Eden* (2011), or *iS: Internal Section* (1999).[21] What's surprising about *Boom Boom Rocket*'s music is that each track in its soundtrack is also a remixed classical work (Table 6.1). When the game was released, its soundtrack consisted of ten classical works remixed by composer Ian Livingstone, each piece retitled with a clever pun. These remixes largely focus on electronic dance music but they also include the ska-influenced "Rave New World" and the disco-funk "Carmen Electric." A downloadable "Rock Pack" enhanced this stylistic range by adding five songs remixed by Chris Chudley in a variety of rock styles.

More than in either *Gyruss* or *FEZ*, these remixes are obviously supposed to be funny, or at least lighthearted. But there's also a bit of a subversive edge, evident both in the new titles and in the music itself. "Game Over Beethoven" recalls Chuck Berry's song "Roll Over Beethoven" (1956), a call for classical music to make way for popular styles. In one way or another, most of the rest of the titles suggest replacing boring classical elements with exciting modern ones. For example, two remixes update the generic title "overture," once with "overdrive" and once with "overload." Some titles even hint at a violent break with tradition, particularly in the "Rock Pack": Pachelbel's infamous Canon in D becomes a "cannon," Beethoven's Ode "explodes," and Rimsky-Korsakov's bumble bee "stings." The end result is both a celebration and a carnivalesque mockery of the remixed classical works. Players aren't forced to choose one interpretation or the other, of course; as Katz notes, a newly created hybrid work "can be understood as derivative *and* novel, exploitative *and* respectful, awkward *and* subtle."[22]

The remixes revel in this liminal space. To my mind, it's a bit similar to the pleasure 1970s DJs took in introducing contradictory elements; Joseph Schloss points out that "many deejays are known to have taken a special delight in getting audiences

---

[21] On soundtrack-based level design in games, see Steven Beverburg Reale, "Transcribing Musical Worlds; or, Is *L.A. Noire* a Music Game?," in *Music and Video Games: Studying Play*, ed. K. J. Donnelly, William Gibbons, and Neil Lerner (New York: Routledge, 2014), 77–103.

[22] Katz, *Capturing Sound*, 160.

TABLE 6.1

Remixed classical music in *Boom Boom Rocket* (2007)

Track Title	Source Composer	Original Source
"Smooth Operetta"	Léo Delibes	"Flower Duet," from *Lakmé*
"Rave New World"	Antonin Dvořák	Symphony No. 9 in E Minor, Op. 95, "From the New World," IV
"William Tell Overload"	Gioachino Rossini	Overture to *William Tell*
"Hall of the Mountain Dude"	Edvard Grieg	"In the Hall of the Mountain King" from *Peer Gynt*
"1812 Overdrive"	Pyotr Tchaikovsky	*1812 Overture*, Op. 49
"Valkyries Rising"	Richard Wagner	"Ride of the Valkyries," from *Die Walküre*
"Tail Light Sonata"	Ludwig van Beethoven	Piano Sonata in C-sharp Minor, Op. 27, No. 2 ("Moonlight"), I
"Carmen Electric"	Georges Bizet	Overture to *Carmen*
"Game Over Beethoven"	Ludwig van Beethoven	Symphony No. 5 in C Minor, Op. 67, I
"Toccata and Funk"	J. S. Bach	Toccata and Fugue in D Minor, BWV 565

DLC "ROCK PACK"

"Sting of the Bumble Bee"	Nikolai Rimsky-Korsakov	"Flight of the Bumble Bee" from *The Tale of Tsar Saltan*
"Explode to Joy"	Ludwig van Beethoven	Symphony No. 9 in D Minor, Op. 125, IV
"Sugar High"	Pyotr Tchaikovsky	"Dance of the Sugar Plum Fairy," from *Nutcracker*
"Eine Kleine Rochtmusik"	Wolfgang Amadeus Mozart	*Eine Kleine Nachtmusik*, K. 525, I
"Cannon in D"	Johann Pachelbel	Canon in D

to dance to breaks that were taken from genres that they professed to hate."[23] Certainly, some of *Boom Boom Rocket*'s players recognize this playfulness. As one user-contributed review to the website *GameFAQs* notes:

> The songs—what I have played—are great and fun to listen to. And this is coming from a person who listens to rap and nothing else. Most of the music in this game is

---

[23] Joseph G. Schloss, *Making Beats: The Art of Sample-Based Hip-Hop* (Middletown, CT: Wesleyan University Press, 2004), 32.

remixed Classical, and Classical bores me . . . but not the music in this game. Why? I honestly don't know. . . . Another thing that makes this game fun for a person like me that enjoys Rap, RnB, and music of that nature is that the songs actually have somewhat of a beat (for the most part) and the fireworks flow with that.[24]

More than any other game I explore in this chapter, *Boom Boom Rocket* illustrates the pleasure derived from combining supposedly incompatible musical styles.

And yet its message was a bit muddled. In this sort of remix, audiences eventually have to be in on the joke. Critics and players alike, however, were for the most part unsure what to make of *Boom Boom Rocket*. Its few media reviews reveal a profound ambivalence toward its score in particular. Some found the music and gameplay repetitive, its initial ten-song soundtrack insufficient to hold their attention for long. (For comparison's sake, *Rock Band*—also released in 2007—included fifty-eight songs on the disc and regularly introduced new downloadable content up to a total of more than two thousand songs.) The response to the music itself is even more revealing; oddly, most reviewers made almost no mention of the classical-based soundtrack. What little attention critics did pay to the remixes was fairly dismissive. The critic Douglass C. Perry, writing for the prominent gaming website *IGN*, offers a lukewarm assessment, noting that the game was "good but not great, likeable but not loveable, somewhat but not terribly addictive, and doesn't drive home that memorable soundtrack to keep you around for weeks." Perry goes on isolate the score as a major cause of the game's mediocrity: "Part of the problem . . . is the lack of great songs and the simplicity of the song design. These tunes are decent takes on familiar songs, but they don't grab you the way songs in *Guitar Hero* do. The addictive quality inherent in *BBR* quickly rubs off, then, because as a music game it's short on the quality and quantity of songs."[25]

Perry's review is worth a bit of unpacking. A few themes emerge: a lack of interest in the specifics of the music, an uncertainty even in how to describe it, and yet—most interestingly—a reluctance to directly deride it. Of course, game journalists aren't usually music experts, and they rarely have the time or inclination to explore it beyond a cursory appraisal. It is nonetheless remarkable, however, that I have yet to find even one review of *Boom Boom Rocket* that mentions a single composer's name (aside from Livingstone, who was identified on occasion). Critics mostly just

---

[24] Cuzit, "Boom Boom Fun!," *GameFAQs* (April 17, 2007), available online at http://www.gamefaqs.com/xbox360/937889-boom-boom-rocket/reviews/review-112746 (accessed July 18, 2014).

[25] Douglass C. Perry, "*Boom Boom Rocket* Review," *IGN* (April 12, 2007), available online at http://www.ign.com/articles/2007/04/12/boom-boom-rocket-review (accessed July 12, 2014).

describe the works as familiar, or well known. Tom Bramwell of *Eurogamer.net* comes the closest to discussing the classical works, identifying some of the pieces but not their composers: "Each level is built around one piece of music, and while they're all new, composed by a Mr. Livingstone . . . , they're all derived from well-known classical tunes. There's *William Tell*, the *1812 Overture, Ride of the Valkyries*, and seven others."[26] Like other reviewers, Bramwell puts more emphasis on the remixes than on the original classical works.

Then again, maybe critics ignoring the classical works and their composers isn't that surprising. Thanks to their constant appearances in media and generic orchestral pops concerts—the kind that often accompany fireworks displays in the United States—these works become part of our collective musical unconscious. One user-contributed review on the website *GameFAQs*, for example, intriguingly notes that the soundtrack "consists of 10 remixed classical songs, [that] everyone knows (even if you don't want to admit it)."[27] In other words, they're not as much individual works as they are representations of classical music in general.

As put off as critics and players were by *Boom Boom Rocket*'s soundtrack, however, few openly questioned the music's quality or appropriateness. Bramwell, for example, equivocates—writing that "aurally it's novel, but you won't be rushing out to buy the songs."[28] Perry, too, hoped that the game's "new downloadable stuff equates to more and preferably licensed tracks."[29] In other words, he thought licensed pop music would vastly improve *Boom Boom Rocket*, but he hesitated a bit to say so directly. Game critics aren't known for pulling punches when a key gameplay element is lacking. So why were critics of *Boom Boom Rocket* so confused by the game's soundtrack, and why were they so timid about lambasting it? The answer to both questions, I think, is tied to classical music's cultural position. Nobody wants to seem uncultured, so critics may have been reluctant to suggest that these classical tracks just weren't that enjoyable to listen to. At the same time, players are faced with the cognitive dissonance of so-called masterpieces being playfully combined with popular styles, and all for a simple game about fireworks. How could critics and players make sense of this conflicting information—and how, for that matter, can we? Jeff Gerstmann of *GameSpot* suggests that "these updated takes on classical music are pretty cheesy, though they're exactly the sort of tracks you'd expect to hear

[26] Tom Bramwell, "*Boom Boom Rocket*," *Eurogamer.net* (April 12, 2007), available online at http://www.eurogamer.net/articles/boom-boom-rocket-review (accessed July 12, 2014).

[27] ULTSF [username], "Enough Boom for Your Buck?," *GameFAQs* (April 16, 2007), available online at http://www.gamefaqs.com/xbox360/937889-boom-boom-rocket/reviews/review-112746 (accessed July 13, 2014).

[28] Bramwell, "*Boom Boom Rocket*."

[29] Perry, "*Boom Boom Rocket* Review."

at a fireworks show. . . . The soundtrack isn't bad, but it's all a little goofy."[30] "Cheesy" and "goofy" are hardly high praise. But those words do tell us something about the game: *Boom Boom Rocket* pulls high art off its pedestal. But why?

In search of some answers about a game based on fireworks displays, it feels appropriate to turn to the cultural theorist Mikhail Bakhtin's concept of "carnival." Named for the raucous period of pre-Lenten celebration in Western Christian traditions, Bakhtin's carnival describes any time when traditional values are suspended or inverted, creating a safe place to laugh at even the most serious topics. By viewing issues through a lens of humor, Bakhtin tells us, "the world is seen anew, no less (and perhaps more) profoundly than when seen from the serious standpoint. Therefore, laughter is just as admissible in great literature, posing universal problems, as seriousness."[31] By learning to laugh at these classical works in their goofy new setting, we can see them in a different light, visualizing the music (as the carnivalesque fireworks do) in a unique way. Through laughter, carnival breaks down the walls between the high and low arts through laughter. As literary scholar Renate Lachmann has pointed out:

> The inventory of carnival acts, symbols, and signs derives its meaning from this parodistic and profane inversion of canonized values, but also from the utopian dimension of the myth. . . . The provocative, mirthful inversion of prevailing institutions and their hierarchy as staged in the carnival offers a permanent alternative to official culture—even if it ultimately leaves everything as it was before.[32]

Applying that concept to the literally carnivalesque context of *Boom Boom Rocket* causes some underlying meanings to emerge. Seen through the lens of carnival, the game highlights the arbitrary nature of cultural hierarchies. The soundtrack pokes fun at classical music, yes, but not to denigrate it. Instead, the remixes reveal the compatibility of classical and popular styles—and seeks to bridge the perceived gaps between them. One obscure video game can't permanently upend centuries-old cultural hierarchies, of course. Yet *Boom Boom Rocket* allows for a brief moment in which the playful spirit of carnival can remove the barriers between art and entertainment.

---

[30] Jeff Gerstmann, "*Boom Boom Rocket* Review," *GameSpot* (April 11, 2007), available online at http://www.gamespot.com/reviews/boom-boom-rocket-review/1900-6168919/ (accessed July 13, 2014).

[31] Mikhail Bakhtin, *Rabelais and His World*, trans. Hélène Iswolsky (Bloomington: Indiana University Press, 1984), 66.

[32] Renate Lachmann, "Bakhtin and Carnival: Culture as Counter-culture," *Cultural Critique* 11 (1988–1989): 125.

TABLE 6.2

Remixed classical music in *Parodius: The Octopus Saves the Earth* (1988)

Track Title (as listed on soundtrack)	Original Composer(s)	Original Source(s)
"Crime of Century"	Pyotr Tchaikovsky	Piano Concerto No. 1 in B-flat Major, Op. 23
"Light of Octopus"	Ludwig van Beethoven	Piano Sonata in C-sharp Minor, Op. 27, No. 2 ("Moonlight"), III
"Illusion of Octopus"	(1) Edvard Grieg (2) Frédéric Chopin	(1) "In the Hall of the Mountain King" from *Peer Gynt* (2) Fantaisie-Impromptu, Op. 66
"Crazy World"	(1) Antonin Dvorak (2) Leon Jessel	(1) Symphony No. 9 in E Minor, Op. 95, "From the New World," IV (2) "The Parade of the Tin Soldiers," Op. 123
"The Waltz of the Octopus"	Pyotr Tchaikovsky	Finale from *Swan Lake*, Op. 20
"Fate of Octopus"	(1) Richard Wagner (2) Ludwig van Beethoven	(1) "Ride of the Valkyries" from *Die Walküre* (2) Symphony No. 5 in C Minor, Op. 67, I
"Sweet Emotion"	(1) Georges Bizet (2) Franz Liszt	(1) "March of the Toreadors" from *Carmen* (2) Hungarian Rhapsody No. 2, S. 244
"Crisis 4th Movement"	Ludwig van Beethoven	Symphony No. 9 in D Minor, Op. 125, IV
"Boss BGM"	Nikolai Rimsky-Korsakov	"Flight of the Bumblebee" from *The Tale of Tsar Saltan*

Boom Boom Rocket isn't alone in tackling these issues in a carnivalesque way. Consider, for example, the *Parodius* games. If that doesn't sound familiar, it might be because unlike most of the games I discuss in this book, the *Parodius* series has never been released outside Japan—the games are just too idiosyncratic and bizarre. Konami created the first game in the series, *Parodius: The Octopus Saves the Earth* (*Parodiusu: Tako wa Chikyū o Sukū*, 1988) as a parody of one of its own games: the hit shooter *Gradius* (1985). The humor in *Parodius* largely emerges from sheer absurdity. Players fight not only aliens borrowed from other Konami games, but also characters drawn from Japanese culture and mythology, as well as cartoonish animals—including, on one notable occasion, what appears to be a giant space anteater. This formula proved unexpectedly (inexplicably?) popular. There are five *Parodius* sequels to date, expanding the parodic aspects of the original by introducing references to other Konami games, ranging from the *Castlevania* series to the arcade shooter *Lethal Enforcers* (1992).

The music of the *Parodius* series is every bit as bizarre and referential as its other aspects. Each of the original game's nine looped tracks remixes classical works, mostly in a progressive rock style (Table 6.2). Supposedly, the classical-based soundtrack resulted from a rushed development process—although the complexity of the arrangements makes me doubt that claim—but the quality and quirkiness of the music were crucial to the game's success.[33] Original music is combined with elements of one or more classical pieces, often requiring significant alterations to pitches and rhythms. Later entries in the series added even more complexity, incorporating music from other Konami games, folk songs, popular music, and classical music—sometimes all in the same remix. For example, in *Sexy Parodius* (1996) we find cues like "Welcome, Kid," a mash-up of a track from the original *Castlevania* (1986) with Johannes Brahms's *Hungarian Dance*, No. 5, WoO 1 (1869). Another track, "Tanuko's Destiny," combines Beethoven's Fifth Symphony (1808), with both Mozart's *Eine Kleine Nachtmusik* (1787) and a Japanese children's song.[34]

Why has classical music become such an integral part of *Parodius*'s identity? For one thing, the musical combinations echo the surreal hodgepodge of visual elements drawn from other games, popular culture, mythology, and more. *Parodius* only works if players understand it's a parody; likewise, its soundtrack only works if players recognize the diversity of musical sources. Well-known classical pieces fit that bill nicely. Furthermore, by reflecting *Parodius*'s anarchic design, the music taps into another aspect of the carnivalesque: the grotesque. In contrast to *Gyruss, Fez,* or even *Boom Boom Rocket*, the remixes in *Parodius* transform and distort in an almost manic, slapstick fashion. Like the ridiculous caricatures of characters from other games and from Japanese culture, *Parodius*'s music renders classical works comically absurd. These games are neither mean-spirited nor particularly profound—they draw the line at playful, madcap transgression. And yet this grotesqueness contains a hint of something unsettling. The next chapter is devoted to following that thread, investigating the darker possibilities hidden within the musical carnivalesque.

---

[33] Jeremy Parish, "An Interview with Konami's Hidenori Maezawa, Pt 3," *1up.com* (January 15, 2009), available online at http://www.1up.com/do/blogEntry?bId=8978659&publicUserId=5379721 (accessed June 23, 2016.).

[34] For a complete listing of the music in the *Parodius* series, see "*Parodius* music," *Wikipedia*, https://en.wikipedia.org/w/index.php?title=Parodius_music&oldid=726410513 (accessed June 23, 2016).

7   Love in Thousand Monstrous Forms

"THE GROTESQUE," LITERARY critic Wolfgang Kayser once wrote, "is an attempt to control and exorcise the demonic elements in the world."[1] Kayser was writing in the 1950s, but his definition seems tailor-made for *Catherine* (2011), one of the most thoroughly unusual video games I've ever encountered. Despite its pedigree from the developer Atlus, the edgy and experimental *Catherine* feels more like an independent computer game than a major console release. Players take on the role of Vincent, a thirty-something slacker in the midst of a major life crisis. His longtime girlfriend, the professionally successful but somewhat emotionally distant Katherine, is pressuring him to improve his job prospects and to get married—with both demands only intensifying after a pregnancy scare. In the midst of his internal struggles, Vincent meets the young, attractive, fun-loving Catherine, with whom he enters a second relationship (Figure 7.1). That much alone is enough to separate *Catherine* from the vast majority of games—but that's not even close to its most unusual aspect.

Here's where the demonic element comes into play: after he starts seeing Catherine, whenever Vincent goes to sleep he's transported to a nightmare world. In this bizarre dreamscape, "cheating" men have to solve puzzles to survive the night. Late in the game, players learn that demons are to blame, and that Catherine is a succubus tasked with luring Vincent away from Katherine. Based on the player's

---

[1] Quoted in Philip Thomson, *The Grotesque* (London: Methuen, 1972), 18.

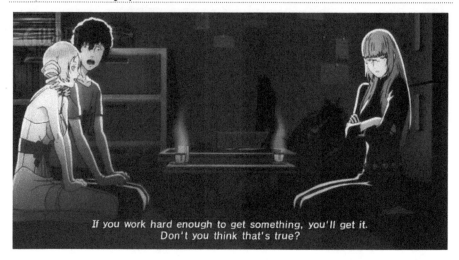

If you work hard enough to get something, you'll get it.
Don't you think that's true?

FIGURE 7.1 To Vincent's dismay, Catherine (left) meets Katherine (right) in *Catherine* (2011).

choices, there are ten potential endings to *Catherine*, covering a range of possibilities. Vincent might atone for his philandering and marry Katherine, for instance—or he might decide to rule the underworld together with Catherine instead. Or, maybe he rejects both women and becomes the first space tourist. For all its tongue-in-cheek moments, though, *Catherine* also addresses a number of serious issues regarding the transition into adulthood: marriage, parenthood, and disappointment, to name a few. I argue that the chief way *Catherine* engages with these topics is through the grotesque—what Philip Thomson succinctly describes as "the unresolved clash of incompatibles."[2]

It's by exploring that "clash of incompatibles" that *Catherine*'s unusual structure starts to make sense. In implicit and explicit ways, *Catherine* deals in dualities—diametric opposites that yield grotesque results when forced into interaction. This construction is evident even in basic gameplay, which is divided into two starkly contrasting parts. In the day and early evening, players guide Vincent through his everyday life, which unfolds in conversations, text messages, and so on. In the evenings, players wind up at the Stray Sheep, Vincent's regular bar, where he can, for example, order drinks, play a minigame, or engage in conversations. This part of the game is essentially a "dating simulation," a (typically Japanese) genre focused on using clever tactics to win over potential partners.[3] *Catherine* shares a number of

---

[2] Thomson, *The Grotesque*, 27.

[3] On dating sims, see, for example, Emily Taylor, "Dating-Simulation Games: Leisure and Gaming of Japanese Youth Culture," *Southeast Review of Asian Studies* 29 (2007): 192–208; and Patrick W. Galbraith, "Bishōjo Games: 'Techno-Intimacy' and the Virtually Human in Japan," *Game Studies* 11, no. 2 (May 2011), available online at http://gamestudies.org/1102/articles/galbraith (accessed July 19, 2014).

FIGURE 7.2 Vincent climbing in *Catherine*.

features with dating sims, in fact—a focus on binary choices, the existence of multiple endings, and the obvious influence of Japanese anime. In this portion of the game there is no need to hurry, and there are no right or wrong choices. The only goal is advancing the narrative.

The dreamworld sequences, however, are an entirely different story—almost literally. Instead of a dating sim, players instead experience yet another generic hybridization: a blend of horror and puzzle games.[4] Players ascend towers by pulling blocks to create stairs, a timed puzzle mechanic that provides the most obviously "gamey" experience in *Catherine*, complete with points, level names (3-1, 3-2, etc.), and so on (Figure 7.2). The pace is frenetic. In place of the slow-paced feel of *Catherine*'s daytime, here a few small mistakes could end in a gruesome death, followed by the game-over screen (which ominously reads "Love Is Over"). As if that weren't nerve-racking enough, at the end of each level players face a macabre version of one of Vincent's waking preoccupations. The final boss of the fourth stage, for instance, is "The Child," a repulsive symbol of Vincent's fear of fatherhood (Figure 7.3). Hopefully at this point it's becoming clear how playing *Catherine* feels like an exercise in trying to synthesize—or at least survive—seemingly irreconcilable gameplay elements.

---

[4] The blending of horror and puzzle genres in *Catherine* isn't entirely without precedent. The PC title *The 7th Guest* (1993), its sequel *The 11th Hour* (1995), and titles such as *Phantasmagoria* (1995) and its sequel *Phantasmagoria: A Puzzle of Flesh* (1996) each combined a horror narrative with puzzles that would advance the plot. In a more humorous and not strictly "puzzle" vein, in 1999 Sega remade its popular arcade shooter/horror game *House of the Dead 2* into *The Typing of the Dead*, an edutainment game in which players defeated zombies by quickly typing words on a keyboard. It has thus far spawned two improbable sequels: *The Typing of the Dead 2* (2007) and *Typing of the Dead: Overkill* (2013).

FIGURE 7.3 "The Child," the culminating boss of the Fourth Night in *Catherine*.

Not only is each night's combination of puzzle and horror mechanics unusual, but *that* combination gets combined with the daytime dating sim elements, and so on. This fundamental duality manifests throughout the game with almost fractal repetition: dating simulation versus puzzle/horror; day versus night; the effervescent, blond Catherine (dressed in white) versus the older, serious, brunette Katherine (dressed in black); and more, stretching into infinity.

Given the prevalence of duality as a motif in *Catherine*, it's no surprise that composer Shoji Meguro's musical score illustrates these same structures. Music for the daytime and evening portions of the game (the dating sim part, in other words) favors a piano-heavy smooth jazz idiom. As Vincent is carried to his dreamworld each night, the music takes on a much darker tone, with dissonant strings and piano evocative of horror films. More interesting for my purposes, however, is the music that accompanies each of the puzzle sequences. With a few exceptions and repetitions, each level features a different piece of remixed classical music. The music selections are all well known, similar to those in the previous chapter—works you might hear in any concert hall (Table 7.1). This juxtaposition of classical and popular styles is another of *Catherine*'s many dualities—and one that has significant ramifications for how we understand both the nightmarish nighttime scenes and the game more broadly.

The play of dualities within *Catherine*'s use of classical music is a testament to the complexity of the game's structure. Every element focuses on creating a compelling narrative, and as a result the musical selections become deeply integrated into its story. Particular classical pieces, rather than simply works that serve as general signifiers of classical music, assume significantly more importance. Some

TABLE 7.1

Classical music in *Catherine* (2011)

Placement in Game	Original Composer	Original Source
Levels 1 and 2	Gustav Holst	"Jupiter" and "Mars," from *The Planets*
Level 3	Ludwig van Beethoven	Symphony No. 5, III
Levels 3 (boss), 4 (boss), and 8	Modest Mussorgsky	"The Hut on Fowl's Legs" ("Baba Yaga"), from *Pictures at an Exhibition*
Level 4	J. S. Bach	"Little" Fugue in G Minor
Level 5	Antonin Dvořák	Symphony No. 9, "From the New World," I
Level 6	Gioachino Rossini	Overture to *William Tell*
Level 7	Alexander Borodin	Polovtsian Dances, from *Prince Igor*
Level 9	Georges Bizet	"Farandole," from *L'Arlésienne* suite
Final Boss	Frédéric Chopin	"Revolutionary" Étude
Victory of each level (not remixed)	G. F. Handel	"Hallelujah," from *Messiah*
Death (arranged, but not remixed)	Pablo de Sarasate	"Zigeunerweisen" ("Gypsy Airs")
Break-Ups (in "real world")	Frédéric Chopin	Piano Sonata No. 2, "Funeral March"

of the musical selections in *Catherine* were chosen for relatively straightforward reasons. Handel's "Hallelujah Chorus" (which, while obviously synthesized, is not actually remixed) symbolizes triumph, appearing at the finish line of every level. Chopin's "Funeral March" is only slightly more complicated, representing not the death of an individual but the death of a relationship. Uniquely among the remixed classical music in *Catherine*, Chopin's music appears in the daytime real world on two occasions: when Vincent breaks up with Catherine, and when Katherine breaks up with *him*. In both cases, it's remixed into a piano-jazz idiom, blending in with the typical underscore for the game's daytime segments. In reflecting the concepts of triumph and death, the "Hallelujah Chorus" and "Funeral March" echo their uses in countless films, television programs, and video games. Chopin's "Revolutionary" Étude, which appears in the game's final level, works in a similar way. Vincent effectively revolts against the demonic forces responsible for his nightly torments—an echo of the political overtones of Chopin's étude.

Other classical works illustrate *Catherine*'s central ideas much more subtly. Sometimes, for instance, the selections appear to be alluding to other media products. I'll focus here on two strikingly different examples. The nineteenth-century

French composer Georges Bizet's "Farandole"—remixed in *Catherine* as a kind of stadium-rock anthem—is best known today as a purely instrumental work, but it originated as incidental music for Alphone Daudet's play *L'Arlésienne* (1872). In the play, a young man is torn between two women, one more sexually liberated and one more reserved. After becoming (briefly) engaged to the first of these two, he's driven mad by her involvement with another man and ultimately commits suicide by throwing himself from a high balcony. Clearly, this situation parallels Vincent's in several ways: the protagonist struggles to choose between two very different women, infidelity is a central a plot device (although in *Catherine* the infidelity is Vincent's own), and both feature the motif of death by falling.

The violinist/composer Pablo de Sarasate's *Zigeunerweisen* for *Catherine*'s game-over screens suggests an equally obscure source.[5] Sarasate's piece appears prominently on several occasions in Suzuki Seijun's 1980 Japanese cult film of the same name. Though the film's quasi-surrealist plot is nearly impossible to summarize, it deals with many of the same issues found in *Catherine*, especially complicated sexual relationships—polyamory and infidelity, for example—as well as death. Moreover, as Japanese studies scholar Rachel Dinitto notes, *Zigeunerweisen* (the film, that is) explores duality and "double vision," a concept that extends to the same actress portraying two separate (and contrasting) roles as love interests. "In addition to the obvious doppelgänger effect," Dinitto suggests, "Suzuki reuses or doubles images, scenes, dialogue, and sounds. These replications, be they false or true, tie the film together."[6] *Catherine* evokes Suzuki's film in both plot themes and narrative structure, using concepts of duality to frame a complex and occasionally unintelligible work. These examples from Bizet and Sarasate illustrate how the selection of a particular piece of music may deepen our understanding of the game's central narrative themes. To be clear, I do not expect that most players would approach *Catherine* with a frame of reference encompassing nineteenth-century French plays and Japanese cult films of the 1980s. I certainly didn't when I first played it. For that matter, I don't believe it necessary for the game designers to have consciously intended these references. Yet in both cases, *Catherine*'s play of dualities extends even to these minute details.

On a larger scale, the musical choices and their remixes join with the visual and narrative aspects of *Catherine* to almost obsessively dwell on the grotesque. Though grotesque elements appear throughout *Catherine*'s imagery and narrative, nowhere

---

[5] The *Zigeunerweisen* is, like the "Hallelujah Chorus," not stylistically remixed in *Catherine*, but its resonance with the game's narrative merits some mention here.

[6] Rachel Dinitto, "Translating Prewar Culture into Film: The Double Vision of Suzuki Seijun's *Zigeunerweisen*," *Journal of Japanese Studies* 30 (2004): 46.

are they more apparent than during the battles at the culmination of each level. As mentioned earlier, each of these bosses is a twisted, grotesque incarnation of Vincent's waking preoccupations: the allure of the female body, marriage to Katherine, incipient fatherhood—or, more generally, a fear of adulthood and a sense of self-loathing. These manifestations are certainly hideous and misshapen, but they're also grotesque in the sense of being composed of irresolvable contradictions. Some bosses are made up of a collection of assorted parts, both animate and occasionally inanimate. Others are both living and dead—suggesting, perhaps, that Vincent fears that marriage or fatherhood would in a sense end his old life. In the following section, I turn to how these grotesque elements play out in the remixed classical works.

Catherine/Katherine

In the previous chapter, I explored how Mikhail Bakhtin's theory of carnival might apply to the playful remixes of classical music in games like *Boom Boom Rocket* and *Parodius*. The musical selections in *Catherine* echo some of the same issues. Yet in this new context, juxtapositions that seemed humorous in other games instead contribute to an atmosphere of horror, revulsion, and disgust. The musical results often feel like a collection of disparate elements that are uncomfortably, perhaps violently, fused. For example, composer Shoji Meguro seems to have been drawn to classical works that contain some type of internal dichotomy. His remix of Rossini's overture to *William Tell*, for example, contains the most dramatic and most serene moments of the original work: "The Storm" and the "Ranz des Vaches" (a kind of pastoral Swiss folk tune). In the same way, the remix of Holst's orchestral suite *The Planets* incorporates elements of two radically different sections of the larger work: "Jupiter" ("The Bringer of Jollity") and "Mars" ("The Bringer of War"). In the Rossini and Holst examples, there are extreme contrasts in both musical and extramusical content—the notes themselves, in other words, as well as the larger story being told. The act of remixing thus creates a nested duality. Two contrasting portions of the original classical work are combined, but then what results gets remixed with popular styles, creating a second level of juxtaposition. This kind of multilayered musical design resonates strongly with the game's visual and narrative construction—dualities within dualities within dualities.

The history of classical music offers a number of instances of high and low arts brought grotesquely into dialogue. Claude Debussy's piano prelude *Golliwog's Cakewalk* (1913), for instances, distorted the central musical theme of Richard Wagner's opera *Tristan and Isolde* (1865) into ragtime, evoking the the grotesquely racist doll for which the piece is named. The effect is remarkable, rendering one of the most influential musical moments of the nineteenth century into a comic parody (and, intentionally or not, one suggestive of Wagner's own racism). The music theorist Yayoi Uno Everett has located a similar use of the grotesque in the Hungarian composer György Ligeti's opera *Le grand macabre* (1977, rev. 1996), which borrows and distorts supposedly highbrow and lowbrow musical styles.[7] In one scene, Ligeti twists a theme from Beethoven's "Eroica" Symphony, Op. 55 (1804) into an almost unrecognizable form, then combines it with elements of ragtime, Brazilian samba, and Greek Orthodox chant. Everett's description of the final scenes of *Le grand macabre*, in fact, resonates strongly with *Catherine*:

> By combining music drawn from high and low styles into a massive collage, this passage turns into an ultimate macabre dance, . . . in which the ludicrous and horrifying states co-mingle. As a musical corollary to Bakhtin's grotesque body . . . [as] the procession of incongruous tunes unfolds, chaos reigns on stage as people fight, eat, drink, copulate, and so forth, in coping with the final moments of life.[8]

Combining the classical works with their electronic or rock remixes in *Catherine* achieves much the same effect, creating a dizzyingly incomprehensible musical accompaniment to Vincent's frantic block pulling.

In both Ligeti's opera and *Catherine*, the irreconcilably diverse musical styles reflect the same tendency to juxtapose carnal excess with the specter of death, whether literal, metaphorical, or—as in Vincent's nightmares—both. In *Catherine*, moreover, that aspect of the grotesque becomes a fixation on equivocating death with the female body. That uncanny combination is in keeping with what scholars have identified the "female grotesque," building on Bakhtin's considerations of ancient Greek terra cotta figurines depicting pregnant old women:

> This is typical and very strongly expressed grotesque. It is ambivalent. It is pregnant death, a death that gives birth. There is nothing completed, nothing calm and stable in the bodies of these old hags. They combine senile, decaying, and deformed flesh with the flesh of new life, conceived but as yet unformed.[9]

---

[7] Yayoi Uno Everett, "Signification of Parody and the Grotesque in György Ligeti's *Le Grand Macabre*," *Music Theory Spectrum* 31 (2009): 26–56. On how the grotesque figures into classical music, see also Esti Sheinberg, *Irony, Satire, Parody, and the Grotesque in the Music of Shostakovich: A Theory of Musical Incongruities* (Aldershot, UK: Ashgate, 2000); and Julie Brown, *Bartók and the Grotesque: Studies in Modernity, the Body and Contradiction in Music* (Aldershot, UK: Ashgate, 2007).

[8] Everett, "Signification of Parody and the Grotesque," 43.

[9] Mikhail Bakhtin, *Rabelais and His World*, trans. Hélène Iswolsky (Bloomington: Indiana University Press, 1984), 25. For a discussion of this passage in the context of the female grotesque, see Mary Russo, *The Female Grotesque: Risk, Excess, and Modernity* (New York: Routledge, 1994), chap. 2.

TABLE 7.2

Bosses in *Catherine* and possible interpretations of their meaning

Level	Boss Name	Description
Level 2	Fist of Grudge	Two female hands with a fork, silver hair; represents fear of commitment to Katherine (with whom he has just had an uncomfortable dinner)
Level 3	Immoral Beast	Picasso-esque amalgamation of female body with Catherine's eyes, vagina dentata; represents affair with Catherine
Level 4	The Child	Huge "undead" newborn; represents fears of parenthood, appears the night Katherine reveals possible pregnancy
Level 5	Doom's Bride	Huge, nude "undead" Katherine with wedding veil and knife "bouquet"; represents fear of marriage to Katherine
Level 6	Child with a Chainsaw	Newborn as mechanical doll with cybernetic attachments; represents continued fear of fatherhood coupled with fear the child is not his
Level 7	Shadow of Vincent	Shadowed, masked version of Vincent himself; represents self-loathing and the conflict of inner and outer selves
Level 8	Catherine	Fanged, nude, demonic version of Catherine; represents fears of Catherine's reprisal after Vincent ends their relationship
Level 9	The Demon Dumuzid (final boss)	Demonic final boss; concrete manifestation of Vincent's own wrongdoing and fears of judgment

Vincent's dream-monsters frequently embody this female grotesque, corrupting either female forms or infants—combining the death/life binary that Bakhtin identifies in the terra cotta figurines (Table 7.2). In level 5, for instance, he confronts "Doom's Bride," a repulsive, decaying version of Katherine clad only in a wedding veil and wielding a knife covered in flowers (Figure 7.4).

This focus on the female grotesque also manifests musically. Only one of *Catherine*'s remixes appears more than once: "The Hut on Fowl's Legs," also known as "Baba Yaga," from Russian composer Modest Mussorgsky's *Pictures at an Exhibition* (1874). What about "Baba Yaga" singles it out this way? Although Mussorgsky's ominous music certainly fits the game's macabre tone, I think the answer once again lies in the score's extramusical meanings. Baba Yaga is a recurring figure in Russian folklore, whose identity and motivations always remain cloaked in mystery. She appears

FIGURE 7.4 "Doom's Bride," the boss of level 5 in *Catherine*.

as a beautiful young woman in some tales and as an old hag in others. Sometimes she helps lost travelers or murders them, seemingly with no rhyme or reason.[10] Already Baba Yaga's grotesqueness is apparent in her dualities: youth and old age, kindness and malice. But Baba Yaga is also significant for her role as a manifestation of femininity. The Russian folklorist Joanna Hubbs, for example, identifies Baba Yaga as an embodiment of "feminine power": "the expression of realized potential fulfillment of the cycle of life associated with woman. . . . In her the cycles of feminine life are brought to completion, and yet she contains them all."[11] Like Bakhtin's terra cotta figurines, Baba Yaga is pregnancy and decay—life and death, and life *from* death. But although she may seemingly embody the "cycles of feminine life," upon closer inspection Baba Yaga is, like Vincent's nightmares, a grotesque perversion of the feminine and the maternal.

Vincent's nightmare monsters illustrate the same concerns—and, tellingly, it is there that players encounter Mussorgsky's music. For instance, "Baba Yaga" plays when Vincent faces the "Immoral Beast." An amalgamation of female body parts, the Beast is disturbing. Catherine's eyes are relocated to what Bakhtin would call the "lower bodily stratum," associated with "degradation, filth, death, and rebirth."[12] The Beast conveys Vincent's animalistic lust for Catherine, combined with his conflicting

[10] For an overview of Baba Yaga's history and interpretations, see Andreas Johns, *Baba Yaga: The Ambiguous Mother and Witch of the Russian Folktale* (New York: Peter Lang, 2004).

[11] Joanna Hubbs, *Mother Russia: The Feminine Myth in Russian Culture* (Bloomington: Indiana University Press, 1988), 39, 37.

[12] Bakhtin, *Rabelais and His World*, 20; Russo, *The Female Grotesque*, 8.

shame and excitement. The depiction of the Beast itself is also strikingly reminiscent of Baba Yaga's home—"The Hut on Fowl's Legs"—which is often represented in stories and artworks as "composed of parts of the human body, with legs for doorposts, hands for bolts, and a mouth with sharp teeth as a lock."[13] Likewise, The Beast's fanged mouth is placed in such a way as to suggest a vagina dentata, recalling the lock on Baba Yaga's door. "The Child" which Vincent faces in the next level, functions in much the same way. The new life promised by Katherine's pregnancy instead heralds to Vincent a kind of death of the self. Again, the presence of Mussorgsky's music suggests a connection to Baba Yaga, who combines birth with death: "Yaga is a mother, but a cannibal mother. She whose children are many . . . is also the hungry one who devours them."[14] Finally, Mussorgsky's music reappears near the end of the game, when Vincent squares off against a giant, demonic incarnation of Catherine. As Vincent flees, she tries to consume him with her razor-sharp teeth, echoing both the Immoral Beast and Baba Yaga's propensity for eating unwary travelers.

Remixed into its new form, Mussorgsky's music sonically reflects the grotesque dualities that recur in so many ways throughout *Catherine*. Yet through its evocation of Baba Yaga, it also contextualizes Vincent's fears as something akin to fairy tales—which is to say, manifestations of lingering, if often subconscious, cultural obsessions.[15] Embedded in these grotesque musical remixes is a set of cultural values that goes far beyond the confines of *Catherine*, and beyond even video games as a whole, revealing underlying beliefs about the nature of classical music.

Classical/Klassical

In *The Female Grotesque*, literary theorist Mary Russo succinctly summarizes the differences between artistic depictions of the idealized human body and its grotesque counterpart:

> The classical body is transcendent and monumental, closed, static, self-contained, symmetrical and sleek; it is identified with the "high" or official culture of the Renaissance and later, with the rationalism, individualism, and

---

[13] Hubbs, *Mother Russia*, 38.

[14] Hubbs, *Mother Russia*, 39.

[15] The literature on fairy tales as reflections of social pressures and/or fears is vast. Best known, perhaps, is Bruno Bettelheim's controversial book *The Uses of Enchantment: The Meaning and Importance of Fairy Tales* (New York: Knopf, 1976). See the several monographs on the topic by Jack Zipes, most recently *The Irresistible Fairy Tale: The Cultural and Social History of a Genre* (Princeton, NJ: Princeton University Press, 2012). See in particular chapter 4, on Baba Yaga.

normalizing aspirations of the bourgeoisie. The grotesque body is open, pro-truding, irregular, secreting, multiple, and changing; it is identified with the non-official "low" culture or the carnivalesque, and with social transformation.[16]

Substituting a word here and there, these descriptions are in many ways similar to the stark contrasts between the social position of high art and popular culture. In *Catherine*, that contrast is made clear through juxtaposing classical music with pop-ular music—but the same concepts apply throughout this book in the relationship between classical music and video games as a whole. Classical music, like Russo's "classical body," is "transcendental and monumental," associated with the upper classes and with intelligence. That's why classical music in media frequently signi-fies that a product or character is "adult oriented," "serious," "refined," or "complex." Or, in a less positive light, classical music also frequently indicates something out of touch, a product that has outlived its usefulness (assuming it had any to begin with). Popular music, on the other hand, often indicates that someone or something is "youth oriented," "fun," "unpretentious," "exciting," or—more cynically—"super-ficial." Like the grotesque body, it pushes constantly for transformation, discarding the cultural shackles of the old guard.

This constantly reinforced dichotomous relationship between classical music and popular culture is something most players will have encountered long before pick-ing up a controller to play *Catherine*. In this setting, however, these old meanings assume new significance. The game's central duality, around which all the others seem to revolve, is the contrast between Katherine and Catherine. Even the game's title seems to place more focus on the love interest(s) rather than on the protagonist. It's fitting, then, that the same ingrained meanings so frequently ascribed to classi-cal and popular music styles map neatly onto Katherine and Catherine, who—like the music itself—become jumbled in Vincent's dreaming mind. Katherine embodies Vincent's anxiety at the onrushing responsibilities of adulthood: his concerns over settling down, finding financial stability, and becoming a boring middle-class adult. The vibrant and significantly younger Catherine, however, provides an antidote to these fears, offering Vincent a fun, if superficial, relationship that reinforces his youthful irresponsibility.[17] The music thus offers us another window into Vincent's

---

[16] Russo, *The Female Grotesque*, 8.

[17] We may think here of Matthew Brown's suggestion (building on several studies) that adolescents turn to pop-ular music "as a means of controlling their moods. It does so in several ways: by relieving them of tension or boredom, by distracting them from their troubles, and even by pumping them up for important social events." Matthew Brown, *Debussy Redux: The Impact of His Music on Popular Culture* (Bloomington: Indiana University Press, 2012), 97.

troubled psyche, revealing—sometimes on multiple levels—his internal conflicts between adulthood and youth, or responsibility and freedom. Players may view the contrasting musical styles in any way they choose: the game gives no indication of whether the original classical piece or its newly found popular style is more desirable. *Catherine*'s remixed music presents a challenge: like many aspects of the game, the music forces players to create their own meaning.

I conclude this chapter by suggesting one final meaning of the grotesque dualities that occur in *Catherine*—and, indeed, in many of the more artistically oriented games in this book. Whatever we might think of its aesthetic merits, *Catherine* is an unlikely fusion of high-minded artistic aspirations and social commentary with low-art sensationalism and basic puzzle-style gameplay mechanics. It is Aristotle meets *Angry Birds*, Tennyson meets *Tetris*. It strives, in short, to be simultaneously art and entertainment. Its soundtrack of uncomfortably juxtaposed classical and popular styles thus becomes a symbol of this larger conflict—a mirror of the precarious and arguably impossible space many video games inhabit. This music, like the game, blends art with entertainment. Yet its narrative effect ultimately relies on that combination remaining unconvincing; the grotesque must always be repulsive. The music only makes sense if the player still perceives classical music and popular music as one of the game's dualities, like day and night, adulthood and youth, stability and freedom, or Catherine and Katherine. Tellingly, players can't have everything at once: there is no synthesis to the dialectic *Catherine* presents, no perfect ending. Eventually, players have to stop juggling and choose one (or neither) of the options before them. What does that ultimate choice mean for players? Can *Catherine* and its remixed music exist at once as art and entertainment—or must they, like Vincent, choose one path or the other? These are questions with no easy answers, yet exploring them illustrates in unique ways the complex nexus of meanings inherent in any combination of classical music and video games.

8   Violent Offenders and Violin Defenders

AS THE PREVIOUS chapters illustrate, classical music crops up frequently in even the most unexpected of video games. Yet in most of the games described in this book, this music lingers in the background—always important but seldom directly acknowledged. On rare occasions, however, games bring classical music and all its cultural baggage into the spotlight, explicitly calling it to the player's attention. This might be something as simple as mentioning the name of a composer or acknowledging a piece of music playing on a radio. But the games considered in this chapter go much further, personifying classical music by incorporating musicians into their narratives. Each in its own way, these titles self-consciously call attention to the music's artistic value, often placing it in opposition to games' typical status as commercial products. Despite—or perhaps because of—their rarity, depictions of classical musicians in games effectively encapsulate discussions of music and the arts in postmodern culture. Through bringing players into direct contact with the musicians of these fictional worlds, these varied games encourage players to engage with the meanings of art.

This use of classical musicians to personify larger artistic concepts has antecedents in film and television. Consider, for example, the protagonist of Roman Polanski's film *The Pianist* (2002), who comes to symbolize the struggle to preserve art and beauty amid the unthinkable brutality of World War II.[1] As the musicologist

---

[1] On Chopin's music in *The Pianist*, see Lawrence Kramer, "Melodic Trains: Music in Polanski's *The Pianist*," in *Beyond the Soundtrack: Representing Music in Cinema*, ed. Daniel Goldmark, Lawrence Kramer, and Richard D. Leppert (Berkeley: University of California Press, 2007), 66–85.

Lawrence Kramer notes, "The film's plotting and frame structure idealize classical music. As a pianist, [Władysław] Szpilman is marked for survival by everyone though there is nothing to distinguish him otherwise from anyone else. If he lives, the music lives."[2] As *The Pianist* illustrates, classical music and its practitioners are frequently reflected in media as bastions of civilization—cultural bulwarks against cruelty, ignorance, and violence. The post-apocalyptic role-playing game *Fallout 3* (2008) offers an example of how this exploration of classical music's humanizing role makes the transition to video games.

Pleasure in the Pathless Woods

Fallout 3 is a game about making choices and accepting the consequences. Set in the centuries after a massive nuclear war in 2077, the *Fallout* series presents players with a retrofuturistic blend of science fiction and ironic 1950s optimism—a brave new world filled with angry mutants, persistent radiation, and rampant cruelty. *Fallout 3* explores the lives of settlers who eke out meager lives in the post-apocalyptic "Wasteland" that used to be the Washington, DC, area. In the course of their travels, players may stumble across Agatha, a senior citizen living modestly in a secluded area. Like many other characters in the game, Agatha needs the player's help. In this case, she wants a family heirloom—a Stradivarius violin—returned to her. This surprisingly daunting task requires players to undertake a lengthy and perilous journey to Vault 92, a shelter designed with the intent to preserve artistic talent for future generations. In an example of the painful irony of the *Fallout* universe, however, Vault 92 was actually a psychological experiment. Instead of providing sanctuary, it was designed to barrage its musician inhabitants with constant subliminal messages, to which their advanced listening skills supposedly made them more susceptible. The experiment triggered extreme paranoia in the residents, eventually causing them to violently turn on one another. Classical music's ability to bring peace amid war is flipped on its head; the innocent musicians themselves were turned into tools of violence.

Retrieving Agatha's violin gives the player a chance to symbolically restore classical music and its civilizing powers to the Wasteland. Completing the quest is a tacit acknowledgment that music's presence improves the Wasteland in important, if invisible, ways. The material reward for completing Agatha's request is fairly paltry—a unique handgun that had supposedly belonged to Agatha's late husband. Yet the intangible rewards are more significant. *Fallout 3*'s soundtrack consists mostly of

---

[2] Kramer, "Melodic Trains," 68.

mid-twentieth-century popular music, which in this case emerges from radios and a computer attached to the protagonist's arm. The computer picks up several in-game radio stations, to which the player can tune in any time the signal is available. If the player helps Agatha, she creates a new radio station featuring several pieces of classical music and a few of her own (obviously precomposed) improvisations. If requested, she'll even perform a piece "live" for the player, visibly—if inauthentically—holding and bowing the instrument as the music is produced (Figure 8.1).

Agatha's music calls attention to its own existence as art, and to her status as its protector. As in *The Pianist*, through a solitary practitioner, classical music somehow survives amid the desolation of war-torn ruins. Yet here that survival is entirely up to the player. While in a film viewers watch helplessly as events unfold on-screen, in *Fallout 3* the music's existence depends on the player's willing participation. Perhaps that act even in some way helps players atone for the many acts of violence they commit in the game. Because even if its violence is often tongue-in-cheek, *Fallout 3* is a gory game. As Tom Bissel points out in *Extra Lives: Why Video Games Matter*, "When Bethesda [Studios] posted a video showcasing *Fallout 3*'s in-game combat . . . many could not believe the audacity of its cartoon-Peckinpah violence. Much of it was rendered in slo-mo as disgusting as it was beautiful: skulls exploding into the distinct flotsam of eyeballs, gray matter, and upper vertebrae; limbs liquefying

FIGURE 8.1 Agatha and her violin in *Fallout 3* (2008).

into constellations of red pearls; torsos somersaulting through the air."[3] Agatha and her music offer us a brief respite from this hyperviolent world—an island of sanity in a sea of blood.[4]

In his study of music and morality in *Fallout 3*, musicologist William Cheng considers some possible meanings of Agatha's music.[5] He recalls a moment when, while recording some game footage for academic presentations, he inadvertently had an artistic experience:

> I remember thinking that, for the purposes of my presentations, this setting would make an elegant showcase for Agatha's music, free of violence, dialogue, and excessive ambient noise. The sky started out dark, but as the station's music played on—cycling through more Bach, a couple of improvisations, Dvořák—my surroundings got brighter by the minute. It eventually dawned on me that I was witnessing sunrise. Slowly, some light—bright, but for once, not too bright.
>
> As this morning glow yawned across the horizon, I realized that, in all my hours wandering the wasteland so far, this was the first time I was listening to the radio while definitely *not* playing the game in a conventional sense. In that half hour, I hardly touched my mouse or pressed a key.[6]

Cheng's reasons for this interlude may be unusual—most players probably don't record themselves doing nothing—but his experience seems fairly common. In fact, I had several such experiences myself while playing the game. But while I agree with Cheng about the importance of Agatha's radio station in understanding the hazy morality of *Fallout 3*, for me the game's emotive success is rooted in the idea of its liveness. As Cheng acknowledges, Agatha is the only character actually performing live music in the game, or participating directly in the creation of an artwork. As Philip Auslander reminds us, the concept of liveness depends entirely on the possibility

---

[3] Tom Bissell, *Extra Lives: Why Video Games Matter* (New York: Vintage Books, 2011), 6. The descriptor "Peckinpah" here refers to Sam Peckinpah, a director notorious for his Westerns (particularly *The Wild Bunch* [1969]) and their unflinching and unromanticized depictions of violence.

[4] Interestingly, *Fallout 4* (2015) features (without explanation) a classical radio station available to the player from the beginning of the game. It turns out, however, that the radio station is a tool of The Institute, an "enlightened" and scientifically advanced organization that views most dwellers of the post-apocalyptic world as savages. In a way, then, the use of classical music here is both similar to and divergent from its appearance in *Fallout 3*; it is a "civilizing" force, but of a patriarchal and arguably nefarious kind rather than Agatha's benevolent influence.

[5] William Cheng, *Sound Play: Video Games and the Musical Imagination* (Oxford: Oxford University Press, 2014), chap. 1.

[6] Cheng, *Sound Play*, 52.

of recording; it gains a special cachet through its ephemerality.[7] In the age of mechanical reproduction, even simulated liveness is often perceived as a central aspect of artistry. Walter Benjamin, for example, invoked the "presence" of live music, a long-lasting suggestion that there is something fundamentally meaningful about live performance as opposed to recordings.[8] As musicologist Emanuele Senici summarizes, for Benjamin, "live performance . . . promises a psychologically and emotionally authentic experience . . . while the video can only offer a fake or at best feeble substitute."[9] In other words, players can't help but connect the liveness of Agatha's performance with the relative sociocultural importance of the music she plays.

Ironically, the oldest music in the game, performed by one of the oldest human characters, is also the newest. Apparently, little or no new music is being created in the world of *Fallout*. Only the vestiges of the Old World remain, musical ruins that—like the statue of Ozymandias in Shelley's poem—exist as memorials to both humanity's boundless hubris and art's ability to withstand the ravages of time. In a literal sense, then, Agatha embodies art's tenacity even in the most adverse of circumstances. Her liveness (admittedly a suspension of disbelief on our part) stands in stark contrast to the "dead" records we hear on other radio stations. And if the music lives—as Agatha's does—then civilization survives, humanity endures, and hope persists.

Rapture on the Lonely Shore

On the other hand, not all video game classical musicians are heroic, and art doesn't always resist violence. Scattered throughout this book are examples of film, television, and game villains whose love of art stands in stark contrast with their depraved acts. The villain *as* musician, however, ratchets this dichotomy to a higher level. The demonic organist is a remarkably hardy trope in horror film, for example, from Boris Karloff's Bach-playing madman in *The Black Cat* (1934) to more recent films and media, such as the organ-playing creature Davy Jones in the *Pirates of the Caribbean* films, or a satanic killer in a 1993 episode of the *Inspector Morse* television series.[10] We can't just blame organists, however. There's also the Haydn piano sonata performed

---

[7] Philip Auslander, *Liveness: Performance in a Mediatized Culture* (London: Routledge, 1999), chap. 2.

[8] Walter Benjamin, "The Work of Art in the Age of Mechanical Reproduction," in *Illuminations*, trans. and ed. Hannah Arendt (New York: Harcourt, Brace, and World, 1968), 217–252. "Even the most perfect reproduction of a work of art is lacking in one element: its presence in time and space, its unique existence at the place where it happens to be" (220).

[9] Emanuele Senici, "Porn Style? Space and Time in Live Opera Videos," *Opera Quarterly* 26 (2010): 66.

[10] On the prevalence of the organ in horror film, see Julie Brown, "*Carnival of Souls* and the Organs of Horror," in *Music in the Horror Film: Listening to Fear*, ed. Neil Lerner (New York: Routledge, 2010), 1–20; and Isabella van Elferen, "The Gothic Bach," *Bach Perspectives* 7 (2012): 7–20. My reference to *Inspector Morse* is drawn from van Elferen's article.

by the diabolical Lestat in *Interview with the Vampire* (1994) or, to keep the vampire-musician theme, the deranged Ernessa's Chopin nocturne in *The Moth Diaries* (2011). In both of those instances, the characters' command of classical music makes their utter disregard for human life all the more chilling. The same kinds of musical villainy appear in video games, albeit less frequently, with *BioShock* (2007) as one particularly notable example. I've already spent some time exploring the *BioShock* series in this book—chapter 3 was devoted entirely to *BioShock Infinite*—and some of the same musical characteristics explored in that chapter are present here as well. Yet the original *BioShock* stands apart for its on-screen representation of musicians.

A first-person shooter with a highly developed narrative, *BioShock* takes place in 1960, in an underwater dystopia called Rapture. Its plot is a dire warning of the dangers of rampant capitalism, depicting a self-contained society where Ayn Rand's Objectivist philosophy has gone horribly wrong. In addition to original music, *BioShock*'s soundtrack makes frequent use of popular music of the midcentury. As I have argued elsewhere, these popular songs carry a great deal of narrative weight, underscoring Rapture's dystopian atmosphere while commenting ironically on the game's action.[11] *BioShock* contains only one example of classical music, but it appears at a particularly significant moment. In the course of the game, players must traverse "Fort Frolic," Rapture's entertainment center. Once replete with high-end shopping and arts venues—a theater, concert hall, art galleries, and so on—by 1960 Fort Frolic is a war-torn shell of its former glory, inhabited by murderous psychopaths. The warden of this asylum is Sander Cohen, a visual artist, filmmaker, and composer driven mad by his pursuit of aesthetic perfection. The game critic Leigh Alexander astutely captures Cohen's essence as "Rapture's poster child for the creative elite": "Cohen held court in Fort Frolic, his musical scores the toast of the city, his artwork held up as the standard of genius. In his battered suit, his hair a nest of pomade and his face a white pancake mask, holding court now over none but a grim army of plaster-cast statues . . . a city that should have become his joy became his madness."[12]

BioShock reveals Cohen's artistic bona fides before players ever interact with him directly. In a gruesome display, players witness Cohen forcing a captive pianist to perform one of his compositions over and over before eventually murdering the unfortunate musician for insufficient artistry. To secure passage through Fort Frolic, however, players must strike a Faustian bargain. They agree to help Cohen create his

---

[11] William Gibbons, "'Wrap Your Troubles in Dreams': Popular Music, Narrative, and Dystopia in *BioShock*," *Game Studies* 11, no. 3 (2011), available online at http://gamestudies.org/1103/articles/gibbons.

[12] Leigh Alexander, "The Aberrant Gamer: An Evening with Sander Cohen," *GameSetWatch* (September 6, 2007), available online at http://www.gamesetwatch.com/2007/09/column_the_aberrant_gamer_an_e.php (accessed July 26, 2014).

FIGURE 8.2   Cohen and his "masterpiece" in *BioShock* (2007).

masterpiece, the Quadtych, which requires killing and photographing Cohen's former protégés (Figure 8.2). At a certain point near the end of this unsettling mission, however, the capricious artist flies into a rage, ordering his followers to attack the player.

The confrontation that follows features an unlikely piece of music: the "Waltz of the Flowers," from Tchaikovsky's *Nutcracker* (1892). That musical choice works here on several levels. Classical music sets Fort Frolic apart from the rest of Rapture, and Cohen from the rest of the villains who populate it. Just as the game's initial antagonist, Andrew Ryan, represents the dangers of ultra-free-market capitalism and Randian philosophies, Cohen illustrates the dangers of art without conscience. Tchaikovsky's elegant, ethereal waltz runs counter to the action it accompanies, a grotesquely misplaced bit of refinement.[13] Yet, as Tchaikovsky's music makes us aware, there is also something balletic about the combat in *BioShock*, a gracefulness to the wanton acts of destruction and the graphic(al) beauty with which they are depicted on the screen. This transformation of violence into art recalls, for example, the films of Quentin Tarantino. The critic Xavier Morales lauds the director's *Kill Bill, Vol. 1* (2003) for "elegantly blurring the distinction between beauty and violence"—a description that applies equally well to *BioShock*.[14]

Music plays an important role in that aestheticization of violence. In a study of Tarantino's uses of popular music in his film scores, the musicologist Lisa Coulthard

---

[13] We might find parallels here with the use of Tchaikovsky's music in Darren Aronofsky's film *Black Swan* (2010). in which the gracefulness of the ballet *Swan Lake* is frequently juxtaposed with violence and psychosis.

[14] Xavier Morales, "*Kill Bill*: Beauty and Violence," *Harvard Law Record* (October 16, 2003), available online at http://hlrecord.org/?p=11285.

identifies an example from *Reservoir Dogs* (1992) as an "instance of a new mode of self-knowing, reflexive, and excessively graphic violent representation." She continues, "Sometimes called the 'new brutality' or 'Hollywood ultraviolence,' this kind of ironic representation of on-screen graphic film violence in the last two decades of American cinema has been characterized as evincing a new atmospheric and aesthetic cinematic trend toward cynical, dystopic, extreme, and explicit violence."[15] In Tarantino's films and elsewhere, this trend is often marked by popular music. Yet the "Waltz of the Flowers" in *BioShock* creates a similar moment of self-reflexivity, ironically calling attention to art amid the violence. This uncomfortable juxtaposition mirrors Cohen's horrific Quadtych and perhaps even reminds players of their own complicity in its creation. But it also raises questions about *BioShock* itself, and whether games like it should be considered artworks.

Despite fully deserving its "Mature" rating, *BioShock* frequently arises in discussions of video games as art.[16] The critic Harold Goldberg, for instance, notes that *BioShock* "made people who eschewed videogames see the art in an entertainment that dealt with profound ideas and twisted emotions."[17] Cohen's artistic goal of transforming violence into art is, in a sense, *BioShock*'s own mission, and the Quadtych episode represents a microcosm of the game as a whole. The "Waltz of the Flowers" scene is obviously a performance—after the Quadtych's completion, Cohen descends a flight of stairs in a spotlight, with confetti streaming from the ceiling. All of Fort Frolic is a grisly variety show of his own devising, much as the developers created the ultraviolent Rapture as a game space for the players' amusement. From that perspective, the "Waltz of the Flowers" scene becomes analogous to players' relationship with the game; they find art amid *BioShock*'s violence just as Cohen finds beauty in death.

A Wide Realm of Wild Reality

For all their fantastic science fiction trappings, both *Fallout 3* and *BioShock* take pains to connect their musicians to classical music history. *Fallout*'s Agatha plays a Stradivarius violin, for instance, and she performs actual classical works. And

---

[15] Lisa Coulthard, "Torture Tunes: Tarantino, Popular Music, and New Hollywood Ultraviolence," *Music and the Moving Image* 2, no. 2 (2009): 1.

[16] Though discussions of *BioShock* as "art" peaked in the months after its initial release, they continue even a decade later, as a recent article in *Vox* illustrates. Peter Suderman, "*BioShock* Proved That Video Games Could Be Art," *Vox* (October 3, 2016), available online at http://www.vox.com/culture/2016/10/3/13112826/bioshock-video-games-art-choice (accessed October 3, 2016).

[17] Harold Goldberg, *All Your Base Are Belong to Us: How Fifty Years of Videogames Conquered Pop Culture* (New York: Three Rivers Press, 2011), 287.

BioShock's Cohen was based on two real-world figures: George M. Cohan—who like Cohen in *BioShock* was involved in many fields of the arts—and the surrealist artist Salvador Dalí. These connections reveal a desire to connect these obviously fictional characters with real-world music culture. Yet in some ways, the closer games get to reality, the more challenging representing musicians becomes. That becomes particularly evident in the representation of actual historical musicians. The idea seems straightforward; film audiences, after all, have long been entertained by depictions of famous composers. Beethoven, as one example, has been depicted on-screen a staggering number of times beginning as early as the 1920s.[18]

Yet real-world historical figures—let alone musicians—are much less common in video games. Or, to be more precise, it's rare for them to be incorporated into a game's narrative successfully. Consider *Shaq Fu* (1994), in which the basketball player Shaquille O'Neal travels to another dimension where he defeats an evil mummy with his martial arts prowess. Or *Dante's Inferno* (2010), which "for gameplay reasons" reimagined the medieval poet as a vengeful Knight Templar rampaging through hell.[19] In both cases, critics and players found the premises laughable. In their quest to create a viable premise for a video game, the developers stretched reality too thin.

Popular musicians are also subjected to these kinds of quasi-parodic representations, usually as a kind of market synergy between the recording and gaming industries.[20] In addition to direct musical tie-ins—band-specific titles like *Beatles Rock Band* (2009), for instance—popular musicians have also appeared in narrative games, from *Journey Escape* (1982) to *Michael Jackson's Moonwalker* (1990) and *50 Cent: Bulletproof* (2005).[21] These games all feature the same superheroic

---

[18] See, for example, Michael Broyles, *Beethoven in America* (Bloomington: Indiana University Press, 2011).

[19] On the adaptation of Dante for the game, the game's producer, Jonathan Knight, summarized the approach, nothing that "whenever we could do something that was more in line with what happens in the poem or had to make a choice about this character or that or this environment or that, we always tried to do what was in the poem first. But sometimes you have to change things for gameplay reasons." The most notable departure from the source material, of course, was the transformation of the main character into a warrior archetype as opposed to a poet; presumably the same attitude would carry over to representations of composers, as well. Quoted in David Wildgoose, "From Poetry to Playability: How Visceral Games Reimagined Dante's *Inferno*," *Kotaku* (February 2, 2010), available online at http://www.kotaku.com.au/2010/02/from-poetry-to-playability-how-visceral-games-reimagined-dantes-inferno/ (accessed July 20, 2014).

[20] On the commercial synergy between the popular music and gaming industries, see, for example, Holly Tessler, "The New MTV? Electronic Arts and 'Playing' Music," in *From Pac-Man to Pop Music: Interactive Audio in Games and New Media*, ed. Karen Collins (Aldershot, UK: Ashgate, 2008): 13–25; and Antti-Ville Kärjä, "Marketing Music through Computer Games: The Case of Poets of the Fall and *Max Payne 2*," in *From Pac-Man to Pop Music: Interactive Audio in Games and New Media*, ed. Karen Collins (Aldershot, UK: Ashgate, 2008), 26–44.

[21] Karen Collins briefly outlines the appearance of these musician-themed games in her book *Game Sound: An Introduction to the History, Theory, and Practice of Video Game Music and Sound Design* (Cambridge, MA: MIT Press, 2008), 111–112.

transformations as *Shaq Fu*, a way of playing with the lines between historical truth and fiction.[22] In *Michael Jackson's Moonwalker* the performer defeats his foes with a combination of physical attacks and dancing abilities; *50 Cent: Bulletproof* sees the rapper and his crew take down criminal organizations in epic action scenes reminiscent of James Bond or *Die Hard* films.[23] These kinds of tongue-in-cheek portrayals are almost always a bit silly, which is all part of the fun. Yet when cultural icons are perceived as more serious, the balance between history and metafiction can be more difficult to achieve, and games often lean toward deference to historical reality. *Assassin's Creed III* (2012) offers one such example. Set in and around the events of the American Revolution, the game lets players take part in events like the Boston Tea Party and to interact with historical figures, including George Washington, Thomas Jefferson, Paul Revere, and Samuel Adams (Figure 8.3).[24] Two design choices are crucial to making this unusual historicity work: these characters are not playable, and the events of the game don't deviate too far from established history—by which I mean the kind of fictionalized history found in media adaptations. If players could perform overtly antihistorical acts like, say, assassinating George Washington, the resulting cognitive dissonance might be counterproductive to the gameplay experience.[25]

Probably because of restrictions like these, classical musicians have fared poorly in games. For that matter, even composer-based films have often struggled to navigate the fine line between dramatic viability and historical fidelity.[26] Taking Beethoven as an example again, films vary widely in their approach, all "working within the Beethoven story but never hesitant to enhance or invent entire situations for

---

[22] Literary theorists describe that kind of artwork as historiographic metafiction—a genre in which historical truths are included in a fictional context. On historiographic metafiction in general, see Linda Hutcheon, "Historiographic Metafiction: Parody and the Intertextuality of History," in *Intertextuality and Contemporary American Fiction*, ed. Patrick O'Donnell and Robert Con Davis (Baltimore: Johns Hopkins University Press, 1989), 3–32.

[23] On Michael Jackson in video games, see Melanie Fritsch, "*Beat It!*—Playing the 'King of Pop' in Video Games," in *Music Video Games: Performance, Politics, and Play*, ed. Michael Austin (New York: Bloomsbury, 2016), 153–176.

[24] *Assassin's Creed III* is not the first game in the series to incorporate historical figures; *Assassin's Creed II* and its sequels *Assassin's Creed: Brotherhood* and *Assassin's Creed: Revelations* featured characters from the Italian Renaissance, including several members of the Borgia family, Leonardo da Vinci, Catarina Sforza, and so on.

[25] Notably, however, *Assassin's Creed III*'s multipart expansion pack *The Tyranny of King Washington* explores a version of the 1780s in which Washington has become a brutal dictator. This narrative deviates enough from history to be easily recognizable as an example of "alternative history" fiction, and furthermore it is identifiable as "separate" from the main (more historically oriented) game.

[26] On Hollywood's obsession with the past, see Robert Brent Toplin, *Reel History: In Defense of Hollywood* (Lawrence: University Press of Kansas, 2002); and Toplin, *History by Hollywood: The Use and Abuse of America's Past* (Urbana: University of Illinois Press, 1996).

FIGURE 8.3 George Washington (right) in *Assassin's Creed III* (2012).

dramatic purposes," in the words of musicologist Michael Broyles.[27] These neces-sary liberties have frustrated some scholars and critics, however. In his provoca-tively titled article "Film Biography as Travesty: *Immortal Beloved* and Beethoven," the musicologist Lewis Lockwood wrote of the 1994 Beethoven biopic that "the pablum this film doles out to the masses is not just of poor quality but should carry a warning to say that it is deleterious to their health."[28] Nor is such vitriol unique to Beethoven's defenders. The changes to Mozart's life (and death) in the film *Amadeus* (1984) were endlessly decried in musicological circles as well as popular press arti-cles, where every "inaccuracy" was seized upon as evidence of Hollywood's insensi-tivity to classical music and its cultural contributions.[29]

More sensible voices might suggest, as Broyles does, that "to expect or complain about historical accuracy would be to misunderstand the film genre itself."[30] No film, game, or biography, after all, can ever present a complete account of a composer's life—and even if it could, who would want to watch it? And yet this fanatical con-cern for fidelity highlights the reverence with which classical composers are often

---

[27] Broyles, *Beethoven in America*, 168.

[28] Lewis Lockwood, "Film Biography as Travesty: *Immortal Beloved* and Beethoven," *Musical Quarterly* 81 (1997): 192.

[29] See, for example, the meticulously prepared lists of *Amadeus*'s "inaccuracies" in Jane Perry-Camp, "*Amadeus* and Authenticity," *Eighteenth-Century Life* 9 (1983): 116–118. For more judicious discussions of the film, see Robert Marshall, "Film as Musicology: *Amadeus*," *Musical Quarterly* 81 (1997): 173–179; and Jeongwon Joe, "Reconsidering *Amadeus*: Mozart as Film Music," in *Changing Tunes: The Uses of Pre-existing Music in Film*, ed. Phil Powrie and Robynn Stilwell (Ashgate, UK: Ashgate, 2006), 57–73.

[30] Broyles, *Beethoven in America*, 191.

viewed. Admittedly, video game players are not known for their dedicated perusal of musicological literature. Yet the underlying perception of classical music as a serious subject explains why few games would take the risk of featuring a well-known composer. Reinterpretations of composers' lives might meet with skepticism, confusion, or outright animosity—but more historically grounded depictions would be highly unlikely to make entertaining gameplay.

In fact, I know of only one game featuring a real-world composer presented in an even relatively straightforward style: *Mozart: Le Dernier secret* (2008), a relatively unknown French title. *Mozart* places the composer in Prague in the days leading up to the premiere of his opera *Don Giovanni* (1787), where a series of mysterious murders forces him to unravel an assassination plot hatched by a malevolent secret society. Needless to say, these events didn't actually occur. Given his supposedly vast intellect and propensity for solving puzzles, Mozart is a natural fit for this kind of *Da Vinci Code* intrigue, so this seems like a successful recipe for a composer-based game if ever there was one. Yet despite a small European fan base, *Mozart* never garnered much success. Perhaps players were unwilling to accept the cognitive dissonance of a classical composer solving crimes, or maybe the whole concept just smacked of bad edutainment. In any case, it seems clear that successfully including real-world composers in video games would require a drastically new approach—one that could draw on a composer's cultural cachet while avoiding the narrative shackles of history.

9   Playing Chopin

FRÉDÉRIC CHOPIN MAKES an unlikely video game hero. Dubbed the "poet of the piano," the nineteenth-century composer seems a far cry from the hypermasculine heroes that still populate many video games. Against all odds, however, video games have offered players several chances to step into Chopin's shoes, first in the Japanese role-playing game *Eternal Sonata* (2007), and a few years later in the mobile games *Frederic: Resurrection of Music* (2011) and its sequel, *Frederic 2: Evil Strikes Back* (2014).[1] This chapter explores the first two of these titles, which raise intriguing questions about the cultural value of classical music in the twenty-first century. Both make an effort to update Chopin's image for modern players, introducing the composer and his music to a generation more familiar with Mario than Mahler. In doing so, however, these games also grapple with the complex and often contradictory cultural meanings of art.[2] As is often the case with well-known composers, a number of myths have coalesced around Chopin's life. In particular, the musicologist Jim Samson has outlined three identities that have profoundly shaped how audiences have understood Chopin's life and music: the salon composer, the

---

[1] Although throughout this chapter I will be referring to the original 2011 release, *Frederic* was rereleased in a director's cut in 2016, adding several new levels. The overall narrative, however, remains unchanged.

[2] For more on stylistic and chronological juxtapositions as aspects of musical postmodernity, see, for example, Jonathan Kramer, "The Nature and Origins of Musical Postmodernism," in *Postmodern Music/Postmodern Thoughts*, ed. Judy Lochhead and Joseph Auner (New York: Routledge, 2002), 13–26.

Romantic composer, and the Slavonic composer.[3] Each of these three mythic identities plays a role in *Eternal Sonata* and *Frederic*, either aiding or hindering Chopin's transformation into a mainstream game character.

After Chopin left his politically troubled native Poland, he sought his fortunes as a pianist and composer in Paris. He eschewed the public concert life adopted by many piano virtuosos, such as his friend and rival Franz Liszt, preferring instead the intimacy of salons—smaller musical gatherings in the homes of wealthy Parisian patrons. These salons were predominantly feminine social and musical spaces, and Chopin's association with them encouraged a view of him as "a composer 'for the ladies,'" as Samson puts it—a perception that was "reinforced not just in critical writing but in portraits, drawings and pictorial representations on nineteenth-century editions."[4]

At the risk of understatement, the classical music world has long been rife with gender bias, and women's musical activities and contributions were (and unfortunately still are) often met with derision. Thus, for many years, Chopin's association with the feminine drawing room raised questions about his status as a serious composer.[5] The historian Whitney Walton, for example, has traced some of the challenges Chopin's feminization posed for his reception, a problem exacerbated by his relationship with the writer George Sand, who provoked scandals with her propensity for stereotypically masculine behavior.[6] Walton succinctly summarizes how Chopin and Sand flipped traditional gender roles: "Sand did . . . dress in men's clothes, smoke little cigars, live an independent life, and succeed in literature—all practices that violated feminine norms of behavior in her time. And Chopin was . . . usually in poor health, thin, weak, and careful about his dress and interior decoration—all characteristics associated with femininity rather than masculinity."[7] In short, Chopin was effeminized though his musical and personal lives, as the composer of trivial salon music and as the stereotypically feminine half of a romantic relationship.

---

[3] Jim Samson, "Myth and Reality: A Biographical Introduction," in *The Cambridge Companion to Chopin*, ed. Jim Samson (Cambridge: Cambridge University Press, 1992), 1–8.

[4] Samson, "Myth and Reality," 3. Samson expands on these ideas somewhat in his "Chopin Reception: Theory, History, Analysis," in *Chopin Studies 2*, ed. John Rink and Jim Samson (Cambridge: Cambridge University Press, 1994), 1–17.

[5] On the gendering of the salon (and Chopin), see, for example, Jeffrey Kallberg, "The Harmony of the Tea Table: Gender and Ideology in the Piano Nocturne," *Representations* 39 (1992): 102–133.

[6] Whitney Walton, "Gender and Genius in Postrevolutionary France: Sand and Chopin," in *The Age of Chopin: Interdisciplinary Inquiries*, ed. Halina Goldberg (Bloomington: Indiana University Press, 2004), 224–243.

[7] Walton, "Gender and Genius in Postrevolutionary France," 230–231. Walton argues compellingly that these transgressions of gender norms complicated perceptions of Sand—and, to a lesser degree, Chopin—as artistic geniuses.

These gender issues are further complicated by Chopin's reputation as a somehow otherworldly figure—an angel or a fairy. As the musicologist Jeffrey Kallberg notes, "These terms . . . engaged a complex of unstable meanings having to do with sex and gender, and so ultimately helped forge a changing image of Chopin as an androgynous, hermaphroditic, effeminate and/or pathological being."[8] Kallberg suggests that Chopin's critics may have (perhaps subconsciously) found evidence of these qualities in his physical frailty and disease—a corporeal manifestation of his deviation from sexual and gender norms.

The question of his physical frailty brings up the second Chopin myth: the Romantic suffering artist. Quoting Samson again:

> From childhood his heath was delicate and at the end of his short life consumption took a cruel toll on his creative energies. Yet the image of Chopin the consumptive, with "the pallor of the grave," came to take on additional significance, interpreted almost as a philosophy of life and even as an explanation of his creative output. Through music he "discloses his suffering."[9]

Thankfully, in recent years video games have begun to embrace a more diverse range of protagonists. Yet the idea of a physically weak, vaguely androgynous game hero still stands sharply at odds with the standard archetypes.[10] In fairness to games, even films struggle to depict Chopin as a compelling leading character, although he has been the subject of several biopics: *A Song to Remember* (1945), *Impromptu* (1991), the French film *La note bleue* (1991), and the Polish-English *Chopin: Desire for Love* (2002). Not surprisingly, to satisfy the dramatic necessities of a cinematic narrative, each of these films manipulates or wholly fabricates events from the composer's life—but even the relatively successful *Impromptu* leaves moviegoers with the impression that Chopin was, again in Kallberg's words, "an enervated weakling."[11]

To avoid falling prey to the same obstacles, *Eternal Sonata* and *Frederic* lean disproportionately on Chopin's third identity: the Slavonic composer. Despite the fact that the composer was actually quite apolitical, "the issue of Chopin as a Polish 'national' composer" has become "one of the central features of our perception of

---

[8] Jeffrey Kallberg, "Small Fairy Voices: Sex, History, and Meaning in Chopin," in *Chopin Studies 2*, ed. John Rink and Jim Samson (Cambridge: Cambridge University Press, 1994), 57.

[9] Samson, "Myth and Reality," 5.

[10] Japanese role-playing games in particular have a disturbing history of characters whose androgyny is an indicator of their villainy, as with, for example, Kefka in *Final Fantasy VI* (1994), Flea in *Chrono Trigger* (1995), and Kuja in *Final Fantasy IX* (2000).

[11] Jeffrey Kallberg, "Nocturnal Thoughts on *Impromptu*," *Musical Quarterly* 81 (1997): 200.

Chopin," as musicologist Jolanta Pekacz writes.[12] Pekacz argues that biographers and interpreters have unduly emphasized Chopin's nationalistic impulses in an effort to bring him into conformity with heroic stereotypes. That strategy is readily apparent in both *Eternal Sonata* and *Frederic*. The former, for example, prominently touts Chopin's desire to "use the piano as a weapon to fight for Poland."[13] Yet even emphasizing (or inventing) the composer's nationalist motivations seems insufficient to compensate for his frail, effeminate reputation. And so both games employ innovative narrative and musical strategies to wholly transform Chopin, dramatically reinventing the composer for the benefit of twenty-first-century gaming audiences.

Sleep Hath Its Own World

Even among the wacky plots of Japanese role-playing games (or JRPGs), *Eternal Sonata*'s premise seems a bit bizarre. To quote from the ad copy on the back of the game's box: "On his deathbed, the famous composer, Chopin, drifts between this life and the next. On the border between dreams and reality, Chopin discovers the light that shines in all of us in this enduring tale of good and evil, love and betrayal." As this description suggests, the plot involves several narrative levels, which I describe as "real," "fictional," and "metafictional." The first two of these appear only sporadically and never involve player interaction. The real world—our reality, in other words—interjects itself through slideshows depicting important locations and events in Chopin's life. The fictional world, by contrast, appears in a series of cutscenes set in 1849 Paris, where Chopin lies on his deathbed.

---

[12] Jolanta T. Pekacz, "Deconstructing a 'National Composer': Chopin and Polish Exiles in Paris, 1831–49," *19th Century Music* 24 (2000): 161.

[13] The slideshow that opens *Eternal Sonata*'s chapter 2 ("Revolution") contains the following text, directly connecting the "Revolutionary" Étude to Polish independence and projecting profoundly martial impulses onto Chopin: "On November 29th, 1830, an insurrection occurred in Warsaw, the capital of Poland. It was the November Uprising. At the time, most of Poland was Russian territory, and the desire for independence had been growing. About four weeks before the insurgence, on November 2nd, Chopin left the increasingly dangerous Warsaw and headed for Vienna. It is said that Chopin's friends encouraged him to leave the country, because they knew rebellion was certain. But Chopin was unaware of this, and his trip had been planned many months in advance. Chopin was unusually talented, as well as physically weak, so his friends wanted him to use the piano as a weapon to fight for Poland. On November 23rd, approximately twenty days later, Chopin arrived in Vienna. And six days after that, the insurrection in Warsaw started. It went on for almost a year. Then, on September 8th, 1831, Warsaw fell. Ten months of fighting had ended in defeat. Chopin, then age twenty-one, learned of the insurrection's failure while in Stuttgart, Germany. The feelings with which he played the piano at this time took the form of this composition, 'The Revolutionary Étude.' To Chopin, who genuinely loved his homeland of Poland, the insurrection's failure was difficult to bear. But perhaps he found it even more difficult to bear the fact that he was safe in a foreign country. Chopin would never set foot in his native land again."

No. it's true. Everything around us is all a part of my dream. Even you are just a product of my imagination.

FIGURE 9.1 Screenshot of a cutscene in *Eternal Sonata* (2007, metafictional Chopin at right).

The majority of the game, however, takes place in the metafictional dreamworld inside the fictional Chopin's mind—a colorful fantasy realm filled with quirky characters, hordes of monsters, and ample melodrama. Metafiction can mean a number of things, but here I mean what literary theorist Patricia Waugh describes as "fictional writing which self-consciously and systematically draws attention to its status as an artifact in order to pose questions about the relationship between fiction and reality."[14] For reference, examples of that kind of reality-bending metafiction might include William Goldman's novel *The Princess Bride* (1973) or Michael Ende's novel *The Neverending Story* (1979) and its film adaptation. In *Eternal Sonata*'s metafictional world, a highly stylized version of Chopin—fully aware that this world exists only in his mind—joins a ragtag group of youths in a rebellion against an oppressive government (Figure 9.1). This fantasy clearly draws on Chopin's experiences as a musician—towns and characters are all named after musical terms, and many of the characters fight with weapons based on instruments. The political struggles also evoke the composer's life: as the game repeatedly implies, the oppression he fights is reminiscent of that in Chopin's native Poland. By actively contributing to the battle, the metafictional Chopin engages with conflict in a direct way that the real composer never could.

By keeping the three versions of Chopin separate, *Eternal Sonata*'s elaborately multilayered narrative serves an important structural purpose. This isolation cleverly sidesteps issues of historical fidelity, allowing the metafictional Chopin to become

---

[14] Patricia Waugh, *Metafiction: The Theory and Practice of Self-Conscious Fiction* (London: Routledge, 1984), 3.

a video game hero without negating his real-world biography.[15] In this fantasy, the game seems to say, Chopin can appear as he wants to be—or, perhaps, as *we* want him to be. The game minimizes the effeminacy and illness that might have prevented his video game success, but without denying their existence. The text that accompanies chapter 1 ("Raindrops"), for example, describes his relationship with George Sand— "a somewhat masculine woman who wore pants and smoked cigars in public"—and notes that "Chopin was not in the best of health." Yet neither of those biographical realities seems to influence his metafictional incarnation in the slightest.

Eternal Sonata also avoids the salon composer problem by diverting attention instead to his nationalism. From the opening to chapter 4 ("Grande Valse Brillante"):

> Chopin appeared at salons and dinner parties, performing music for small audiences. It is said that after these performances, Chopin returned to his room and played his piano furiously.
>
> He must have felt a frustrating anger towards himself, forced to suppress his true feelings, put on a mask, and perform music to please people. In contrast to the cheerful style of this piece, Chopin's heart was most likely not nearly as high-spirited.

Chopin might have played in salons, the text implies—but that was a repression of his true, masculine self, which he expressed later through his "furious" playing. The nationalist tinge recurs in many of the real-world slideshows. Five of the seven, in fact, make explicit reference to political turmoil in Poland, with the final chapter ("Heroic") being the most blatant:

> Perhaps [the "Heroic" Polonaise in A-flat Major, Op. 53] is a culmination of the feelings that Chopin had for his homeland. . . . It's almost as if one can feel the invisible power of the entire nation of Poland behind it. If one ever wondered just how proud Chopin was of his home country, this piece answers that question eloquently.[16]

On the other hand, although these passages fall prey to stereotypes that are all too common in Chopin reception, *Eternal Sonata*'s designers also made extensive

---

[15] Interestingly, in the Japanese version of *Eternal Sonata*, the "real-world" slideshows take place with a single static image throughout, perhaps to reduce distractions from the music and text.

[16] Samson and others have observed the Romantic tendency to ascribe autobiographical meaning to Chopin's music, a desire to "seek out either a specific referential meaning in this musical work . . . or a hidden emotional content." Samson, "Myth and Reality," 5.

efforts at historical realism. As a blog entry by one staff member reveals, the game's localization team was in close communication with the Frederick Chopin Society for "double checking our facts related to Chopin, as a historical figure, and his music."[17] The end result of this complex navigation between reality, fiction, and metafiction is that *Eternal Sonata* has its cake and eats it, too. Players get a suitably heroic metafictional version of Chopin, while the real Chopin is left more or less intact.

One possible downside to that strategy, however, is that in practice the multiple narrative levels might be confusing. That's where the game's soundtrack becomes particularly important. Music helps keep this complex structure understandable, providing players with sonic cues that differentiate the narrative levels. The fictional Paris scenes take place in musical silence, meaning players hear only the noises the characters hear: voices, and an ominous ticking clock that reinforces the inexorable approach of Chopin's death. The metafictional world features newly created music by Motoi Sakuraba, a veteran JRPG composer. Indeed, the score could just as easily be from any other JRPG. Aside from the prominence of piano—a frequent feature of Sakuraba's music—nothing in *Eternal Sonata*'s score hints at the game's subject matter. The placement of the music is equally typical, with most towns and dungeons in the game associated with an endlessly looped musical cue unique to that location.[18]

Chopin's compositions appear in *Eternal Sonata* only during the real-world slideshows between game chapters. During each of these transitional interludes, players hear one of the composer's piano works in its entirety, featuring new recordings made for the game by the Russian pianist Stanislav Bunin (Table 9.1). The treatment of music in these sections differs strikingly from the rest of the game. In the metafictional world, the game music mostly stays in the background. The slideshow interludes, on the other hand, treat the music reverentially. The flood of aural and visual information players receive during most of the game is dramatically reduced,

---

[17] The author notes: "Communicating with the Frederick Chopin Society provided us with a resource for double checking our facts related to Chopin, as a historical figure, and his music. We sent them a copy of all the text we were going to include in the game that related to Chopin. They reviewed everything and pointed out any information that was erroneous or misleading. So, of course, we made any changes they requested or suggested until all of our text met with their approval. We wanted our facts to be as historically accurate as possible without diverting too much from the text as it was originally written . . .. As you can imagine, we were very grateful to get help like that from such a knowledgeable source!" Stephanie Fernandez, "Lost in Translation," *IGN* (September 12, 2007), available online at http://www.ign.com/blogs/eternalsonata/2007/09/12/lost-in-translation (accessed September 15, 2015).

[18] On typical music placement in JRPGs, see, for example, William Gibbons, "Music, Genre, and Nationality in Postmillennial Fantasy Role-Playing Games," in *The Routledge Companion to Screen Music and Sound*, ed. Miguel Mera, Ron Sadoff, and Ben Winters (London: Routledge, 2017), 412–427.

TABLE 9.1

Chapters of *Eternal Sonata* (2007) with musical selections

Game Chapter	Title of Piece
Chapter 1: Raindrops	Prelude in D-flat Major ("Raindrop"), Op. 28, No. 15
Chapter 2: Revolutions	Étude in C Minor ("Revolutionary"), Op. 10, No. 12
Chapter 3: Fantaisie-Impromptu	Fantaisie-Impromptu, Op. 66
Chapter 4: Grande Valse Brillante	Grande Valse Brillante, Op. 18
Chapter 5: Nocturne	Nocturne in E-flat Major, Op. 9, No. 2
Chapter 6: Tristesse	Étude in E Major, Op. 10, No. 3
Chapter 7: Heroic	Polonaise in A-flat Major ("Heroic"), Op. 53

muted photographs replace the usual cartoonishly colorful graphics, and written text replaces recorded dialogue—all changes that encourage players to give the music their full attention.

The split narrative levels also help explain why classical music plays no part in the metafictional world. Unlike the newly composed music, players recognize Chopin's works as products of the real world—as such, they're reserved for that portion of the game. Yet this treatment of classical music seems to make a larger statement: art shouldn't be reduced to background music. *Eternal Sonata* positions classical music as something special, to be protected and isolated from the game around it. For most of the game, these barriers remain impermeable—yet even the strongest walls eventually develop cracks. Near the end of the game, once Chopin and his group liberate his dreamworld, the composer muses at length on the unknowable nature of reality. In a final bid to return to his version of reality, the metafictional Chopin attempts to destroy the world his mind has created. As this final struggle pits him against his former friends, the boundaries between reality and fiction that have held *Eternal Sonata*'s narrative together begin to collapse—Chopin the composer merges with Chopin the video game hero.[19]

This breach manifests dramatically in the music. As the worlds collide, Chopin forcibly imposes his reality onto the other narrative levels. As he does so, his music, previously kept isolated from the game's original score, begins to bleed over into the

---

[19] There is, debatably, a smaller and quite subtle moment of rupture earlier in *Eternal Sonata*. After one of the game's interludes, players hear applause, and as the next chapter begins, the metafictional Chopin has just performed a concert of his music. One plausible interpretation is that these two scenes are connected, implying that Chopin diegetically performed the work players just heard. Interpreting the scene this way means that the real and metafictional worlds briefly overlap.

metafictional world. The result is an underscore that blends the "Revolutionary" Étude with Sakuraba's musical style just as the two Chopins intersect. This startling moment of rupture draws connections between the dichotomies of reality/fiction and art/not-art. As the narrative levels implode, the game calls attention to the metafictional Chopin's hierarchical constructions of reality. Ultimately, the defeated composer rejects his simplistically dualistic perspective, sacrificing his real life to save the lives of his imaginary (?) friends. In the same way, juxtaposing Chopin's music with Sakuraba's video game score raises questions about the nature of art, suggesting that perhaps the privileging of classical music that the game previously encouraged might be equally naive.

Chopin, Hero

The walls surrounding art come tumbling down only in the final moments of *Eternal Sonata*, at the culmination of a forty-plus-hour journey. The Polish-produced mobile title *Frederic: Resurrection of Music*, in contrast, embraces that chaos from the outset, reveling in musical and narrative juxtapositions. *Frederic* is a music-based game in which players perform Chopin's music by touching the correct part of an on-screen keyboard at the right time (Figure 9.2).[20] A series of cutscenes between stages hold together a tongue-in-cheek plot: in a cartoonish version of modern-day Paris, a mysterious hooded figure resurrects the long-dead Chopin and quickly departs the scene.[21] Befuddled, the composer receives some much-needed guidance from the three Muses, who reveal the sorry state of today's music. Case in point: as the composer ponders his next move, a self-declared master of electronic music challenges him to a musical duel. After a decisive victory, Chopin sets off across the globe in search of answers. Who brought him back, and why? And, even more important, what role does his art play in this new world?

Like *Eternal Sonata*'s metafictional narrative, *Frederic*'s premise avoids a need for game designers to stick to historical fact. That being said, in stark contrast to

---

[20] The game mechanics function similarly to the display for the keyboard in *Rock Band 3*, although that game features an actual keyboard controller rather than a touchscreen. *KeyboardMania* (Konami, 2000) was an earlier keyboard-based music game, which allowed players to use MIDI keyboards connected to PCs for input.

[21] Joseph Leray, reviewing the game for *Touch Arcade*, noted that *Frederic* "isn't a game so much as it is a rewriting of Chopin's cultural identity . . . .. *Resurrection* ultimately leads him back to a culturally reinvigorated Warsaw, but only after he uses his musical gifts to destroy the stereotyped, corporate shills that populate the rest of the world. Chopin is cast as the savior of music, but it's odd that he uses modern remixes, not his traditional compositions, to further his cause." Joseph Leray, "*Frederic: Resurrection of Music* Review," *Touch Arcade* (February 1, 2012), available online at http://toucharcade.com/2012/02/01/frederic-resurrection-of-music-review/ (accessed October 3, 2015).

FIGURE 9.2 Gameplay screenshot from *Frederic: Resurrection of Music* (2011).

the historical vignettes of *Eternal Sonata*'s slideshow sequences, *Frederic* is far less concerned with educating its audience about Chopin's life than it is with revitalizing his image. Initially he appears in nineteenth-century clothes and with a sickly blue pallor that makes him appear "undead" compared with the modern musicians. Combined with his antiquated speech and mannerisms, these characteristics cause Chopin to come across as a man entirely out of his element. Near the end of the game, however, he undergoes a transformation, rebranding himself with a new rock-star persona (Figure 9.3). Any suggestion of the effeminate or sickly Chopin is absent—*Frederic* unabashedly aims to maximize its protagonist's appeal even at the risk of historical inaccuracy. The composer literally wields music as a weapon, with lightning bolts or other pyrotechnics frequently exploding from his piano to wreak havoc on his opponents. *Frederic*, clearly, is a game about the power of art.

In contrast to the strict separation of musical styles in *Eternal Sonata*, much of the appeal of *Frederic*'s entirely remixed soundtrack stems from crossing those barriers. *Frederic* follows Chopin to a number of locations around the world, each one featuring an opponent to defeat. (That premise will sound familiar to players of fighting games like *Street Fighter II: The World Warrior* [1991]—and indeed it's helpful to understand *Frederic* as a hybrid music/fighting game.) Each of these musical duels

FIGURE 9.3 Chopin "updated" in *Frederic: Resurrection of Music*.

features one of Chopin's works remixed with stereotypical musical styles from its graphical location: Celtic music in Ireland, reggae in the Caribbean, hip-hop in New York, and so on (Table 9.2). Each time, Chopin and his music triumph—symbolically demonstrating not only his virtuosity as a performer but also, by implication, the superiority of classical music.

Like *Eternal Sonata, Frederic* initially privileges classical music, but later complicates that position. In this case, what starts as a celebration of classical music's power eventually becomes a manifesto against the dangers of commodifying art. Players eventually learn that the man who resurrected Chopin was Mastermind X—the most powerful record-company executive in the world. All along, his nefarious goal was to trick Chopin into defeating the world's last independent musicians, thus forever eliminating the scourge of noncommercialized music. After this dramatic revelation, *Frederic* abruptly pivots from a celebration of classical music into an indictment of capitalist society's aesthetic bankruptcy. In this dark outlook on the present day, even the Muses aren't immune to crass pandering: they cut short their conversation with Chopin to film a commercial for a fast-food Greek salad.

It's tempting to attribute *Frederic's* surprising change of tone to the lack of a clear thematic vision—a claim not without some merit. But the shift also acts as a kind of metacommentary on musical prejudice. Players have presumably been perfectly

TABLE 9.2

Classical remixes in *Frederic: Resurrection of Music*

Track Title	Musical Style	Title of Original Piece
Midnight Flight to Paris	EDM	Prelude in E Minor, Op. 28, No. 4
Jamaican Coconuts	Reggae	Polonaise in A Major ("Military"), Op. 40, No. 1
New Deputy in Town	Country/Western	Piano Sonata No. 2 in B-flat Minor, Op. 35, III ("Funeral March")
The Big Wild Apple	Hip-hop	Nocturne in F Minor, Op. 55, No. 1/ Polonaise in A-flat Major ("Heroic"), Op. 53
Exploding Star	EDM	Waltz in A Minor (Op. post)
Classical Feelings	Easy listening/classical	Nocturne in E-flat Major, Op. 9, No. 2
Chasing the Leprechaun	Ambient/Irish	Étude in G-flat Major ("Butterfly"), Op. 25, No. 9
Whales in the Sky	EDM	Lithuanian Song, Op. 74, No. 16
The Epic Battle	Chiptunes	Étude in C Minor ("Revolutionary"), Op. 10, No. 12
Oriental (Bonus track)	JPop (Japanese pop)	Prelude in A Major, Op. 28, No. 7

willing to accept what the Muses told us in the game's opening moments: Chopin is a composer whose talents have yet to be equaled. The enjoyable but generally unsophisticated musical juxtapositions that accompany each level encourage this belief in his superiority, giving the impression that popular styles are simple, derivative, and repetitive. Likewise, in contrast with Chopin's earnest politeness, his opponents are depicted as buffoons, incapable of treating music seriously—not to mention the ways in which they sometimes raise uncomfortable racial and cultural stereotypes.[22] When Mastermind X's plan is revealed, *Frederic* pulls the rug from under these assumptions, and by the end of the game, the idea of music as an art

---

[22] The critic for *Slide to Play*, for example, writes: "What isn't necessarily . . . respectful . . . is the game's illustrations of different kinds of people. Frederic doesn't feel like an encyclopedia of stereotypes, but it does have some questionable depictions in its narrative. For example, Ireland is represented by a leprechaun-like man, and Jamaica's avatar is a Rastafarian who's way into certain psychoactive plants. At some point these kinds of images can cross lines of decency, but we're not sure if Frederic is guilty of such an offense or not. It's worth considering, but we'll leave it up to you to decide if Forever Entertainment was tactless or not in this regard." Devin Wilson, "*Frederic—Resurrection of Music* Complete Review," *Slide to Play* (February 17, 2012), available online at http://www.slidetoplay.com/review/frederic-resurrection-of-music-complete-review/ (accessed October 1, 2015).

form is effectively detached from the concept of classical music. Art, *Frederic's* protagonist and players learn, encompasses *all* music created apart from commercial consideration.[23]

But even that message isn't totally clear. *Frederic's* story suggests that Chopin's art is inherently superior to commercialized music (whatever *that* means). Yet a large part of the game's appeal emerges from enjoying how classical music can be transgressively remixed with nonclassical styles. This playfully postmodern approach to Chopin's works might help engage players who don't typically listen to classical music—yet it runs completely counter to the game's central message. Despite its idealistic, if off-kilter, ruminations on the nature of art and commercialization, *Frederic* is itself a commercial product that earns revenue through the commodification of Chopin's music. Viewed in this light, *Frederic* becomes a self-reflexive contemplation of its own emptiness. It's an unresolvable contradiction, simultaneously celebrating and satirizing music's cultural authority. It lures players into believing in the powers of art, then mocks them for their naiveté.

Classical music in video games often destabilizes the status quo, disrupting players' understandings of art and entertainment. Its presence erodes cultural boundaries, subverting generic expectations of video games and shaping new understandings of where, when, and how it is appropriate to engage with classical music. It's by playing *as*, and playing *with* Chopin and composers like him that games can alter cultural perceptions of classical music. Although *Eternal Sonata* and *Frederic* feature an unusual protagonist, their treatment of classical music reflects many of the trends explored throughout *Unlimited Replays*. Both games to a greater or lesser extent embrace postmodern stylistic remixes, at once defamiliarizing classical music and rendering the other genres more artistic. Each also offers a reinterpretation of music history, combining Chopin's music with scenes of his heroism, rewriting his persona to suit the necessities of gameplay. These games try to make classical music look cool, or at least mitigate its profound lack of coolness—hence *Frederic's* rock-star Chopin.[24] Reimagining Chopin is a way of rewriting music history, transforming the foreign country of the past into a more familiar locale.

---

[23] *Frederic 2: Evil Strikes Back* returns to these issues. The gameplay is identical to that of the original *Frederic*, but here Frederic challenges caricatures of well-known pop musicians around the world (Michael Jackson and Lady Gaga, for example) who are supposedly destroying music with their soulless, mass-produced hits. The game's soundtrack, consequently, parodies popular songs by these artists ("Bad" and "Poker Face," respectively) rather than remixing Chopin's music.

[24] Here again there are parallels with media dictions of Beethoven, who Broyles notes often appears "somewhere between a Romantic god and a rock star." Michael Broyles, *Beethoven in America* (Bloomington: Indiana University Press, 2011), 195.

Importantly, this reinterpretation emerges from an educational impulse. In an interview with the popular gaming website *GameSpot*, *Eternal Sonata*'s director, Hiroya Hatsushiba, opined:

> People who play games and people who love classical music are not necessarily sharing [the] same type of interests. Most people in Japan know the name of Chopin; however, most of the people who know of Chopin think he is just some kind of a great music composer without knowing any more about him. Most of them have heard Chopin's music but not a lot could put his name to it immediately. . . . I was hoping that people would get into this game easily and also come to know how great Chopin's music is.[25]

In other words, *Eternal Sonata* encourages players to explore music history by bringing art and entertainment together, and can thus make a claim that it serves an important cultural function. A number of critics certainly took note of this educational potential. One reviewer for *IGN*, for example, suggested it "teaches music appreciation and history"—stressing the educative value by invoking the names of two standard college courses. But this music, the reviewer makes clear, doesn't hamper players' enjoyment: "It uses his music and life to bring context to what is happening in front of you. . . . It's educational, but it's also incredibly fun and interesting."[26]

Players have noticed the same kinds of educational aspirations, suggesting that Hatsushiba at least partially realized his lofty goals.[27] In a user-submitted review for *Eternal Sonata* on the website *GameFAQs*, MizuruTakagi writes: "For once you can think of video games as 'educational' with this one. I personally, was amazed at how much I learned. Seeing photographs about Chopin's life telling his story, really got me hooked. And for most of you, it will do the same."[28] Another reviewer identifying as ShadowAspect echoed the same thoughts but added an intriguing connection: "Amazingly, you can actually LEARN something about the man while you

---

[25] "Eternal Sonata Director Q&A," *GameSpot* (August 7, 2007), available online at http://www.gamespot.com/xbox360/rpg/trustybellchopinnoyume/news.html?page=1&sid=6176358 (accessed January 15, 2016).

[26] Erik Brudvig, "Eternal Sonata Review," *IGN* (September 13, 2007), available online at http://www.ign.com/articles/2007/09/13/eternal-sonata-review-2 (accessed January 16, 2016).

[27] Raising awareness of the subject is, of course, a major goal for any kind of biographical cinematic project. As cinema historian Robert Brent Toplin writes (summarizing the views of historical documentary producers), "A film can only introduce a subject . . .. If it is successful, it will bring a subject to the attention of people who did not know much about it before, and it will encourage them to ask questions and seek further information through reading." Robert Brent Toplin, "The Filmmaker as Historian," *American Historical Review* 93 (1988): 1213.

[28] MizuruTakagi, "An Ingenious Masterpiece Portrayed with Innovative Art and Beauty," *GameFAQs* (June 30, 2008), available online at http://www.gamefaqs.com/console/xbox360/review/R126318.html (accessed January 17, 2016).

play the game. It's really refreshing to see and adds a lot to classifying this [game] as 'art.'"[29] For this reviewer, evidently, including educational aspects in games elevates them to artworks. This complex and revealing process—entertainment becoming art, and art becoming entertainment—is the subject of this book's final pair of chapters.

---

[29] ShadowAspect, "A Masterful Example of Artistry in Gaming.," *GameFAQs* (September 28, 2007), available online at http://www.gamefaqs.com/console/xbox360/review/R118148.html (accessed January 17, 2016).

10 Gamifying Classical Music

THIS WAS IT—THE ultimate showdown. Several minutes of intense thought had gone into this final challenge, but now I was nearing the goal. Looking down at my iPad, I triple-checked that everything was ready to go. Then, holding my breath, I tentatively tapped the screen, and . . . victory! As a musical fanfare played, I let out a satisfied sigh and watched a tally of how many experience points I'd earned. But who was this dread foe? Not the usual evil wizard, mad scientist, or supervillain. This time, I was locked in a battle of wills with—French. The language. More specifically, the past tense of the conditional, which I still can't quite master. (Fortunately, so far I've been able to survive without being able to say "I would have been going to go to the museum.") Rather than a game in the traditional sense, I was playing Duolingo, a language-learning program that combines a web-based learning platform with gamelike apps.

Duolingo is an example of gamification—the application of concepts drawn from games to other activities. The increasing prevalence of computer technology has allowed gamification to profoundly affect almost every aspect of our daily lives, from personal fitness, to education, to how we choose to purchase products. In her book *Reality Is Broken: Why Games Make Us Better and How They Can Change the World*, Jane McGonigal argues that gamification (or "alternate realities," as she prefers) can exert a powerful, and positive, influence on humanity.[1] "The great

---

[1] Jane McGonigal, *Reality Is Broken: Why Games Make Us Better and How They Can Change the World* (New York: Penguin, 2011); see also McGonigal's follow-up, *SuperBetter: The Power of Living Gamefully*

challenge for us today, and for the remainder of the century," McGonigal suggests with some urgency, "is to integrate games more closely into our everyday lives, and to embrace them as a platform for collaboration on our most important planetary efforts."[2] The general process of gamification is fairly simple. Developers take the things players like about games—earning points, leveling up, getting rewards, and so on—and use those elements of positive reinforcement to encourage people to do things they might otherwise find tedious or challenging.

The idea of applying aspects of games to other activities has a long history, not least in music. Eighteenth-century Viennese musicians, for example, sometimes composed new music using dice-based games, and nineteenth-century students could choose from several different board games to improve their music theory skills.[3] And as several recent studies have explored, there are obvious and subtle connections between playing video games and musical performance. Both require manual dexterity and a sense of rhythm, for instance. On a deeper level, like games, for the most part music operates by adhering to sets of rules. Composers and performers are often successful based on their ability to be creative within given structures and frameworks. As a result of their shared emphasis on playfulness, video games have drawn on music as a design element from their earliest days.[4] Consider, as one example, the musical memory—based *SIMON* (1978), an electronic game created in part by Ralph Baer, the man often described as "the father of video games."[5]

In the same vein, the entire popular genre of music-based games is predicated on gamifying music, from the rock-based *Guitar Hero* series to a diverse range of

---

(New York: Penguin, 2015). The latter book even pairs with an accompanying app aimed at putting the author's strategies for self-improvement through gamification into practice.

[2] McGonigal, *Reality Is Broken*, 354.

[3] See, for example, Stephen A. Hedges, "Dice Music in the Eighteenth Century," *Music and Letters* 59 (1978): 180–187; and Carmel Raz, "Anne Young's 'Musical Games' (1801): Music Theory, Gender, and Game Design" (paper presented at the annual meeting of the American Musicological Society, Vancouver, British Columbia, November 3–6, 2016).

[4] Notable explorations of the shared notion of playfulness between music and games include Ian Bogost, *How to Do Things with Video Games* (Minneapolis: University of Minnesota Press, 2011), chap. 4; Anahid Kassabian and Freya Jarman, "Game and Play in Music Video Games," in *Ludomusicology*, ed. Michiel Kamp, Tim Summers, and Mark Sweeney (Sheffield, UK: Equinox, 2016), 116–132; and, most significantly, Roger Moseley, *Keys to Play: Music as a Ludic Medium from Apollo to Nintendo* (Berkeley: University of California Press, 2016). For a general introduction and helpful summary, see also Michael Austin, "Introduction—Taking Note of Music Games," in *Music Video Games: Performance, Politics, and Play*, ed. Michael Austin (New York: Bloomsbury, 2016), 1–22. Many of the essays in this edited volume, in fact, deal in one way or another with issues of play in music and games.

[5] On *SIMON* as the forerunner of the current music game genre, see William Knoblauch, "*SIMON*: The Prelude to Modern Music Video Games," in *Music Video Games: Performance, Politics, and Play*, ed. Michael Austin (New York: Bloomsbury, 2016), 25–42.

lesser-known titles, like *PaRappa the Rapper* (1996), *Space Channel 5* (1999), and *Samba de Amigo* (1999).

The majority of music games focus on popular music of one style or another. A surprising number, however, explore classical styles, such as *Boom Boom Rocket* (2007) and *Frederic: Resurrection of Music* (2011), both of which were explored in previous chapters. Other notable examples would include the narrative-driven iOS game *Symponica* (2012), which tells the story of a young conductor in a world where nearly everything revolves around classical music. Each of these classical music games focuses on combining the fun parts of classical music and video games to create an entertaining experience.

A core concept of gamification is that it leads to betterment—encouragement toward self-improvement. All music games fall into that category in one way or another. Anahid Kassabian and Freya Jarman, for example, have argued that all music-based games are educational, because

> they "teach" or "improve" some kind of skill, be it memory, hand-eye-ear co-ordination, the liberty to shape and create patterns of sound, or an entry into (a) musical culture(s). That is not to say that the didactic function is a primary, or even necessarily intended, outcome of gameplay, but rather that the player necessarily learns something or acquires or improves a skill.[6]

I fully agree with this understanding of music games, and with the potential of these games to improve music education. In this chapter, however, I'm interested in instances where that "didactic function" assumes a different role, enhancing players' cultural education as much as or more than their technical skills. In contrast to the overwhelming dominance of popular music styles in music-based games, these types of edutainment products often focus on classical music—which is itself frequently associated with self-improvement. The musicologist Mark Katz, for example, has traced how the widespread availability of recorded music in the early twentieth-century United States led to a push for education in so-called good music, a civilizing force many believed would lead to massive improvements in American culture.[7]

Hopes for gamified classical music remain somewhat less lofty at present. Nevertheless, the underlying—though usually unspoken—assumption is that developing an appreciation for classical music is inherently beneficial. In the two

---

[6] Kassabian and Jarman, "Game and Play in Music Video Games," 123.

[7] See Mark Katz, *Capturing Sound: How Technology Has Changed Music*, rev. ed. (Berkeley: University of California Press, 2010), chap. 2.

examples that follow—both mobile-based apps from the 2010s—a classical work is transformed from being a piece of concert music into being an interactive experience. In the first instance, the iOS app *Young Person's Guide to the Orchestra by Benjamin Britten* (2013), we find gamelike elements applied to a classical work as a form of music appreciation. In the second, *Steve Reich's Clapping Music—Improve Your Rhythm* (2015), performing a classical work becomes in itself a tool for self-improvement.

Music App-reciation

Initially composed for the documentary film *Instruments of the Orchestra* (1946), Benjamin Britten's *Young Person's Guide to the Orchestra* (1945) has become much better known as a stand-alone concert piece for children. Like many other classical works for youth audiences, the *Young Person's Guide* is explicitly educational.[8] Through a set of variations on a theme by the seventeenth-century composer Henry Purcell, it introduces listeners to instrument groups (woodwinds, strings, and so on) and to musical forms, such as the fugue. Britten's piece is a guide in two senses. It's a manual for understanding the orchestra, similar to a guidebook to a foreign country that contains helpful hints for new travelers. But it's also a guide *to* the orchestra, directing new audiences to the concert hall just as a guide dog might lead its owner. By educating children about the orchestra, in other words, the piece aims to create a new generation of people who not only understand classical music but also actually want to hear it.

Britten's *Young Person's Guide* emerged at a time when the so-called music appreciation movement was well underway in the United Kingdom, the United States, and elsewhere, creating lasting effects that reverberate in the educational system even today.[9] After World War I, governments, broadcasters, arts organizations, and publishers made concerted efforts to drive audiences to classical music through the edification of the masses. That effort was particularly concentrated on children. Secure in the belief that classical music had a positive impact on the mind and character of its devotees, they sought to develop children's ears in ways that would ensure a new generation of eager audience members. As the musicologist Kate Guthrie points out, "The music appreciation movement was founded on the belief that the 'normal listener' would appreciate 'good' music (that is, Western art music)

---

[8] Another example of a similarly didactic orchestral work would be Sergei Prokofiev's *Peter and the Wolf* (1936), with which Britten's *Young Person's Guide* is frequently paired, both in recordings and in live performance.

[9] On the impact of print and broadcast music appreciation efforts, see, for example, Joseph Horowitz, *Classical Music in America: A History of Its Rise and Fall* (New York: Norton, 2005), chap. 5.

more if they approached it with a knowledge of the rudiments of music theory and interpretation."[10]

Britten's music aimed to educate young people about classical music in ways that were both meaningful and measurable. And, intentionally or not, this mission reinforced distinctions between serious classical music, which required education and study, and other implicitly lesser forms of music, which did not. To again quote Guthrie:

> Being able to name the instruments of the orchestra or describe a piece of music's form were comparably quantifiable measures of serious engagement. The notion that listening to such music was an acquired skill reinforced the high art canon's elite status. Thus, *Instruments of the Orchestra* sought to defend art music against a denigrating association with mass culture, even as it promoted this repertoire to a broad audience.[11]

In other words, one goal of music appreciation programs was to convince large swaths of the population to accept the propositions that (1) classical music exerts a positive influence on the listener, and (2) an understanding of classical masterworks indicates a person of sophisticated taste.

Emergent media technologies have played an enormous role in the success of music appreciation programs. The widespread availability of classical recordings in the early twentieth century led to hopes for a massive surge in the popularity of "good music." Radio programs enabled huge segments of the population to tune in to regular broadcasts—at one time NBC's *Music Appreciation Hour* allegedly had eleven million listeners (seven million students and four million adults).[12] Televisual media were equally important. *Instruments of the Orchestra* illustrates the early impact of film, as did other efforts, like Disney's *Fantasia* (1940) and a spate of composer biopics. On television, the impact of programs like the American composer-conductor Leonard Bernstein's televised *Young People's Concerts*—broadcast on CBS and syndicated around the world from 1958 to 1972—was enormous. More recent examples would include the *Keeping Score* series of PBS documentaries sponsored by the San Francisco Symphony, each of which provides historical and musical background on a major work of Western classical music. Each of these media products aims to disseminate classical music to a wide audience in the hopes of building audiences through education.

---

[10] Kate Guthrie, "Democratizing Art: Music Education in Postwar Britain," *Musical Quarterly* 97 (2014): 595–596.
[11] Guthrie, "Democratizing Art," 603.
[12] Horowitz, *Classical Music in America*, 404.

In the digital era, these media are joined by apps. The iOS app version of *The Young Person's Guide to the Orchestra* (which I'll refer to as *YPG* for simplicity's sake) works much like many of the older media products I just named. Sponsored by the Royal Northern College of Music (Manchester, UK) and the Britten-Pears Foundation, *YPG* is a well-designed, engaging program with a clear mission: introducing children to the *Young Person's Guide* and, more generally, to the symphony orchestra. From the app's home screen, users can choose a number of options (Figure 10.1). Tapping the large arrow in the center takes users to a performance of Britten's work accompanied by an annotated score that highlights important musical moments and provides commentary. By touching "The Orchestra," users can uncover details about the history of the instruments and how they're grouped into families, as well as listen to examples. And the "B.B." logo takes users to a wealth of information about the *Young Person's Guide* and its composer, including samples of other Britten works. For all intents and purposes, the app is a young person's guide to *The Young Person's Guide*.

Many of *YPG*'s features aren't really games, or even gamified. The recording and score, for example, might best be described as interactive musical experiences. *YPG* is not unique in that respect—in fact, there are quite a few apps that provide such experiences. The developer Amphio (previously known as Touchpress), for instance,

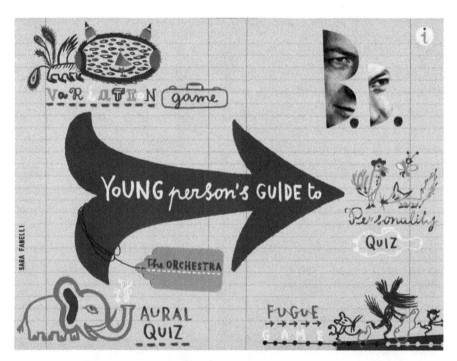

FIGURE 10.1 The home screen of the *Young Person's Guide to the Orchestra* app (2013).

has produced several iPad apps that focus on interactive classical music, such as *Vivaldi's Four Seasons* (2014) and *Beethoven's 9th Symphony* (2014). Along with historical background, these apps typically provide multiple recordings of classical works, which can be viewed with video-recorded performances, musical scores, and other forms of music visualization. Outside classical music, there are also some parallels with the Icelandic composer and performer Björk's "app album" *Biophilia* (2011), which allowed listeners to interact with some aspects of the music.[13] Despite their inclusion of elements that allow users to "play" with the music in some respects, each of these apps studiously avoids using game-related terminology. There is a sense, perhaps, that while adopting some interactive elements helps broaden the music's appeal to digital natives, too much gamification runs the risk of cheapening the experience, trivializing serious musical works.

In contrast, and likely because it's aimed at children, there are four activities in *YPG* that we can clearly identify as gamified: two "games" and two "quizzes." The quizzes are fairly straightforward. The simpler of the two is the Personality Quiz, an experience seemingly influenced by the unending flow of social media personality quizzes ("Which *Star Wars* character are you?"). Users answer a few questions about themselves—"The school bell rings! Are you in your seat ready for class or do you arrive just at the last minute?"—and the app suggests orchestral instruments that supposedly fit that personality type. Much more complex, however, is the Aural Quiz, which presents players with a short musical excerpt and asks them to choose which instrument they think they heard. Although it starts off simple, eventually the challenge ramps up considerably. The satisfaction of getting a perfect score encourages players to hone their listening abilities and to develop an understanding of how the various instrumental timbres work together in an orchestra. This is a straightforward example of gamification: encouraging a desirable behavior by establishing win/loss conditions and awarding points based on good player performance.

Ironically, the two components of *YPG* that are explicitly labeled games are much less overt in their gamification. Both are sandbox games, in the sense that there is no right or wrong way to play; they simply let players experiment with music while learning about musical forms. The Variation Game offers players the chance to compose a short piece by rearranging and embellishing a simple melody (Figure 10.2). The game begins with four measures of music, presented as pictures roughly graphing out the shape of the melody (although players can choose to view sheet music instead). The four measures may be dragged into any order, and a plus or minus

---

[13] On the "gamelike" nature of Björk's album, see Samantha Blickhan, "'Listening' through Digital Interaction in Björk's *Biophilia*," in *Ludomusicology*, ed. Michiel Kamp, Tim Summers, and Mark Sweeney (Sheffield, UK: Equinox, 2016), 133–151.

FIGURE 10.2 The "Variation Game" in the *Young Person's Guide to the Orchestra* app.

button in the corner of each measure swaps between a simple and an ornamented version. Players can also select which of three instruments will play the piece, as well as how they would like the melody to sound in terms of articulation: staccato, normal, or legato. This variety of choice leads to a large number of possibilities for the final piece, even if in practice most end results will sound fairly similar. The Fugue Game works in much the same way. In a fugue—one of the more complex forms in classical music—musical lines enter one at a time, each playing a shared musical theme, before combining into independent melodies. Here again the player has a range of choices. Four animated animals represent the four lines; each animal can play any of four different instruments. As in the Variation Game, the voices can be dragged into any order, meaning that the instruments can enter in whatever order the player wishes. Impressively, all possible iterations work musically, which encourages experimentation. Because there are no wrong answers, evaluating the result is purely a matter of musical taste.

The purpose of these embedded games is to provide children with knowledge about basic musical concepts, which they can then apply through consuming classical works. Initially, that consumption might take the form of listening to the *Young Person's Guide* in the *YPG* app. But that's just the first step. The ultimate goal—instilling an abiding appreciation for classical music—hasn't changed since Benjamin

Britten's time. Like earlier examples of music appreciation in media, there's an undertone of betterment running through this app and others like it. In fact, I initially discovered *YPG* by googling "music apps to make children smarter"—a search that turns up countless lists of apps designed to turn children into the geniuses of tomorrow. Classical music apps frequently appear in these kinds of searches, a consequence of long-lived (if erroneous) beliefs that classical music *does* somehow make children smarter.[14] The *YPG* app succeeds by appealing to consumers' lingering sense that developing an appreciation for "good music" in children is a socially responsible thing for parents and teachers to do.

While these goals seem laudable, they also raise some serious concerns. There's nothing inherently bad about an app designed to foster an appreciation for classical works, but doing so also runs the risk of perpetuating elitist narratives of artistic superiority. Apps like *YPG* imply by their very existence that this music, unlike other genres, requires careful study. Moreover, the involvement of governments, leading universities, and arts organizations suggests that it *should* be studied, just as television broadcasts like Bernstein's concerts or educational films like *Instruments of the Orchestra* did for previous generations. This approach, while arguably somewhat successful in building audiences for classical music, also disproportionately celebrates the contributions of a few so-called "masters"—typically white men—while minimizing the important contributions of others, including women, minorities, and diverse socioeconomic classes. Tellingly, I can find no similar apps that guide young people to even such historically significant artworks as, say, Miles Davis's *Kind of Blue* (1959), Woody Guthrie's *Dust Bowl Ballads* (1940), or Carole King's *Tapestry* (1971), to name only three.[15]

These issues are neither new nor limited to apps. The American composer-critic Virgil Thomson, for instance—a contemporary of Britten—lamented as early as the 1930s the rising authority of what he called the "music appreciation racket." What others perceived as the savior of high culture, Thomson derided as a "fake-ecstatic, holier-than thou" collusion of publishers, conductors, and educators, designed to indoctrinate listeners (especially children) in the superiority of co-called classical orchestral masterworks.[16] "A certain limited repertory of pieces," Thomson writes,

---

[14] See, for example, the discussion of postmillennial classical music programming targeted at children in Mina Yang, *Planet Beethoven: Classical Music at the Turn of the Millennium* (Middletown, CT: Wesleyan University Press, 2014), 29–38.

[15] The closest parallels might be the BBC's *100 Jazz Legends* (2012), which features background history and photography of major figures in jazz.

[16] Virgil Thomson, *The State of Music and Other Writings*, ed. Tim Page (New York: Library of America, 2016), 87. *The State of Music*, from which my quotations emerge, was originally written in 1939 and was reprinted in 1961.

ninety percent of them a hundred years old, is assumed to contain most that the world has to offer of musical beauty and authority. . . . It is further assumed . . . that continued auditive subjection to this repertory harmonizes the mind and sweetens the character, and that the conscious paying of attention during the auditive process intensifies the favorable reaction. Every one of these assumptions is false, or at least highly disputable.[17]

Thomson, who wrote several major symphonic works himself, wasn't opposed to classical orchestral works. But he was deeply troubled by any approach that, in his words, "pretends that a small section of music is either all of music or at least the heart of it."[18] Fortunately, things have changed somewhat since Thomson's time. The university music appreciation course, for instance, which was long a bastion of this type of thinking, has in recent years gradually stepped back a bit from reinforcing myths of classical music's superiority.[19]

I invoke Thomson's writings because they were similar in both period and content to Benjamin Britten's *Young Person's Guide*—and yet diametrically opposed in viewpoint. Both men agreed on the purpose of music appreciation—guiding listeners to the canon of classical masterworks—but they disagreed strongly on the merits of those goals. Some might reasonably argue that apps like *YPG*, despite the newness of their medium and their innovative presentation, simply reinforce this older mentality, not least by encouraging the development of listening skills rather than musicianship. Users can interactively learn about topics such as musical form or instrumental timbres, yet in the end they are only passive observers to Britten's music. To return to Thomson's colorful invective, music appreciation works by convincing listeners to "feel that musical non-consumption is sinful," compelling them to purchase concert tickets, recordings, or preferably both. Those results aren't in themselves musical. Rather, "They are at best therapeutic actions destined to correct the customer's musical defects without putting him through the labors of musical exercise."[20] Yet the draw of video games, and of gamification

---

[17] Thomson, *The State of Music*, 85.

[18] Thomson, *The State of Music*, 88.

[19] Even that change, however, has been much to the chagrin of some traditionally minded music appreciation instructors (and students), many of whom remain resolute in their beliefs that classical music is more worthy of academic study than popular (or even non-Western) genres. In outlining a more inclusive approach, Steven Cornelius and Mary Natvig, for example, have suggested regarding the traditional classical-only model of music education that "too strong a focus on Western art music does a disservice by ignoring most of the world's music while simultaneously devaluing students' own musical experiences. Such an approach makes little sense in a society as culturally pluralistic as ours." Steven Cornelius and Mary Natvig, "Teaching Music History: A Cultural Approach," *Journal of Music History Pedagogy* 4 (2013): 141.

[20] Thomson, *The State of Music*, 85.

more generally, is interactivity. Nearly three quarters of a century after Britten and Thomson, can gamification bridge the gap between teaching music appreciation and teaching music performance? My second case study is an app targeted at that very goal.

Tapping Music

In a brief article from 2015, one of *Business Insider*'s executive editors, Matt Rosoff, called attention to a new smartphone app: "Last Friday, a fellow music-nut friend of mine sent me a link to an iPhone app based on composer Steve Reich's *Clapping Music*. I've become totally obsessed with beating it."[21] That may not seem like a particularly noteworthy attitude toward a mobile game. Many of us, after all, have fallen prey to the addictive charms of, say, *Candy Crush* (2012) or *Flappy Bird* (2013). What makes Rosoff's statement unusual is that, in this case, "beating the game" essentially translates to "correctly performing twentieth-century avant-garde classical music." Another collaboration between game developers, arts organizations, and higher education—in this case the London Sinfonietta, Queen Mary University of London, and the developer Touchpress (now Amphio)—*Steve Reich's Clapping Music* aims to create just the kind of obsession-inducing experience that Rosoff describes. And it does. The *New York Times* critic Michael Cooper, for instance, found the app "maddeningly addictive."[22] I have been a music educator in various forms for most of my adult life, from teaching beginning piano to advising doctoral students, and I feel comfortable asserting that I have *never* heard anyone describe the often tedious process of learning a complex musical work as "maddeningly addictive." So how is this response possible?

Part of the answer lies with the nature of Reich's piece. *Clapping Music* (1972) is a deceptively simple minimalist work, requiring only two performers, both of whom produce sound by clapping their hands. The end result creates a rich and musically rewarding experience from a very small amount of musical material, a feat it accomplishes through a process not entirely unlike a video game. It starts with a basic premise and a simple set of rules that players follow to create the piece. In this case, one performer repeats the same pattern for the entire piece, while the other performer slowly changes the pattern, displacing it by one beat every few

[21] Matt Rosoff, "I'm Obsessed with This Fiendishly Difficult App That Separates Real Musicians from Wannabes," *Business Insider* (July 16, 2015), available online at http://www.businessinsider.com/steve-reich-clapping-music-app-2015-7 (accessed November 11, 2016).

[22] Michael Cooper, "Steve Reich, Game Designer," *New York Times* (July 9, 2015), available online at http://artsbeat.blogs.nytimes.com/2015/07/09/steve-reich-game-designer/ (accessed November 11, 2016).

repetitions. Other aspects of *Clapping Music* also help make it uniquely suited to gamification. Like a game, Reich's piece begins with a tutorial—both performers clapping the same rhythm—before ramping up the difficulty. Because it consists only of clapping, *Clapping Music* is reduced to one musical element, rhythm, which is the one aspect of music that video games are best equipped to handle. The vast majority of music games are based entirely on rhythm, from older titles such as *PaRappa the Rapper* (1996) to *Guitar Hero Live* (2015)—you just push the right button at the right time.[23] These types of games have also made their way to the iPad, as in *Groove Coaster* (2011) and *Tone Sphere* (2012), adapting the popular genre to touch-based controls.[24] Yet while many rhythm games give players the *sense* of performing more musical elements than they actually are, in *Steve Reich's Clapping Music* (hereafter *SRCM*) the player actually performs every musical element of the work.[25]

Upon opening *SRCM*, an eye-catching Tap to Play graphic greets players, with somewhat less enticing options underneath: About the Music, About the App, and Research Project. After starting a game, players see a string of dots that represent the rhythmic pattern, with filled-in dots representing claps, and empty dots indicating rests (Figure 10.3). Each horizontal line is one iteration of the pattern, and upon its completion the bottom line drops off the screen, the other lines drop down one space, and the pattern continues. Although this system differs from traditional music notation, players are given all the information necessary for a complete performance of the work—only the clapping sound is fake, generated each time the player taps the screen (a necessary conceit, since tapping is nearly silent). One of the

---

[23] I also find some meaningful parallels between *SRCM* and the *Rhythm Heaven* series of games from Nintendo. Both involve the interaction of two musical parts and focus on the development of the player's rhythmic skills, for instance. See Peter Shultz, "Rhythm Sense: Modality and Enactive Perception in *Rhythm Heaven*," in *Music Video Games: Performance, Politics, and Play*, ed. Michael Austin (New York: Bloomsbury, 2016), 251–273.

[24] On tablet-based rhythm games, as well as other approaches to mobile music games, see Nathan Fleshner, "Pitching the Rhythm: Music Games for the iPad," in *Music Video Games: Performance, Politics, and Play*, ed. Michael Austin (New York: Bloomsbury, 2016), 275–296.

[25] Because *Clapping Music's* unique structure and instrumentation make the piece so suited for this type of gamification, we might question how many other works could be usefully gamified in this way. Although *SRCM* is certainly the most gamified, it is worth noting that there are several other apps dedicated to performing, or at least exploring, contemporary classical works. The most notable of these include the *4'33"—John Cage* app, produced by the John Cage Trust and his publisher (C. F. Peters), which allows listeners to "perform" Cage's famous work by recording the ambient sounds around them, which can then be uploaded for the enjoyment of others. There are also several apps from the ensemble Third Coast Percussion, allowing players to explore and to some extent (re)compose works by Cage and Reich, as well as Augusta Read Thomas's work *Resounding Earth* (2012). Though not strictly a game, we may also think of the *John Cage Piano* app (2012), which provides samples of the timbres of Cage's experimental music for prepared piano.

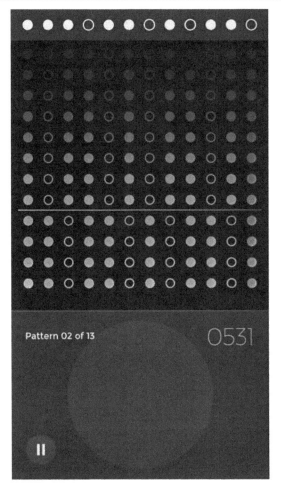

FIGURE 10.3 Screenshot of *Steve Reich's Clapping Music* (2015).

advertisements for *SRCM* includes a brief interview with the composer about both his work and the app. The voice-over in full:

Hi, I'm Steve Reich. In 1972 I composed a piece called *Clapping Music*, and all it needs is your two hands. It's a simple piece. There's just one rhythmic pattern; one person plays it over and over again, and the second person gradually changes their part one note at a time. This app is very helpful in teaching you the piece, and it will prepare you to play it live. The goal is to follow the dots, play the patterns exactly as presented, but if you miss— game's over for a minute, and then you can try again. And when you're all done, just in case you're interested, you might check out a few other pieces I've written that you might enjoy. Do give the *Clapping Music* app a try. It's a bit of a challenge, but it's an interesting one, and you can download it for nothing.[26]

Although there's quite a bit to unpack in this short statement, it is noteworthy that the composer clearly views *SRCM* not only as an enjoyable (and "interesting") experience but also as a gateway to live performance of this piece. Upon completing the game on a high difficulty setting—which is quite a challenge—players are ready to perform *Clapping Music*. And all without ever intending to develop their musical skills.

Despite its conceptual simplicity, *Clapping Music* is not easy to perform. As one of its original performers recently noted, the piece "demands a different kind of virtuosity from its performers. It showcases their concentration, endurance, rhythmic precision, consistency, phrasing within repetition, and comfort with metrical and perceptual ambiguity."[27] The app cleverly facilitates the development of exactly these skills. Musical elements like rhythmic accuracy are easy to assess and quantify as a numerical score, and indeed, being able to trace improvement in these skills over time is partly why the app was created in the first place. Users who explore the Research Project option from the main menu are sent to a website (accessible outside the app) detailing a set of goals. Aside from creating an enjoyable experience for players, the app was designed to answer two questions:

1. How are musical performance skills acquired through a digital game interface?
2. Can audience engagement with a new music genre be increased by a game based smartphone app?[28]

This second question is a new-music variation on the old music appreciation approach we saw with the *YPG* app. Other aspects of the app also reflect the same mentality. The About the Music section on the main menu contains program notes

---

[26] This video is available on the London Sinfonietta's YouTube channel. LondonSinfonietta, "Steve Reich's Clapping Music," published July 9, 2015, available online at https://www.youtube.com/watch?v=7Z23EmPsoto (accessed November 15, 2016).

[27] Russell Hartenberger, "*Clapping Music*: A Performer's Perspective," in *The Routledge Research Companion to Minimalist and Postminimalist Music*, ed. Keith Potter, Kyle Gann, and Pwyll ap Siôn (Surrey, UK: Ashgate, 2013), 379.

[28] "Research," *Steve Reich's Clapping Music* website. available online at http://cogsci.eecs.qmul.ac.uk/clapping-musicresearch/Research.html (accessed November 11, 2016). Though the app designers have yet to provide definitive answers to these questions, some preliminary results are available in a research study available at http://music-cognition.eecs.qmul.ac.uk/papers/Steve_Reichs_Clapping_Music_App_RandD_report_QM.pdf (accessed November 12, 2016).

from Reich, for instance, as well as an interview with Reich about the work and a live performance. Users can also delve into Reich's other works, several of which are featured in the app, with video examples and links to purchase the music on iTunes. Still other links contain information about the app's sponsors—the London Sinfonietta and Queen Mary University of London—presumably with the aim of encouraging players who have enjoyed the app to attend concerts and events, or to financially support these institutions through donations. *SRCM* differs significantly from most music appreciation apps, however, in its focus on the development of not only listening skills but also practical musical abilities. The chance to "improve your rhythm" is even highlighted in the title of the app as it appears on Apple's App Store (though not in the app itself).

SRCM's focus on teaching music skills isn't unique. A number of studies have addressed music games' potential impact on the development of musical skills, such as music theory or sight-reading.[29] Yet *SRCM* is something different, in degree if not necessarily in kind—the line between developing musical skills and actually performing a musical work becomes blurred into unrecognizability. At some point, for both players and listeners, playing a game becomes indistinguishable from a musical performance. And because playing *SRCM* is effectively a performance of *Clapping Music*, the app also avoids some of the critical hurdles that music games often face. Kiri Miller, for example, has detailed the scorn many *Guitar Hero* players endured from naysayers who found the instrument-based controllers to be unconvincing simulacra of traditional musical instruments.[30] Despite *SRCM*'s playful, gamified approach, however, its players create the work almost as it was originally conceived. Even the most classically minded of players—some of whom might otherwise have deemed the exercise pointless, frivolous, or even disrespectful—could rest at ease that the work was being taken seriously. Tapping music, after all, is hardly less inherently musical than *Clapping Music*.

Steve Reich's Clapping Music—Improve Your Rhythm and the *Young Person's Guide to the Orchestra* app gamify classical music with the same fundamental goal: bettering

---

[29] See, for example, Fleshner, "Pitching the Rhythm." The early 2010s saw a spate of articles on the topic in music education publications, presumably as a result of the boom in popularity of *Guitar Hero*, *Rock Band*, and similar games. See in particular Lily Gower and Janet McDowall, "Interactive Music Video Games and Children's Musical Development," *British Journal of Music Education* 29 (2012): 91–105; Patrick Richardson and Youngmoo E. Kim, "Beyond Fun and Games: A Framework for Quantifying Music Skills Developments from Video Game Play," *Journal of New Music Research* 40 (2011): 277–291; and Evan S. Tobias, "Let's Play! Learning Music through Video Games and Virtual Worlds," in *The Oxford Handbook of Music Education*, vol. 2, ed. Gary McPherson and Graham Welch (Oxford: Oxford University Press, 2012), 531–548.

[30] Kiri Miller, *Playing Along: Digital Games, YouTube, and Virtual Performance* (Oxford: Oxford University Press, 2012), chap. 3.

their users by incentivizing positive behaviors. Yet the differences between these two gamified visions of betterment are profound, raising fundamental questions regarding the performance and consumption of classical music in the digital era. What role, if any, should emergent digital technologies play in reinforcing arguably outdated notions of classical music consumption? How gamified can classical music become before it ceases to be classical (or even music!) at all? These questions are also the focus of the next chapter, although they are transformed in significant ways, as well. As video game music becomes a staple of concert halls across the world, it creates meaningful dialogues regarding the interaction between the classical music sphere and gaming culture. Thus I shift from studying how apps gamify classical music to an investigation of equally enthusiastic efforts to classify game music.

11 Classifying Game Music

I BEGAN THIS book with the suggestion that classical music and video games are, by definition, fundamentally incompatible. The former is a nebulous cultural construct that lumps together disparate musical styles on the basis of shared artistic status; the latter are popular-culture products that exist to provide entertainment to the masses. As I hope the previous chapters have illustrated, the reality is substantially more complex. The frequent contact between these two cultural forces reveals cracks in the conceptual facades, exposing the art in the game, and the game in the art. Many of the examples in earlier chapters have traced the ways in which classical music in games subverts expectations of highbrow and lowbrow arts. This final chapter considers whether that distinction has collapsed altogether. What if, as many listeners are coming to believe, some video game music *is* classical? Concert performances of works by game music composers like Koji Kondo, Nobuo Uematsu, and Jeremy Soule reflect a fundamental shift in how some audiences understand classical music. That change offers a fascinating glimpse into how music becomes classical in the digital age and raises substantial questions about musical legitimacy and authenticity. Although concerts of video game music have taken a variety of forms—running the gamut from marching band halftime shows, to solo piano concerts, to chamber music—I'm particularly interested here in live symphonic concerts. These not only are among the best attended of game music concerts but also interact in complex ways with the symphony orchestra's traditional role as bastion of high art.

It's no secret that many professional orchestras have struggled financially in recent years. Dwindling audiences, insufficient charitable giving, and a myriad of other complex issues have resulted in labor disputes and even bankruptcies. Over the past decade or so, video game concerts have proved popular with orchestras eager for new audiences and artistic identities. Although the first orchestral game music concerts took place in Japan in the 1990s, in the decades since they have become equally prominent in Europe and North America.[1] Germany's long-running *Symphonic Game Music Concerts* (*Symphonische Spielmusikkonzerte*) series began in 2003, for example, and since relocating to Cologne in 2008 has regularly resulted in recordings and live concerts using the WDR Radio Orchestra.[2] The popularity of this series inspired similar programs, including both one-off national tours such as *Dear Friends: Music from Final Fantasy* (North America, 2004) and long-running and constantly updated programs like *Play! A Video Game Symphony* (North America, 2006–2010) and *Distant Worlds: Music from Final Fantasy* (worldwide, 2007–present).

Once dismissed as fringe events—gimmicks, really—orchestral game music concerts have quickly become a staple of ensembles ranging from local community orchestras to elite professional ensembles. In terms of press coverage and critical awareness, the year 2015 seems to have been a watershed. One widely circulated article in the *Wall Street Journal*, for example, noted that game music is inspiring "a new generation of symphony patron that is invigorating the bottom-line performance of concert halls across the U.S."[3] The author, Sarah Needleman, offers examples from orchestras and performance venues from across the country, noting that tickets for game music concerts often sell for double the amount as normal pops concerts, and audience members also purchase substantially more merchandise. Aside from yielding this short-term burst of much-needed income, however, the strategy seems to be using game music to lure younger and more culturally diverse audiences—some of whom, theoretically, go on to become regular patrons. As a classical-trained musician suggested of game concerts in a different article from 2015, "It's impressive and intimidating for gamers to step into this [classical music] world. But will they come back for a Beethoven or Mozart? That's our goal. We need to blur the lines a little more to expose the gamer

[1] The Tokyo-based series "Orchestral Game Music Concerts" took place between 1991 and 1996 and set the tone of mixing the music of "classic" games with new releases. Concert programs for these influential performances are available at https://en.wikipedia.org/wiki/Orchestral_Game_Music_Concerts.

[2] "History," *Game Concerts*, n.d., available online at http://www.gameconcerts.com/en/hintergrund/geschichte/ (accessed December 4, 2016).

[3] Sarah E. Needleman, "How Videogames Are Saving the Symphony Orchestra," *Wall Street Journal* (October 12, 2015), available online at http://www.wsj.com/articles/how-videogames-are-saving-the-symphony-orchestra-1444696737 (accessed November 12, 2016).

to Tchaikovsky."[4] Thomas Böcker, a German musician and impresario of game music concerts, expressed much the same hope, albeit in more tempered language:

> Not everybody who comes to video game concerts will listen to Beethoven— of course not, that's not our goal. I know of a few examples of many, many people who have become interested in orchestral music in general and they are now getting into listening to [film composers] John Williams and Jerry Goldsmith. Then they might find their way and think: "Oh wow, Prokofiev also sounds really interesting."[5]

It's still too early to know if such a strategy will ultimately be successful, but the immediate benefits to orchestras and audiences alike are obvious.

Two personal anecdotes: I've attended a number of game music concerts over the past decade, and I'm always struck both by the demographic differences from traditional classical concerts and by the level of audience engagement. For instance, at my first video game concert—a 2009 outdoor concert of *Play! A Video Game Symphony* in Cary, North Carolina—I vividly recall watching a large audience of mostly teenagers and twentysomethings stand enraptured in the pouring rain listening to the North Carolina Symphony perform Martin O'Donnell's music from *Halo*. More recently, in the past few years I've had the delightful opportunity to act as onstage emcee with the professional symphonic band the Dallas Winds during two game concerts. In contrast with the relatively staid responses from audience members when I give talks at traditional symphony concerts, after the Dallas Winds event I was virtually mobbed by enthusiastic audience members who had lingering questions or simply wanted to talk about their favorite music. Statistics tend to bear out my personal experiences. If the aim of these events is simply to attract and engage younger and more diverse (paying) audiences, then game concerts are a rousing success.

Yet not all musicians and concertgoers appreciate the incursion of video games into the sacred concert hall space. Needleman's article includes one such naysayer, whose clearly stated position helpfully summarizes the opposing view:

> "From a business-strategy perspective, it completely devalues the brand," said Roderick Branch, a 39-year-old lawyer in Chicago who attends

---

[4] Jeffrey Fleishman, "Video Game Music Comes to the Orchestra Concert Hall," *Los Angeles Times* (June 12, 2015), available online at http://www.latimes.com/entertainment/herocomplex/la-ca-hc-video-games-music-20150614-story.html (accessed December 2, 2016).

[5] Matthew Jarvis, "Play On: How Video Game Music Is Rocking the Classical World," *MCV* (September 28, 2015), available online at http://www.mcvuk.com/articles/media-pr/play-on-how-video-game-music-is-rocking-the-classical-world (accessed November 18, 2017).

symphony-orchestra performances about once a week. The very idea, he said, is "akin to Mouton Rothschild using its wine to make and sell sangria."[6]

This perspective deserves some consideration at length. Branch presents two related points: one regarding the business side of the orchestra's brand (though one wonders if it's the classical music brand at stake more than any particular orchestra) and the subsequent simile regarding wine. The former statement suggests that performing video game music not only devalues the individual concert on which it is performed but also tarnishes the image of the orchestra itself. How can serious concertgoers trust any ensemble that would demean itself by stooping so low?

Branch's final analogy is particularly revealing. The Bordeaux produced by Château Mouton Rothschild, an estate founded in the nineteenth century, is one of the world's most celebrated—and expensive—wines. Often selling for hundreds of dollars per bottle, the wine is a symbol of both quality and exclusivity, a distinctly old-world European luxury, limited to a select few. Sangria, on the other hand, is a much less exalted drink. Originating in Spain via the Caribbean, this popular (and delicious) beverage is typically made by adding fruit and brandy to less expensive red wines, sweetening them to make them more palatable. Sangria made its way to the United States largely through the immigration of Hispanic peoples, leading many to associate the drink with Mexico and its cuisine. Thus, when Branch suggests that game music concerts are "akin to Mouton Rothschild using its wine to make and sell sangria," he protests the use of an elite European product like the orchestra to produce a less expensive product designed for mass appeal and consumption. Branch is hardly alone in these feelings. A scathing 2013 *New Republic* article on the problems of contemporary orchestral programming by the critic Philip Kennicott, for example, identifies "video-game nights" in a list of "special events" concerts that distract orchestras from their true mission.[7] Rather than focusing on developing diverse audiences, orchestras should instead focus on performing great classical music. If they do that, he implies, the audience will follow. Furthermore, Kennicott believes events such as video game concerts are of no interest to "serious listeners" and actually exert a negative effect by "curtailing the number of nights the orchestra presents classical music."

It's not hard to understand why some conservative audience members and critics might share that perspective on game music. Often the ways game music is presented

[6] Needleman, "How Videogames Are Saving the Symphony Orchestra."

[7] Philip Kennicott, "America's Orchestras Are in Crisis," *New Republic* (August 25, 2013), available online at https://newrepublic.com/article/114221/orchestras-crisis-outreach-ruining-them (accessed November 13, 2016).

live differ dramatically from traditional classical concerts. Consider, for example, *Video Games Live* (VGL). Since its debut in 2005, VGL has remained among the most popular touring orchestral programs of game music. Largely the brainchild of the eccentric composer and impresario Tommy Tallarico, VGL concerts pair local orchestras with a traveling multimedia show featuring celebrity game musicians, including composers, musicians, and conductors. Amid spectacular light shows and fog machines more typically associated with rock concerts, orchestras play arrangements of game music from classics to new releases, while videos from the games are projected in the background. As an article in the *Deseret News* (Utah) dryly noted regarding a 2008 appearance: "With strobe lights, a big video screen, mirror balls and an electric guitar, it was clear that 'Video Games Live!' is not a typical symphony concert."[8] Tallarico's methods don't suit everyone's tastes, even within the game concert community. Jason Michael Paul, for instance, a game-concert producer whose *Play!* concerts competed with *Video Games Live* for several years, was exasperated by Tallarico's approach. Although the *Play!* concerts did involve multimedia, they were considerably less rock influenced. Lamenting the growing popularity of VGL in a 2006 interview with the *Washington Post*, for instance, Paul responded that his "whole goal is to keep the arts alive in a way that is classy."[9]

Games aren't alone in sparking these kinds of fiery debates. There exists similar resistance from some corners of the classical music community to film music, or orchestral collaborations with popular musicians. What I find particularly interesting about game music concerts, however, is how fervently many of its advocates contend that it has crossed some philosophical or artistic line and become classical music. Perhaps surprisingly, Tallarico is one of the most ardent advocates for such a perspective. Despite his lack of classical training, game music's relationship to classical composers is a recurring motif in Tallarico's interviews; one of his most frequent and provocative claims is that Beethoven would have been a game music composer had he been born in our time.[10] Even more directly, in defending game music against detractors, he claims that symphonic game music is "modern day classical music. The only thing that's different is that all of the composers are still

---

[8] Scott Iwaskai, "Concert Review: Symphony Help Breathe Life into Video Games," *Deseret News* (March 29, 2008), available online at http://www.deseretnews.com/article/695265797/Symphony-help-breathe-life-into-video-games.html (accessed December 2, 2016).

[9] Mike Musgrove, "Mario's New World: Symphonies," *Washington Post* (August 3, 2006), available online at http://www.washingtonpost.com/wp-dyn/content/article/2006/08/02/AR2006080201889_pf.html (accessed November 20, 2016).

[10] On the Beethoven claim, see, for example, the profiles of Tallarico in Fleishman, "Video Game Music Comes to the Concert Hall"; Sarah Thomas, "From Beethoven to Bleeps and Bloops: The Symphony of Video Game Soundtracks," *Sydney Morning Herald* (July 27, 2015), available online at http://www.smh.com.au/entertainment/music/from-beethoven-to-bleeps-and-bloops-the-symphony-of-video-game-soundtracks-20150723-giim12.

alive. The truth is, we're just as relevant as Beethoven and Mozart and we're just as good."[11] Tallarico's viewpoint has a number of supporters. A growing number of musicians and listeners believe that symphonic game music either already is, or can be readily transformed into, classical music. I turn now to a few examples of how this process has worked, beginning with how some fans advocate for "classical" status for game music, and then exploring how some orchestral arrangements encourage that view.

Gaming the Vote

The UK-based radio station Classic FM boldly promises its listeners "The World's Greatest Music." Since its creation in the 1990s, the station—also available via streaming—has based its identity on the quality of the masterworks that it broadcasts. Yet its programming veers heavily toward lighter classical—the kind of familiar works seen in many examples throughout this book. The musicologist James Parakilas has suggested, "On the whole, the message of the classics is a message of comfort. . . . Classical music is approved music; it is politically and socially safe."[12] Classic FM plays into this notion of a safe, comfortable classical music, designed to put listeners at ease. Still, as Parakilas notes, "The politics of comfort make many listeners uncomfortable. These listeners include not only some who do not like classical music anyway, but also some of those most deeply involved with it."[13] In the latter category we might place the musicologist Julian Johnson, whose understanding of classical music was explored in some detail in chapter 1. In his book *Who Needs Classical Music?*, Johnson expresses some strong feelings about Classic FM's programming, which he feels "is tied up with classical music functioning as popular music." "Most striking," he continues, "is what is *not* played on Classic FM: anything that risks being less than popular."[14] In Johnson's view, Classic FM is so concerned with catering to the musical comforts of its listeners—rather than challenging and bettering listeners through contemplation or serious study—that it ceases to be classical at all. If, on the other hand, Parakilas is correct that classical music gives

html (accessed December 2, 2016); or Mark MacNamara, "The S.F. Symphony Gets Its Game On," *San Francisco Classical Voice* (July 18, 2013), available online at https://www.sfcv.org/article/the-sf-symphony-gets-its-video-game-on (accessed December 3, 2016).

[11] MacNamara, "The S.F. Symphony Gets Its Game On."

[12] James Parakilas, "Classical Music as Popular Music," *Journal of Musicology* 3 (1984): 10–11.

[13] Parakilas, "Classical Music as Popular Music," 11.

[14] Julian Johnson, *Who Needs Classical Music? Cultural Choice and Musical Value* (Oxford: Oxford University Press, 2002), 75.

comfort to listeners who regard it as art, then perhaps Classic FM is simply a democratization of the concept.

Each year since 1996, Classic FM has given its British audience—more than six million listeners—the opportunity to vote for their favorite classical works. From the results, the station compiles its annual Hall of Fame: the three hundred works receiving the most nominations. In 2016, more than 170,000 aficionados cast their votes, and as usual the resulting list offers a unique perspective on classical music and its masterworks. Although the list for the most part contains popular works by Beethoven, Mozart, Rachmaninov, and so on, many unsuspected readers might be shocked by number 17: Nobuo Uematsu's music from the *Final Fantasy* series. Although still impressive, seventeenth place is actually a drop for Uematsu—in 2013, *Final Fantasy* reached number 3. That same year, Jeremy Soule's music for *The Elder Scrolls* series joined Uematsu in the Top Ten. Both of these works were rated higher than anything by Beethoven or Mozart. The newfound prominence of game music in the Hall of Fame has not gone unnoticed. In fact, the "FAQs" section on Classic FM's website answers the question "How has the chart changed in recent years?" with "Three words: video game music."[15] (See Table 11.1 for a full list of game soundtracks in the Hall of Fame.)

Game music's rapid ascent in the Classic FM Hall of Fame during the 2010s represents a confluence of several factors. For one thing, there's simply a great deal more orchestral game music than has existed before—ever-increasing game budgets and a frequent emphasis on emulating cinematic models often encourage game composers to make use of orchestral textures. Furthermore, game soundtracks are now available through a dizzying variety of media. In the course of writing this book, I have looked up literally hundreds of game soundtracks on YouTube, for instance, ranging from major recent releases to obscure games of the 1980s. There are excellent podcasts devoted to video game music, documentary films on the topic, and a surprising number of playlists on streaming services such as Spotify. Even so, it appears that game music didn't make it to the apex of Classic FM's Hall of Fame without a little help from some devoted fans with a clear agenda.

For several years there has been a concerted effort by game music fans to inundate the online polls with as many votes as possible. As I write, for example, there's a Facebook group with about twenty-five hundred followers called Keep Video Games Music in the Classical FM Hall of Fame. Alongside regular updates on game

---

[15] "The Hall of Fame—The Best Classical Music of All Time," *ClassicFM.com*, n.d. available online at http://www.classicfm.com/hall-of-fame/ (accessed December 1, 2016). The long-standing prominence of Scottish composer Grant Kirkhope on the list, particularly for games that are less well known, may also be partially attributable to Classic FM's UK bias.

TABLE 11.1

Video game soundtracks in the Classic FM Hall of Fame, 2013–2016

Game Title	Composer	2013	2014	2015	2016
Banjo-Kazooie	Grant Kirkhope	–	#50	#13	#98
Blue Dragon	Nobuo Uematsu	–	–	#118	#126
Everybody's Gone to the Rapture	Jessica Curry	–	–	–	#268
Final Fantasy (series)	Nobuo Uematsu	#3	#7	#9	#17
Halo (series)	Martin O'Donnell	–	–	#244	–
Journey	Austin Wintory	–	#289	–	#221
Kingdom Hearts	Yoko Shimomura	–	#177	#30	#31
Kingdoms of Amalur: Reckoning	Grant Kirkhope	–	#75	#59	–
Shenmue	Various	–	–	–	#144
StarCraft II	Glen Stafford	–	–	#163	–
The Elder Scrolls (series)	Jeremy Soule	#5	#17	#11	#120
The Last of Us	Gustavo Santalallo	–	–	#193	–
The Legend of Zelda (series)	Koji Kondo	–	–	#84	#135
Viva Piñata	Grant Kirkhope	#17	#54	#41	#272
World of Warcraft	Various	–	#52	#53	#269
Total number of game/series soundtracks by year		**3**	**7**	**12**	**11**

music concerts, this group issues regular reminders to vote in the Hall of Fame polls, and reports the results. The "About" section for the group identifies it as "an ongoing campaign for the recognition of video game scores as classical music. Fantastic music by incredible composers that deserve to be praised!"[16] Since 2015 the group has had a related Twitter account (@WeLoveGameMusic), the biographical statement of which notes, "We campaign for the recognition of orchestral VGM [video game music]."[17] Run by two UK-based advocates, the account routinely tweets messages concerning upcoming game music concerts and recordings, serving as a communication hub for fans. Similarly, for several months in early 2016, supporters of the ambitious cult favorite *Shenmue* series of games organized a grass-roots campaign on fan websites and across social media to get the soundtracks into the

---

[16] "Keep Video Games Music in the Classical FM Hall of Fame," Facebook page, available online at https://www.facebook.com/ClassicVGMusic/about/ (accessed December 3, 2016).

[17] WeLoveGameMusic, Twitter bio, available online at https://twitter.com/WeLoveGameMusic (accessed December 3, 2016).

Hall of Fame, including detailing how to vote (and how to get around international restrictions on voting). As one poster in a forum on the website *shenmuedojo.net* put it, "Let's make this the year that *Shenmue*'s majestic score takes its rightful place in the Hall of Fame!"[18] The game ultimately made it to number 144 on the list—a much-celebrated triumph.

These groups' central tenet, and that of others like them, is not simply the promotion of video game music. Instead, the groups champion an understanding of orchestral game music as classical, and therefore worthy of serious artistic consideration.[19] Such an idea is at once subversive and traditionalist. On the one hand, it undermines the exclusivity of classical music by arguing for the inclusion of popular-culture products under its umbrella. On the other hand, however, it reinforces the fundamental principle on which classical music as a concept is based: some music is art and some music isn't. Despite what their opponents might claim, it isn't that these fans want to eradicate musical hierarchies—it's that they want to ensure their preferred music makes the cut. The barbarians at the gate aren't tearing down the walls; they just want to come in for tea. Having game music declared classical is thus a moral victory, a validation and vindication of the tastes of its long-suffering (and oft-derided) fans. Even more, understanding game *music* as art goes a long way toward arguing that the games themselves must also be artworks. As a 2015 article in the tech magazine *Wired* noted regarding game music's "strongest showing ever" in the Classic FM Hall of Fame, "For 'new media' such as games to get such representation is a huge accomplishment, and shows the widespread and growing impact of gaming as an art form."[20] But for whom, precisely, is this change a "huge accomplishment"? Fans of game music? Composers? The industry as a whole? Such an attitude encourages the perspective that attaining classical status is an achievement to be unlocked, a necessary step on the path toward legitimization.

---

[18] Sonoshee, "Vote Shenmue Music into the ClassicFM Hall of Fame," shenmuedojo.net (January 16, 2016), available online at http://shenmuedojo.net/forum/viewtopic.php?f=48&t=49575 (accessed December 6, 2016).

[19] There are some clear parallels between the recent critical reception of film and game music. See, for instance, the opposing perspectives on film music concerts in the United Kingdom presented in Tristan Jakob-Hoff, "Can Film Music Ever Be Classical?," *The Guardian* (April 7, 2008), available online at https://www.the-guardian.com/music/musicblog/2008/apr/07/canfilmmusiceverbeclassical (accessed December 3, 2016); and Hannah Furness, "Film Score Composers Should Be Treated as 'Seriously' as Mozart and Tchaikovsky, Royal Albert Hall Director Says," *Telegraph* (July 3, 2014), available online at http://www.telegraph.co.uk/culture/music/classicalmusic/10943665/Film-score-composers-should-be-treated-as-seriously-as-Mozart-and-Tchaikovsky-Royal-Albert-Hall-director-says.html (accessed December 3, 2016).

[20] Matt Kamen, "Video Games Storm Classic FM's 2015 'Hall of Fame,'" *Wired* (April 7, 2015), available online at http://www.wired.co.uk/article/game-music-classic-fm (accessed December 5, 2016).

Orchestrating Change

Dedicated fans aren't the only ones encouraging listeners to perceive game music as classical—that idea is deeply embedded in many of the orchestral concert programs. Game music had been increasingly common in concert halls for nearly a decade before it ever entered Classic FM's Hall of Fame. Yet while the elaborate pyrotechnics and audience interactivity of programs like VGL remain popular, they've been joined in recent years by the increasing prominence of more overtly classical video game concerts. In 2013, for example—the same year *Final Fantasy* hit number 3 on the Classic FM Hall of Fame—the London Symphony Orchestra performed the *Final Symphony* concert at the Barbican Centre. It was the first game concert from that venerable orchestra, and the event led one games writer to declare, "Video game music has pretty officially 'made it.'"[21] Removing game music from its original context and positing it in such an illustrious and classical venue has a profound impact on audience perceptions. To quote James Parakilas again, "When classical music is performed at Avery Fisher Hall [in New York's Lincoln Center] or the Met [i.e., the Metropolitan Opera] there is no more reason to label it 'classical' than there is to label music at the Shubert Theatre 'Broadway' or music at a square dance 'folk.' The place places it."[22] In other words, if a classical orchestra is playing game music in a traditionally classical venue, then the music is necessarily functioning as classical music. There's some degree of truth to that idea, but it's not the end of the story. I would also suggest that game music programs like *Final Symphony* are conceived, arranged, and marketed in such a way as to emphasize their most classical aspects.

Final Symphony is the product of Thomas Böcker's Merregnon Studios, which produces the long-running, Germany-based *Spielekonzerte* (*Game Concerts*) series. Since at least 2003, when Böcker produced the first concert of game music outside Japan, the studio has emphasized its classical-ness, contrasting its programming, venues, and imagery from those of competitors like VGL. Its programs and albums have foregrounded the orchestral aspects of the music, featuring titles like *Symphonic Shades, Symphonic Fantasies, Symphonic Legends*, and *Symphonic Odysseys*. The group's marketing reinforces this connection. From its website: "For the very first time, DECCA, a leading label for classical music, released a live concert recording of video game music. And with this, again for the first time, video game music

---

[21] Connor Sheridan, "Final Fantasy Performance by London Symphony Orchestra in May," *Games Radar* (February 7, 2013) available online at http://www.gamesradar.com/final-fantasy-performance-london-symphony-orchestra-may/ (accessed December 3, 2016).

[22] Parakilas, "Classical Music as Popular Music," 1.

reached the Top 15 in the German classical music charts."[23] By noting these successes alongside images of formalwear-clad musicians in lavish concert halls, the website reinforces the idea that this music is an extension of the European classical tradition. This is particularly the case with *Final Symphony*, the company's most internationally renowned venture do date. Quoting again from the website:

> Another landmark first was set in 2013 as the celebrated London Symphony orchestra performed its first game concert with *Final Symphony*. A triumphant concert . . . , *Final Symphony* marks the tenth and most successful production for Thomas Böcker to date. No other concert has been performed as many times, with sell-out shows in Germany, the United Kingdom, Japan, Denmark, Sweden, Finland, the Netherlands and the USA.[24]

A 2015 recording of *Final Symphony* (also featuring the London Symphony) met with equal success. As the recording's website proudly notes, it reached the top of the iTunes Classical Charts "in more than ten countries" and appeared in "the Classical Album Top 5 of both the Billboard Charts and the Official UK Charts."[25]

These official descriptions stress both the program's international success and its appeal as a specifically classical work. This careful positioning is equally evident in the arrangements themselves. In place of the straightforward transcriptions and medleys featured on many game concerts, *Final Symphony* more thoroughly reimagines the original source material. Unlike the kinds of remixes seen in previous chapters, however, here the arrangers—Jonne Valtonen, Robert Wanamo, and Masashi Hamauzu—adapted the music not to fit popular music models but to conform to the forms and styles of classical orchestral works.[26] *Final Symphony* begins with an original work by Valtonen, a Finnish composer who supervises the arrangements for Merregnon Studios. Although not a *Final Fantasy* arrangement, his *Fantasy Overture—Circle within a Circle within a Circle* sets the tone for the concert. It suggests a bombastic opening fanfare, the generic title "overture" evoking opera, ballet, or perhaps epic films of the 1930s. The "fantasy" part of the title is, perhaps intentionally, a bit unclear. In addition to its reference to the *Final Fantasy* games, a fantasy is also a form of classical music, indicating a kind of free-form structure. (Beethoven's

[23] "History," *Game Concerts.*

[24] "History," *Game Concerts.*

[25] "Final Symphony," *Game Concerts*, available online at http://www.gameconcerts.com/en/concerts/final-symphony/ (accessed December 6, 2016).

[26] My description of the order of works here refers to the 2015 studio recording; live performances may have differed somewhat.

TABLE 11.2

Final Symphony program and titles

Game	Generic Title	Programmatic Titles
–	Fantasy Overture	Circle within a Circle within a Circle
Final Fantasy VI	Symphonic Poem	Born with the Gift of Magic
Final Fantasy X	Piano Concerto	I. Zanarkand
		II. Inori
		III. Kessen
Final Fantasy X	Encore	Suteki da ne
Final Fantasy VII	Symphony in Three Movements	I. Nibelheim Incident
		II. Words Drowned by Fireworks
		III. The Planet's Crisis
Final Fantasy VII	Encore	Continue?
Final Fantasy Series	Encore	Fight, Fight, Fight!

famous "Moonlight" piano sonata of 1801 is subtitled "sonata in the style of a fantasy," for example.) But the linguistic confusion continues: Is Valtonon's work the overture *to* a fantasy, is it a fantasy-overture (the term Tchaikovsky preferred for his orchestral work *Romeo and Juliet*)—or is it both?

This classical formal borrowing endures through the following works. Each piece on the program is identified in three ways: by the *Final Fantasy* game from which it emerges, by a generic title, and by an additional programmatic title or titles (Table 11.2). For example, following Valtonen's *Fantasy Overture*, we hear *Final Fantasy VI—Symphonic Poem (Born with the Gift of Magic)*. Here again the connection with classical traditions is obvious. Symphonic poems, or tone poems, were a genre favored by composers in the nineteenth and early twentieth centuries—and still occasionally today, although composers seldom use the term "symphonic poem" anymore. These are typically one-movement orchestral works with some type of narrative. Paul Dukas's *The Sorcerer's Apprentice* (1896–1897), featured in Disney's *Fantasia* and its related video games, is one well-known symphonic poem. So is Richard Strauss's *Also sprach Zarathustra* (1896), which appeared prominently in Stanley Kubrick's *2001* and in several video game references to that film. In both cases, the title gives the listener a sense of the musical work's narrative content—in essence, the story it tells. To those familiar with the game's plot, *Born with the Gift of Magic* indicates its dramatic trajectory in the same way.

Even more intriguing, however, is the largest work on the program: *Final Fantasy VII—Symphony in Three Movements*. Once again, several aspects of this work strongly reinforce its classical aspirations—more, indeed, than might initially be apparent. Calling a work a "symphony" is in itself a grand claim. As scholars like the musicologist Mark Evan Bonds have pointed out, by the early nineteenth century the symphony had acquired a cultural cachet as "the most prestigious of all instrumental genres," as well as the "most serious."[27] Writing a symphony was a way of demonstrating to listeners and critics that a composer could handle the complexities of a lengthy work for a diverse musical ensemble. "It was not," Bonds notes, "a genre composers could take up lightly."[28] Nor is that the case now; if anything, the intervening centuries have reinforced our assessment of the symphony as the apex of classical music culture. Invoking the term raises the specters of a musical pantheon: Mozart, Beethoven, Brahms, Mahler, and so on. Arranging video game music into a symphony is thus a bold statement—the compositional equivalent of Tommy Tallarico's claim that game composers are "just as relevant as Beethoven and Mozart and . . . just as good."[29] Here, however, I think the comparison is more to another, though hardly less revered, composer: Igor Stravinsky.

Classical symphonies most often have four movements, although by the early nineteenth century other numbers of movements were becoming more frequent, as in, for example, Beethoven's "Pastoral" Symphony (1808) or Hector Berlioz's *Symphonie Fantastique* (1830). Specifically identifying the work as a symphony in three movements, however, strikes me as a reference to Stravinsky's 1945 work of the same name. Stylistically the *Final Fantasy VII* Symphony borrows from the modernist musical style of much of Stravinsky's music—as well as his Russian contemporary Sergei Prokofiev's—and so the title may be a kind of homage. The often dissonant musical language of the *Final Fantasy* Symphony in Three Movements may challenge listeners more accustomed to more straightforward arrangements. Referencing Stravinsky's music could both establish the music's historical pedigree and provide listeners with a musical framework for understanding the work. Another more oblique connection: the second movement of Stravinsky's Symphony in Three Movements originated as part of a score for a 1943 film adaptation of the novel *The Song of Bernadette* (although the music was not ultimately used in the film). Perhaps in invoking Stravinsky's work, the arrangers of *Final Symphony* sought a connection with another classical work that originated as a multimedia underscore—proof that such a transition to art was possible.

---

[27] Mark Evan Bonds, *Music as Thought: Listening to the Symphony in the Age of Beethoven* (Princeton, NJ: Princeton University Press, 2009), 1, 2.

[28] Bonds, *Music as Thought*, 2.

[29] MacNamara, "The S.F. Symphony Gets Its Game On."

The transformation of game music into art is a cornerstone of the *Final Symphony* project. One of the promotional videos for the recording features a revealing interview with composer Nobuo Uematsu, worth quoting at some length:

> The quality of [video game] music has definitely improved along with the development of the game systems, but I think the bigger factor is that, for the past 20 years or so, many kids who played games have grown up wanting to create game music. And they've gone on to study music properly, graduating from music schools to become game music composers. Although there are many game music concerts nowadays, they tend to be quite loyal to the game music style. It doesn't deviate too far, so it feels like game music, and it's often arranged to be easy to listen to. What makes *Final Symphony* so different is that it's interpreted more freely, in an artistic manner. There are even aspects that are closer to contemporary classical music. I find it very interesting that in *Final Symphony*, entertainment music is shifting more toward contemporary music. And I think that's very new.[30]

The musical values embedded in this passage are hard to miss. Despite his own background in rock, Uematsu seems to privilege classical training—or, as he calls it, studying music "properly" in a university setting. And he separates music in a "game music style" from that composed "in an artistic manner," suggesting that there's a fundamental incompatibility between those concepts. That artistic manner, Uematsu implies, results from the arrangements being closer to "contemporary classical music"—which I interpret to mean music composed after about 1900 rather than specifically music being composed today. Finally, to make things absolutely clear, Uematsu points out that this incorporation of classical elements shifts the music away from being entertainment, and presumably toward being art. Certainly, Uematsu's interview is a form of advertisement, and, self-deprecation aside, *Final Symphony*'s success translates into his own cultural and financial profit. Yet his tone reinforces the distinction between game music and art music, even as he lauds the arrangers of *Final Symphony* for transforming his music from the former to the latter. Repeatedly throughout the interview, Uematsu emphasizes the superiority of classical training and musical styles over earlier game styles—including, it seems, his own.

In every aspect of its design, *Final Symphony* is crafted to present game music in a form that is appealing to devotees of both game music and classical music. While

---

[30] Merregnon Studios, "Final Symphony—Interview with Nobuo Uematsu," *YouTube* (March 19, 2015), available online at https://www.youtube.com/watch?v=r1rbdoUmZGI (accessed December 8, 2016).

I have focused here on this particularly fascinating example, *Final Symphony* is hardly alone in that effort.[31] Another of the most popular touring game concerts, for instance, is *The Legend of Zelda: Symphony of the Goddesses*, an ongoing concert program premiered in 2012, featuring a four-movement symphony of the same name.[32] It's difficult to speculate what, if any, long-term effects these more classically inspired adaptations of game music will have on the orchestral repertoire—or whether they will come to be regarded as classical works, as many fans, producers, and critics passionately maintain. In the meantime, however, these programs—alongside efforts like the campaigns for game music in the Classic FM Hall of Fame—raise complex questions about what classical music means for twenty-first-century audiences. The coming years will teach us all whether classical music can embrace this new type of music, and the diverse new audience that comes along with it.

---

[31] To be clear, however, although the novelty of symphonic game music has attracted a significant amount of critical attention—and large audiences—in recent years, this approach is not limited to games. The classical and film composer Howard Shore, for example, created *The Lord of the Rings Symphony: Six Movements for Orchestra and Chorus* (2011), based on his music for the popular *Lord of the Rings* film trilogy (2001–2003). Much as we have seen with *Final Symphony*, Shore adapted his music into something somehow more "classical" than the original product; as the composer's website notes, he "mold[ed] them into a series of tone poems free of the specific visual linkage with the films and adhering more to the traditions of the programmatic orchestral works of [Richard] Strauss, [Franz] Liszt, [Bedřich] Smetana and [Jean] Sibelius." "*The Lord of the Rings Symphony*," *howardshore.com*, n.d., available online at http://www.howardshore.com/works/concerts/the-lord-of-the-rings-symphony/ (accessed December 8, 2016).

[32] Subsequent years' tours have tweaked the formula somewhat but have maintained the core programming concept.

Conclusion
THE END IS NIGH

LIKE A GOOD video game, finishing the writing of this book has been immensely rewarding and uniquely challenging—often at the same time. One aspect that undoubtedly falls into both categories is the sheer speed with which games and their culture are changing. Since I began writing in 2014, there have been remarkable shifts in how contemporary culture understands and values games and their music. From concert halls to art museums, including video games in spaces traditionally reserved for high art has raised substantial questions about the relationship between entertainment and artistry. The reverse is also true: the subtlety and nuance with which games have appropriated art forms like classical music have only increased in recent years. In fact, just as I was putting the finishing touches on my manuscript, a new release stopped me in my tracks: *The End Is Nigh* (2017), a new independent game from the much-lauded developer of *Super Meat Boy* (2010) and *The Binding of Isaac* (2011–2017). The game's title seemed like a sign. Rather than going back and rewriting my previous chapters (again), I decided this conclusion is a fitting place for one final analysis, taking into account the lessons I've learned in writing *Unlimited Replays*.

Although *The End Is Nigh* is a postapocalyptic game, its gaze is focused squarely on the past. Its protagonist, Ash, sits alone in the ruins of civilization, kept company only by his old-school 1980s game console. Only when his favorite game malfunctions does Ash brave the dangers of his destroyed world in search of human companionship (or at least some new games). *The End Is Nigh* is self-consciously "meta."

Ash's broken game is also called *The End Is Nigh*, and the difficult platforming of this nested minigame—essentially Mario for masochists—mirrors what players experience. In other words, Ash re-enacts the retro game he's been obsessively playing, just as *The End Is Nigh* nostalgically builds on the experience of those same types of games. Players can discover cartridges as they play, opening twisted new versions of classic games: *Blaster Massacre* instead of *Blaster Master* (1988), *Dig Dead* instead of *Dig Dug* (1982), *Catastrovania* instead of *Castlevania* (1986), and so on.

The duo Ridiculon's excellent soundtrack to *The End Is Nigh*—a compilation score made up entirely of remixed classical music—echoes this mélange of old and new. Given the game's nostalgic tone, it's not surprising to find many of the same pieces of music that have cropped up in earlier chapters. For example, Grieg's "In the Hall of the Mountain King" underscores the subterranean levels, just as it did in *Maniac Miner* (1983). The remixes likewise evoke the present and the past. In fact, each classical work is remixed twice: once in a quasi-popular styles, as in *Boom Boom Rocket* (2007) and *Catherine* (2011), and once in retro, chiptune style, evoking the remixes of older games like *Gyruss* (1983) or more recent retro independent titles like *FEZ* (2012). The soundtrack, like *The End Is Nigh* as a whole, evokes video games' past as much as their present. Most of all, though, the game and its music seem to comment on our present obsession *with* the past—the nostalgic tendency to value things that are old, even at the expense of the new. In music, narrative, and gameplay, the classic and contemporary elements are blended together until it's impossible to tell them apart. The past shapes the present, which changes the construction of the past—on and on, in an endless feedback loop.

Playing *The End Is Nigh*, I was reminded of the musicologist Susan McClary's description of musical postmodernity as "reveling in the rubble."[1] Just as Ash (like the player) ventures through the crumbling remnants of Western civilization, postmodern music often explores the collapsed edifices of classical music and its ideologically driven narratives of high and low art. Rather than lamenting that loss, however, McClary paints a more optimistic picture, advocating an understanding of music that embraces its "history of perpetual bricolage and fusions of hand-me-down codes and conventions." *The End Is Nigh* creates a new and compelling experience by building on fragments of game history—player experiences and expectations developed over decades. Its soundtrack does the same, gluing together bits of popular and classical musics—half remembered from cartoons, movies, earlier video games, concert experiences, and so on—and building something new from the pieces. The

---

[1] Susan McClary, *Conventional Wisdom: The Content of Musical Form* (Berkeley: University of California Press, 2000), chap. 5, "Reveling in the Rubble: The Postmodern Condition."

music collapses historical and stylistic divides in meaningful and intriguing ways. But much more important, it works to bridge the cultural gap that separates classical music and video games.

That's a gap that already seems to be getting smaller. Games still by and large lack classical music's cultural cachet, but perhaps things are changing. Games are increasingly recognized for their capability to tell meaningful stories, produce insightful political and cultural commentary, and make artistic statements. Less obviously—and at a positively glacial pace—the classical music world is also evolving. In search of financial security and social relevance, some ensembles have earnestly begun to explore ways to reach new audiences, including through the allure of video game music. All these signs point to a future where the artificial distinctions between highbrow and lowbrow are erased, and where games and other entertainment forms can stand alongside the art of classical music. But not just yet. In fact, I remain confident that the interaction of games and classical music will continue to create sites of friction and juxtaposition for some time to come.

However problematic or arbitrary they may be, centuries-old conceptions of art versus entertainment aren't easy to eradicate—if we want to get rid of them at all. Much of this book has been about the artistic aspirations of games and their culture. From *Elite* (1984) to more recent releases like *Grand Theft Auto IV* (2008) and *BioShock Infinite* (2013), ambitious games have explored the medium's unique possibilities as an expressive form. Classical music often serves as a point of reference, a way of demonstrating that quality by inviting comparison with unquestioned artworks. Games have something to prove. I think the designers of *Gyruss* remixed Bach's Toccata and Fugue to prove that the sound hardware could do it. *Eternal Sonata* (2007) and *Versailles 1685* (1997) prove that music history can be entertaining. *Steve Reich's Clapping Music* (2015) proves that contemporary classical music can be accessible. And symphonic programs like *Video Games Live* and *Final Symphony* prove that game music is just as good as Beethoven. Over and over in this book, games have depended on players to know that classical music is high art; without that understanding, the comparison loses its potency. Whether to give them either something to aspire to, or something to position themselves against, video games often *need* classical music to remain on its high-art pedestal.

The situation on the classical music side is remarkably similar. Whatever lip service is paid to increasing accessibility and diversity, from a certain perspective those goals are self-defeating. As the sociologist Pierre Bourdieu might say, a taste for classical music is a self-conscious mark of "distinction."[2] Since at least the nineteenth

---

[2] Pierre Bourdieu, *Distinction: A Social Critique of the Judgement of Taste*, trans. Richard Nice (Cambridge, MA: Harvard University Press, 1984).

century, some performers and audience members have relied on classical music's aura of high-class exclusivity as proof of their own intelligence, sophistication, and often wealth.[3] Unconsciously or not, that bias still lingers. As I write this conclusion, for example, today's issue of the *Washington Post* has an opinion piece from critic Philip Kennicott, the very title of which—"The Kennedy Center Honors Abandons the Arts for Pop Culture"—seems to preclude the coexistence of art and popular entertainment like video games.[4] Consequently, efforts to broaden classical music's appeal through games—particularly by bringing their music into classical concert spaces—seem bound to ruffle a few feathers.

The same is true of using classical music *in* games. Devotees who ardently believe in the artistic value, or even cultural superiority, of Western classical music are often dismayed to find it cheapened through association with less elevated media. As the musicologist Claudia Bullerjahn points out in a study of music in advertising, "When a television commercial for ketchup employs a classical symphony as its background music, lovers of the symphony call it an abomination."[5] Video games may rank higher in cultural cachet than ketchup commercials, but only barely. Many would still agree with film critic Roger Ebert's 2005 assessment that "for most gamers, video games represent a loss of those precious hours we have available to make ourselves more cultured, civilized and empathetic."[6]

My personal experiences as a musicologist have also reinforced my belief in a persistent and willful divide between high and low art in scholarship. There is a growing group of scholars researching game music—many of whose works appear in my bibliography and have profoundly shaped my own thinking—and many scholars in other fields have been interested in and supportive of game music research. Yet in some academic settings there remains a palpable sense that this research is somehow frivolous, less important than the study of established classical music. I once had a

---

[3] Ralph Locke, for instance, notes that in the later nineteenth-century United States, "the art experience was . . . carefully stratified and 'framed' in ways that intimidated or even effectively excluded members of the poor and working classes." Ralph Locke, "Music Lovers, Patrons, and the 'Sacralization' of Culture in America," *19th Century Music* 17 (1993): 149–173.

[4] Philip Kennicott, "The Kennedy Center Honors Abandons the Arts for Pop Culture," *Washington Post* (August 3, 2017), available online at https://www.washingtonpost.com/entertainment/the-kennedy-center-honors-abandon-the-arts-for-pop-culture/2017/08/02/0287e65c-77a0-11e7-8f39-eeb7d3a2d304_story.html?utm_term=.e50e1ff7917c.

[5] Claudia Bullerjahn, "The Effectiveness of Music in Television Commercials: A Comparison of Theoretical Approaches," in *Music and Manipulation: On the Social Uses and Social Control of Music*, ed. Steven Brown and Ulrik Volgsten (New York: Berghahn, 2007), 233. See also Peter Kupfer, "Classical Music in Television Commercials: A Social-Psychological Perspective," *Music and the Moving Image* 10 (2017): 23–53.

[6] Ebert's pronouncement came in response to a letter in which a reader made the case for games as art. Roger Ebert, "Why Did the Chicken Cross the Genders?," *RogerEbert.com* (November 27, 2005), available online at http://www.rogerebert.com/answer-man/why-did-the-chicken-cross-the-genders (accessed August 2, 2017).

presentation scheduled for the final session of a long academic conference because, as one of the organizers cheerfully told me, they "wanted to end with something fun after people were burned out from the serious topics." This was not an isolated incident. A well-meaning colleague from another university once earnestly told me that my application for tenure at my current institution was in good shape "because your legit research balances out the game stuff." In that case, "legit" implied the kind of research that involves painstakingly combing through archives in distant countries in search of data that might eventually make a contribution to a well-established topic. Playing video games as research seems too easy, too entertaining, and too popular to fit comfortably into that model of scholarship.

As long as we struggle to define what art is and what it means, these debates over cultural values will play out over and over. My reaction to that conclusion is equal parts chagrin and delight. Chagrin, because the questions I set out to answer in *Unlimited Replays* are ultimately unanswerable. In the digital age, dichotomies like art and entertainment, and high art and low art mean precisely what they have always meant: everything, and nothing. And delight, because just like my eight-year-old self hearing the Toccata and Fugue in D minor in *The Battle of Olympus* for the first time, I can't wait to try puzzling out the next example of classical music interacting with video games. Asking these questions of ourselves and others is what ultimately gives meaning to the art of classical music in video games.

Thanks a million. Push start to replay.

Bibliography

Aldred, Jessica. "A Question of Character: Transmediation, Abstraction, and Identification in Early Games Licensed from Movies." In *Before the Crash: Early Video Game History*, edited by Mark J. P. Wolf, 90–104. Detroit: Wayne State University Press, 2012.

Alexander, Leigh. "The Aberrant Gamer: An Evening with Sander Cohen." *GameSetWatch*. September 6, 2007. http://www.gamesetwatch.com/2007/09/column_the_aberrant_gamer_an_e.php (accessed July 26, 2014).

Altman, Rick. *Silent Film Sound*. New York: Columbia University Press, 2004.

Apperly, Tom. "Modding the Historians' Code: Historical Verisimilitude and the Counterfactual Imagination." In *Playing with the Past: Digital Games and the Simulation of History*, edited by Matthew Wilhelm Kapell and Andrew B. R. Elliott, 185–198. New York: Bloomsbury, 2013.

ap Siôn, Pwyll, and Tristian Evans. "Parallel Symmetries? Exploring Relationships between Minimalist Music and Multimedia Forms." In *Sound and Music in Film and Visual Media*, edited by Graeme Harper, Ruth Doughty, and Jochen Eisentraut, 671–691. New York: Continuum, 2009.

Auslander, Philip. *Liveness: Performance in a Mediatized Culture*. London: Routledge, 1999.

Austin, Michael. "Introduction—Taking Note of Music Games." In *Music Video Games: Performance, Politics, and Play*, edited by Michael Austin, 1–22. New York: Bloomsbury, 2016.

Ayers, William. "Recomposition of Chopin and Narrative Design in Double Fine's *Stacking*." Paper at the North American Conference on Video Game Music. Youngstown State University, January 17–18, 2014.

Bakhtin, Mikhail. *Rabelais and His World*. Translated by Hélène Iswolsky. Bloomington: Indiana University Press, 1984.

Benjamin, Walter. "The Work of Art in the Age of Mechanical Reproduction." In *Illuminations*, translated and edited by Hannah Arendt, 217–252. New York: Harcourt, Brace, and World, 1968.

Bettelheim, Bruno. *The Uses of Enchantment: The Meaning and Importance of Fairy Tales*. New York: Knopf, 1976.

Bourdieu, Pierre. *Distinction: A Social Critique of the Judgement of Taste*. Translated by Richard Nice. Cambridge, MA: Harvard University Press, 1984.

Bissell, Tom. *Extra Lives: Why Video Games Matter*. New York: Vintage Books, 2011.

Bizony, Piers. *2001: Filming the Future*. London: Aurum, 1994.

Blickhan, Samantha. "'Listening' through Digital Interaction in Björk's *Biophilia*." In *Ludomusicology: Approaches to Video Game Music*, edited by Michiel Kamp, Tim Summers, and Mark Sweeney, 133–151. Sheffield, UK: Equinox, 2016.

Bogost, Ian. *How to Do Things with Videogames*. Minneapolis: University of Minnesota Press, 2011.

Bonds, Mark Evan. *Music as Thought: Listening to the Symphony in the Age of Beethoven*. Princeton, NJ: Princeton University Press, 2009.

Bramwell, Tom. "*Boom Boom Rocket*." *Eurogamer*. April 12, 2007. http://www.eurogamer.net/articles/boom-boom-rocket-review (accessed July 12, 2014).

Brookey, Robert Alan. *Hollywood Gamers: Digital Convergence in the Film and Video Game Industries*. Bloomington: Indiana University Press, 2010.

Brown, Julie. *Bartók and the Grotesque: Studies in Modernity, the Body and Contradiction in Music*. Aldershot, UK: Ashgate, 2007.

———. "*Carnival of Souls* and the Organs of Horror." In *Music in the Horror Film: Listening to Fear*, edited by Neil Lerner, 1–20. New York: Routledge, 2010.

Brown, Matthew. *Debussy Redux: The Impact of His Music on Popular Culture*. Bloomington: Indiana University Press, 2012.

Broyles, Michael. *Beethoven in America*. Bloomington: Indiana University Press, 2011.

Brudvig, Erik. "Eternal Sonata Review." *IGN*. September 13, 2007. http://www.ign.com/articles/2007/09/13/eternal-sonata-review-2 (accessed January 16, 2016).

Bullerjahn, Claudia. "The Effectiveness of Music in Television Commercials: A Comparison of Theoretical Approaches." In *Music and Manipulation: On the Social Uses and Social Control of Music*, edited by Steven Brown and Ulrik Volgsten, 207–235. New York: Berghahn, 2006.

Chang, Vanessa. "Records That Play: The Present Past in Sampling Practice." *Popular Music* 28 (2009): 143–159.

Cheng, William. *Sound Play: Video Games and the Musical Imagination*. Oxford: Oxford University Press, 2014.

Code, David J. "Don Juan in Nadsat: Kubrick's Music for *A Clockwork Orange*." *Journal of the Royal Musical Association* 139 (2014): 339–386.

Collins, Karen. *Game Sound: An Introduction to the History, Theory, and Practice of Video Game Music and Sound Design*. Cambridge, MA: MIT Press, 2008.

———. *Playing with Sound: A Theory of Interacting with Sound and Music in Video Games*. Cambridge, MA: MIT Press, 2013.

Cook, Karen M. "Music, History, and Progress in Sid Meier's *Civilization IV*." In *Music in Video Games: Studying Play*, edited by K. J. Donnelly, William Gibbons, and Neil Lerner, 166–182. New York: Routledge, 2014.

Cooper, Michael. "Steve Reich, Game Designer." *New York Times*. July 9, 2015. http://artsbeat. blogs.nytimes.com/2015/07/09/steve-reich-game-designer/ (accessed November 11, 2016).

Cormack, Mike. "The Pleasures of Ambiguity: Using Classical Music in Film." In *Changing Tunes: The Use of Pre-existing Music in Film*, edited by Phil Powrie and Robynn Stilwell, 19–30. Burlington, VT: Ashgate, 2006.

Cornelius, Steven, and Mary Natvig. "Teaching Music History: A Cultural Approach." *Journal of Music History Pedagogy* 4 (2013): 139–150.

Coulthard, Lisa. "Torture Tunes: Tarantino, Popular Music, and New Hollywood Ultraviolence." *Music and the Moving Image* 2, no. 2 (2009): 1–6.

Dinitto, Rachel. "Translating Prewar Culture into Film: The Double Vision of Suzuki Seijun's *Zigeunerweisen*." *Journal of Japanese Studies* 30 (2004): 35–63.

Donnelly, K. J. *The Spectre of Sound: Music in Film and Television*. London: BFI, 2005.

Donovan, Tristan. *Replay: The History of Video Games*. East Sussex, UK: Yellow Ant, 2010.

Dow, Douglas N. "Historical Veneers: Anachronism, Simulation and History in *Assassin's Creed II*." In *Playing with the Past: Digital Games and the Simulation of History*, edited by Matthew Wilhelm Kapell and Andrew B. R. Elliott, 215–232. New York: Bloomsbury, 2013.

Duggan, Maeve. "Gaming and Gamers." *Pew Research Center: Internet, Science & Tech*. December 15, 2015. http://www.pewinternet.org/2015/12/15/gaming-and-gamers/ (accessed January 5, 2018).

Duncan, Dean. *Charms That Soothe: Classical Music and the Narrative Film*. New York: Fordham University Press, 2003.

Eaton, Rebecca M. Doran. "Marking Minimalism: Minimal Music as a Sign of Machines and Mathematics in Multimedia." *Music and the Moving Image* 7 (2014): 3–23.

Ebert, Roger. "Video Games Can Never Be Art." *RogerEbert.com*. April 16, 2010. http://www. rogerebert.com/rogers-journal/video-games-can-never-be-art (accessed July 21, 2015).

———. "Why Did the Chicken Cross the Genders?" *RogerEbert.com*. November 27, 2005. http:// www.rogerebert.com/answer-man/why-did-the-chicken-cross-the-genders (accessed August 2, 2017).

"Eternal Sonata Director Q&A." *GameSpot*. August 7, 2007. http://www.gamespot.com/xbox360/ rpg/trustybellchopinnoyume/news.html?page=1&sid=6176358 (accessed January 15, 2016).

Everett, Yayoi Uno. "Signification of Parody and the Grotesque in György Ligeti's *Le Grand Macabre*." *Music Theory Spectrum* 31 (2009): 26–56.

Fahy, Thomas. "Killer Culture: Classical Music and the Art of Killing in *Silence of the Lambs* and *Se7en*." *Journal of Popular Culture* 37 (2003): 28–42.

Fernandez, Stephanie. "Lost in Translation." *IGN*. September 12, 2007. http://www.ign.com/ blogs/eternalsonata/2007/09/12/lost-in-translation (accessed September 15, 2015).

"*Fez* Review." *Edge Online*. April 11, 2012. http://www.edge-online.com/review/fez-review/ (accessed July 18, 2014).

Fink, Robert. *Repeating Ourselves: American Minimal Music as Cultural Practice*. Berkeley: University of California Press, 2005.

Fleishman, Jeffrey. "Video Game Music Comes to the Orchestra Concert Hall." *Los Angeles Times*. June 12, 2015. http://www.latimes.com/entertainment/herocomplex/la-ca-hc-video-games-music-20150614-story.html (accessed December 2, 2016).

Fleshner, Nathan. "Pitching the Rhythm: Music Games for the iPad." In *Music Video Games: Performance, Politics, and Play*, edited by Michael Austin, 275–296. New York: Bloomsbury, 2016.

Frasca, Gonzalo. "Videogames of the Oppressed: Videogames as a Means for Critical Thinking and Debate." Master's thesis, Georgia Institute of Technology, 2001.

Fritsch, Melanie. *"Beat It!*—Playing the 'King of Pop' in Video Games." In *Music Video Games: Performance, Politics, and Play*, edited by Michael Austin, 153–176. New York: Bloomsbury, 2016.

Furness, Hannah. "Film Score Composers Should Be Treated as 'Seriously' as Mozart and Tchaikovsky, Royal Albert Hall Director Says." *Telegraph*. July 3, 2014. http://www.telegraph. co.uk/culture/music/classicalmusic/10943665/Film-score-composers-should-be-treated-as-seriously-as-Mozart-and-Tchaikovsky-Royal-Albert-Hall-director-says.html (accessed December 3, 2016).

Gabler, Jay. "What Is Classical Music?" *Minnesota Public Radio*. October 16, 2013, http://minnesota.publicradio.org/display/web/2013/10/15/what-is-classical-music (accessed August 7, 2014).

Galbraith, Patrick W. "Bishōjo Games: 'Techno-Intimacy' and the Virtually Human in Japan." *Game Studies* 11, no. 2 (May 2011). http://gamestudies.org/1102/articles/galbraith.

Gee, James Paul. "Why Game Studies Now? Video Games: A New Art Form." *Games and Culture* 1 (2006): 58–61.

Gengaro, Christine Lee. *Listening to Stanley Kubrick: The Music in His Films*. London: Rowman and Littlefield, 2014.

Gerstmann, Jeff. *"Boom Boom Rocket* Review." *GameSpot*. April 11, 2007. http://www.gamespot. com/reviews/boom-boom-rocket-review/1900-6168919/ (accessed July 13, 2014).

Gibbons, William. "Blip, Bloop, Bach? Some Uses of Classical Music on the Nintendo Entertainment System." *Music and the Moving Image* 2, no. 1 (2009): 40–52.

———. "Music, Genre, and Nationality in Postmillennial Fantasy Role-Playing Games." In *The Routledge Companion to Screen Music and Sound*, edited by Miguel Mera, Ron Sadoff, and Ben Winters, 412–427. London: Routledge, 2017.

———. "'Wrap Your Troubles in Dreams': Popular Music, Narrative, and Dystopia in *BioShock*." *Game Studies* 11, no. 3 (2011). http://gamestudies.org/1103/articles/gibbons.

Goldberg, Harold. *All Your Base Are Belong to Us: How Fifty Years of Videogames Conquered Pop Culture*. New York: Three Rivers Press, 2011.

Goldmark, Daniel. *Tunes for Toons: Music and the Hollywood Cartoon*. Berkeley: University of California Press, 2005.

Gorbman, Claudia. "Auteur Music." In *Beyond the Soundtrack: Representing Music in Cinema*, edited by Daniel Goldmark, Lawrence Kramer, and Richard Leppert, 149–162. Berkeley: University of California Press, 2007.

———. "Ears Wide Open: Kubrick's Music." In *Changing Tunes: The Use of Pre-existing Music in Film*, edited by Phil Powrie and Robynn Stilwell, 3–18. Burlington, VT: Ashgate, 2006.

Gower, Lily, and Janet McDowall. "Interactive Music Video Games and Children's Musical Development." *British Journal of Music Education* 29 (2012): 91–105.

Gribbin, John. *In Search of Schrödinger's Cat: Quantum Physics and Reality*. New York: Bantam, 1984.

Guthrie, Kate. "Democratizing Art: Music Education in Postwar Britain." *Musical Quarterly* 97 (2014): 575–615.

"The Hall of Fame—The Best Classical Music of All Time." *ClassicFM.com*. n.d. http://www. classicfm.com/hall-of-fame/ (accessed December 1, 2016).

Hartenberger, Russell. "*Clapping Music*: A Performer's Perspective." In *The Routledge Research Companion to Minimalist and Postminimalist Music*, edited by Keith Potter, Kyle Gann, and Pwyll ap Siôn, 371–379. Surrey, UK: Ashgate, 2013.

Hedges, Stephen A. "Dice Music in the Eighteenth Century." *Music and Letters* 59 (1978): 180–187.

Hillman, Roger. "Sounding the Depths of History: Opera and National Identity in Italian Film." In *A Companion to the Historical Film*, edited by Robert A. Rosenstone and Constantin Parvulescu, 328–347. Chichester, UK: Wiley Blackwell, 2013.

Hirsch, Lily E. *Music in American Crime Prevention and Punishment*. Ann Arbor: University of Michigan Press, 2012.

Horowitz, Joseph. *Classical Music in America: A History of Its Rise and Fall*. New York: Norton, 2005), chap. 5.

Hubbert, Julie, ed. *Celluloid Symphonies: Texts and Contexts in Film Music History*. Berkeley: University of California Press, 2011.

Hubbs, Joanna. *Mother Russia: The Feminine Myth in Russian Culture*. Bloomington: Indiana University Press, 1988.

Hutcheon, Linda. "Historiographic Metafiction: Parody and the Intertextuality of History." In *Intertextuality and Contemporary American Fiction*, edited by Patrick O'Donnell and Robert Con Davis, 3–32. Baltimore: Johns Hopkins University Press, 1989.

Ivănescu, Andra. "The Music of Tomorrow, Yesterday! Music, Time and Technology in *BioShock Infinite*." *Networking Knowledge* 7, no. 2 (2014). http://ojs.meccsa.org.uk/index.php/netknow/article/view/337/168.

Iwaskai, Scott. "Concert Review: Symphony Help Breathe Life into Video Games." *Deseret News*. March 29, 2008. http://www.deseretnews.com/article/695265797/Symphony-help-breathe-life-into-video-games.html (accessed December 2, 2016).

Jacobus, Enoch. "Lighter Than Air: A Return to Columbia." Paper presented at the North American Conference on Video Game Music. Texas Christian University, January 17–18, 2015.

———. "There's Always a Lighthouse: Commentary and Foreshadowing in the Diegetic Music of *BioShock: Infinite*." Paper presented at the North American Conference on Video Game Music. Youngstown State University, January 18–19, 2014.

Jakob-Hoff, Tristan. "Can Film Music Ever Be Classical?" *The Guardian*. April 7, 2008. https://www.theguardian.com/music/musicblog/2008/apr/07/canfilmmusiceverbeclassical (accessed December 3, 2016).

Jarvis, Matthew. "Play On: How Video Game Music Is Rocking the Classical World." *MCV*. September 28, 2015. http://www.mcvuk.com/articles/media-pr/play-on-how-video-game-music-is-rocking-the-classical-world (accessed November 18, 2017).

Joe, Jeongwon. "Reconsidering *Amadeus*: Mozart as Film Music." In *Changing Tunes: The Uses of Pre-existing Music in Film*, edited by Phil Powrie and Robynn Stilwell, 57–73. Ashgate, UK: Ashgate, 2006.

Johns, Andreas. *Baba Yaga: The Ambiguous Mother and Witch of the Russian Folktale*. New York: Peter Lang, 2004.

Johnson, Julian. *Who Needs Classical Music? Cultural Choice and Musical Value*. Oxford: Oxford University Press, 2002.

Juul, Jesper. *A Casual Revolution: Reinventing Video Games and Their Players*. Cambridge, MA: MIT Press, 2010.

———. *Half-Real: Video Games between Real Rules and Fictional Worlds*. Cambridge, MA: MIT Press, 2005.

Kalinak, Kathryn. *How the West Was Sung: Music in the Westerns of John Ford*. Berkeley: University of California Press, 2007.

Kallberg, Jeffrey. "The Harmony of the Tea Table: Gender and Ideology in the Piano Nocturne." *Representations* 39 (1992): 102–133.

———. "Nocturnal Thoughts on *Impromptu*." *Musical Quarterly* 81 (1997): 199–203.

———. "Small Fairy Voices: Sex, History, and Meaning in Chopin." In *Chopin Studies 2*, edited by John Rink and Jim Samson, 50–71. Cambridge: Cambridge University Press, 1994.

Kamen, Matt. "Video Games Storm Classic FM's 2015 'Hall of Fame.'" *Wired*. April 7, 2015. http://www.wired.co.uk/article/game-music-classic-fm (accessed December 5, 2016).

Kapell, Matthew Wilhem, and Andrew B. R. Elliott, eds. *Playing with the Past: Digital Games and the Simulation of History*. New York: Bloomsbury, 2013.

Karhulahti, Veli-Matti. "Defining the Videogame." *Game Studies* 15, no. 2 (December 2015). http://gamestudies.org/1502/articles/karhulahti.

Kärjä, Antti-Ville. "Marketing Music through Computer Games: The Case of Poets of the Fall and *Max Payne 2*." In *From Pac-Man to Pop Music: Interactive Audio in Games and New Media*, edited by Karen Collins, 26–44. Aldershot, UK: Ashgate, 2008.

Kassabian Anahid, and Freya Jarman. "Game and Play in Music Video Games." In *Ludomusicology: Approaches to Video Game Music*, edited by Michiel Kamp, Tim Summers, and Mark Sweeney, 116–132. Sheffield, UK: Equinox, 2016.

Katz, Mark. *Capturing Sound: How Technology Has Changed Music*. Rev. ed. Berkeley: University of California Press, 2010.

Keefe, Simon P. *Mozart's Requiem: Reception, Work, Completion*. Cambridge: Cambridge University Press, 2012.

Kennicott, Philip. "America's Orchestras Are in Crisis." *New Republic*. August 25, 2013. https://newrepublic.com/article/114221/orchestras-crisis-outreach-ruining-them (accessed November 13, 2016).

———. "The Kennedy Center Honors Abandons the Arts for Pop Culture." *Washington Post*. August 3, 2017. https://www.washingtonpost.com/entertainment/the-kennedy-center-honors-abandon-the-arts-for-pop-culture/2017/08/02/0287e65c-77a0-11e7-8f39-eeb7d3a2d304_story.html?utm_term=.e50e1ff7917c.

Knoblauch, William. "*SIMON*: The Prelude to Modern Music Video Games." In *Music Video Games: Performance, Politics, and Play*, edited by Michael Austin, 25–42. New York: Bloomsbury, 2016.

Kolker, Robert Philip. "Oranges, Dogs, and Ultra-violence." *Journal of Popular Film* 1 (1972): 159–172.

Kramer, Jonathan. "The Nature and Origins of Musical Postmodernism." In *Postmodern Music/Postmodern Thoughts*, edited by Judy Lochhead and Joseph Auner, 13–26. New York: Routledge, 2002.

Kramer, Lawrence. "Melodic Trains: Music in Polanski's *The Pianist*." In *Beyond the Soundtrack: Representing Music in Cinema*, edited by Daniel Goldmark, Lawrence Kramer, and Richard D. Leppert, 66–85. Berkeley: University of California Press, 2007.

———. *Why Classical Music Still Matters*. Berkeley: University of California Press, 2007.

Kupfer, Peter. "Classical Music in Television Commercials: A Social-Psychological Perspective." *Music and the Moving Image* 10 (2017): 23–53.

Lachmann, Renate. "Bakhtin and Carnival: Culture as Counter-culture." *Cultural Critique* 11 (1988–1989): 115–152.

Larsen, Peter. *Film Music*. London: Reaktion, 2005.

Leray, Joseph. "*Frederic: Resurrection of Music* Review." *Touch Arcade*. February 1, 2012. http://toucharcade.com/2012/02/01/frederic-resurrection-of-music-review/ (accessed October 3, 2015).

Lerner, Neil. "Mario's Dynamic Leaps: Musical Innovations (and the Specter of Early Cinema) in *Donkey Kong* and *Super Mario Bros.*" In *Music in Video Games: Studying Play*, edited by K. J. Donnelly, William Gibbons, and Neil Lerner, 1–29. New York: Routledge, 2014.

———. "The Origins of Musical Style in Video Games, 1977–1983." In *The Oxford Handbook of Film Music Studies*, edited by David Neumeyer, 319–347. Oxford: Oxford University Press, 2014.

———. "Reading Wagner in *Bugs Bunny Nips the Nips* (1944)." In *Wagner and Cinema*, ed. Jeongwon Joe and Sander L. Gilman, 210–224. Bloomington: Indiana University Press, 2010.

Levine, Lawrence W. *Highbrow, Lowbrow: The Emergence of Cultural Hierarchy in America*. Cambridge, MA: Harvard University Press, 1988.

Lizardi, Ryan. "*Bioshock*: Complex and Alternate Histories." *Games Studies* 14, no. 1 (August 2014). http://gamestudies.org/1401/articles/lizardi.

Locke, Ralph. "Music Lovers, Patrons, and the 'Sacralization' of Culture in America." *19th Century Music* 17 (1993): 149–173.

Lockwood, Lewis. "Film Biography as Travesty: *Immortal Beloved* and Beethoven." *Musical Quarterly* 81 (1997): 190–198.

Lowe, Melanie. "Claiming Amadeus: Classical Feedback in American Media." *American Music* 20 (2002): 102–119.

MacNamara, Mark. "The S.F. Symphony Gets Its Game On." *San Francisco Classical Voice*. July 18, 2013. https://www.sfcv.org/article/the-sf-symphony-gets-its-video-game-on (accessed December 3, 2016).

Marks, Martin Miller. *Music in Silent Film: Contexts and Case Studies, 1895–1924*. Oxford: Oxford University Press, 1997.

Marshall, Robert. "Film as Musicology: *Amadeus*." *Musical Quarterly* 81 (1997): 173–179.

McClary, Susan, *Conventional Wisdom: The Content of Musical Form*. Berkeley: University of California Press, 2000, chap. 5.

McGonigal, Jane. *Reality Is Broken: Why Games Make Us Better and How They Can Change the World*. New York: Penguin, 2011.

———. *SuperBetter: The Power of Living Gamefully*. New York: Penguin, 2015.

McLeod, Ken. "'A Fifth of Beethoven': Disco, Classical Music, and the Politics of Inclusion." *American Music* 24 (2006): 347–363.

McQuiston, Kate. "The Stanley Kubrick Experience: Music, Nuclear Bombs, Disorientation, and You." In *Music, Sound and Filmmakers*, edited by James Wierzbicki, 138–150. New York: Routledge, 2012.

———. *We'll Meet Again: Musical Design in the Films of Stanley Kubrick*. Oxford: Oxford University Press, 2013.

Meyer, John Mix. "Q&A: Ken Levine's Brave New World of *BioShock Infinite*." *Wired*. April 26, 2012. http://www.wired.com/2012/04/ken-levine-interview/all/ (accessed November 11, 2015).

Miller, Kiri. *Playing Along: Digital Games, YouTube, and Virtual Performance*. Oxford: Oxford University Press, 2012.

Miller, Matt. "Fez: Change Your Perspective." *GameInformer*. April 11, 2012. http://www.gameinformer.com/games/fez/b/xbox360/archive/2012/04/11/change-your-perspective.aspx (accessed July 18, 2014).

Morales, Xavier. "*Kill Bill*: Beauty and Violence." *Harvard Law Record*. October 16, 2003. http://hlrecord.org/?p=11285.

Morris, Mitchell. "Sight, Sound, and the Temporality of Myth Making in *Koyaanisqatsi*." In *Beyond the Soundtrack: Representing Music in Cinema*, edited by Daniel Goldmark, Lawrence Kramer, and Richard Leppert, 120–135. Berkeley: University of California Press, 2007.

Moseley, Roger. *Keys to Play: Music as a Ludic Medium from Apollo to Nintendo*. Berkeley: University of California Press, 2016.

Murray, Soraya. "High Art/Low Life: The Art of Playing *Grand Theft Auto*." *PAJ: A Journal of Performance and Art* 27 (2005): 91–98.

Musgrove, Mike. "Mario's New World: Symphonies." *Washington Post*. August 3, 2006. http://www.washingtonpost.com/wp-dyn/content/article/2006/08/02/AR2006080201889_pf.html (accessed November 20, 2016).

Navas, Eduardo. *Remix Theory: The Aesthetics of Sampling*. Vienna: Springer, 2012.

Needleman, Sarah E. "How Videogames Are Saving the Symphony Orchestra." *Wall Street Journal*. October 12, 2015. http://www.wsj.com/articles/how-videogames-are-saving-the-symphony-orchestra-1444696737 (accessed November 12, 2016).

Newman, James. *Videogames*. London: Routledge, 2004.

Owens, Craig. "The Allegorical Impulse: Toward a Theory of Postmodernism." *October* 12 (1980): 67–86.

———. "The Allegorical Impulse: Toward a Theory of Postmodernism, Part 2." *October* 13 (1980): 58–80.

Parakilas, James. "Classical Music as Popular Music." *Journal of Musicology* 3 (1984): 1–18.

Parish, Jeremy. "An Interview with Konami's Hidenori Maezawa, Pt 3." *1up.com*. January 15, 2009. http://www.1up.com/do/blogEntry?bId=8978659&publicUserId=5379721 (accessed June 23, 2016).

Patterson, David W. "Music, Structure and Metaphor in Stanley Kubrick's *2001: A Space Odyssey*." *American Music* 22 (2004): 444–471.

Pekacz, Jolanta T. "Deconstructing a 'National Composer': Chopin and Polish Exiles in Paris, 1831–49." *19th Century Music* 24 (2000): 161–172.

Perry, Douglass C. "*Boom Boom Rocket* Review." *IGN*. April 12, 2007. http://www.ign.com/articles/2007/04/12/boom-boom-rocket-review (accessed July 12, 2014).

Perry-Camp, Jane. "*Amadeus* and Authenticity." *Eighteenth-Century Life* 9 (1983): 116–118.

Peterson, Rolfe Daus, Andrew Justin Miller, and Sean Joseph Fedorko. "The Same River Twice: Exploring Historical Representation and the Value of Simulation in the *Total War*, *Civilization*, and *Patrician* Franchises." In *Playing with the Past: Digital Games and the Simulation of History*, edited by Matthew Wilhelm Kapell and Andrew B. R. Elliott, 33–48. New York: Bloomsbury, 2013.

Pezzotta, Elisa. "The Metaphor of Dance in Stanley Kubrick's *2001: A Space Odyssey, A Clockwork Orange*, and *Full Metal Jacket*." *Journal of Adaptation in Film and Performance* 5 (2012): 51–64.

Plank, Dana. "'From Russia with Fun!': *Tetris*, 'Korobeiniki,' and the Ludic Soviet." *Soundtrack* 8 (2015): 7–24.

———. "From the Concert Hall to the Console: The 8-Bit Translation of BWV 565." Paper presented at the North American Conference on Video Game Music. Youngstown State University, January 18, 2014.

Pozderac-Chenevey, Sarah. "Breaking the Circle: Analyzing the Narrative Function of Music Manipulation in *BioShock Infinite*." Paper presented at the North American Conference on Video Game Music. Youngstown State University, January 18–19, 2014.

Prendergast, Roy M. *Film Music: A Neglected Art*. Rev. ed. New York: Norton, 1992.

Raz, Carmel. "Anne Young's 'Musical Games' (1801): Music Theory, Gender, and Game Design." Paper presented at the annual meeting of the American Musicological Society. Vancouver, British Columbia, November 3–6, 2016.

Reale, Steven Beverburg. "Transcribing Musical Worlds; or, Is *L.A. Noire* a Music Game?" In *Music and Video Games: Studying Play*, edited by K. J. Donnelly, William Gibbons, and Neil Lerner, 77–103. New York: Routledge, 2014.

Reparaz, Mikel. "The Citizen Kanes of Videogames." *GamesRadar*. July 24, 2009. http://www.gamesradar.com/the-citizen-kanes-of-videogames/ (accessed August 1, 2016).

Richardson, Patrick, and Youngmoo E. Kim. "Beyond Fun and Games: A Framework for Quantifying Music Skills Developments from Video Game Play." *Journal of New Music Research* 40 (2011): 277–291.

Ron Rodman, *Tuning In: American Narrative Television Music*. Oxford: Oxford University Press, 2010, 124

Rosoff, Matt. "I'm Obsessed with This Fiendishly Difficult App That Separates Real Musicians from Wannabes." *Business Insider*, July 16, 2015. http://www.businessinsider.com/steve-reich-clapping-music-app-2015-7 (accessed November 11, 2016).

Russo, Mary. *The Female Grotesque: Risk, Excess, and Modernity*. New York: Routledge, 1994.

Samson, Jim. "Chopin Reception: Theory, History, Analysis." In *Chopin Studies 2*, edited by John Rink and Jim Samson, 1–17. Cambridge: Cambridge University Press, 1994.

———. "Myth and Reality: A Biographical Introduction." In *The Cambridge Companion to Chopin*, edited by Jim Samson, 1–8. Cambridge: Cambridge University Press, 1992.

Santiago, Kellee. "Stop the Debate! Video Games Are Art, So What's Next?" *TED Talk*. March 23, 2009. https://www.youtube.com/watch?feature=player_embedded&v=K9y6MYDSAww (accessed January 5, 2018).

Schiesel, Seth. "*Grand Theft Auto* Takes On New York." *New York Times*. April 28, 2008. http://www.nytimes.com/2008/04/28/arts/28auto.html (accessed July 28, 2016).

Schloss, Joseph G. *Making Beats: The Art of Sample-Based Hip-Hop*. Middletown, CT: Wesleyan University Press, 2004.

Senici, Emanuele. "Porn Style? Space and Time in Live Opera Videos" *Opera Quarterly* 26 (2010): 63–80.

Sharp, John. *Works of Game: On the Aesthetics of Games and Art*. Cambridge, MA: MIT Press, 2015.

Sheinberg, Esti. *Irony, Satire, Parody, and the Grotesque in the Music of Shostakovich: A Theory of Musical Incongruities*. Aldershot, UK: Ashgate, 2000.

Sheridan, Connor. "Final Fantasy Performance by London Symphony Orchestra in May." *Games Radar*. February 7, 2013. http://www.gamesradar.com/final-fantasy-performance-london-symphony-orchestra-may/ (accessed December 3, 2016).

Shultz, Peter. "Rhythm Sense: Modality and Enactive Perception in *Rhythm Heaven*." In *Music Video Games: Performance, Politics, and Play*, edited by Michael Austin, 251–273. New York: Bloomsbury, 2016.

Slowik, Michael. *After the Silents: Hollywood Film Music in the Early Sound Era, 1926–1934*. New York: Columbia University Press, 2014.

Smuts, Aaron. "Are Video Games Art?" *Contemporary Aesthetics* 3 (2005). http://hdl.handle.net/2027/spo.7523862.0003.006

Suderman, Peter. "*BioShock* Proved That Video Games Could Be Art." *Vox*. October 3, 2016. http://www.vox.com/culture/2016/10/3/13112826/bioshock-video-games-art-choice (accessed October 3, 2016).

Suellentrop, Chris. "A New Game Delights in Difficulty." *New York Times*. May 16, 2012. http://www.nytimes.com/2012/05/17/arts/video-games/the-video-game-fez-is-complex-by-design.html (accessed July 17, 2014).

Summers, Tim. "From *Parsifal* to the PlayStation: Wagner and Video Game Music." In *Music in Video Games: Studying Play*, edited by K. J. Donnelly, William Gibbons, and Neil Lerner, 199–216. New York: Routledge, 2014.

———. *Understanding Game Music*. Cambridge: Cambridge University Press, 2016.

Taruskin, Richard. "The Musical Mystique." *New Republic*. October 21, 2007. https://newrepublic.com/article/64350/books-the-musical-mystique (accessed January 5, 2018).

Tavinor, Grant. *The Art of Videogames*. Malden, MA: Wiley-Blackwell, 2009.

Tavinor, Grant. "Definition of Videogames." *Contemporary Aesthetics* 6 (2008). http://www.contempaesthetics.org/newvolume/pages/article.php?articleID=492&searchstr=tavinor (accessed August 7, 2014).

Taylor, Emily. "Dating-Simulation Games: Leisure and Gaming of Japanese Youth Culture." *Southeast Review of Asian Studies* 29 (2007): 192–208.

Tessler, Holly. "The New MTV? Electronic Arts and 'Playing' Music." In *From Pac-Man to Pop Music: Interactive Audio in Games and New Media*, edited by Karen Collins, 13–25. Aldershot, UK: Ashgate, 2008.

Thomas, Matt. "Give Me That Old-Time Religion: American Folk Music in the Video Game *BioShock: Infinite*." Paper presented at the annual meeting of the Society for American Music. Sacramento, CA, March 4–8, 2015.

Thomas, Sarah. "From Beethoven to Bleeps and Bloops: The Symphony of Video Game Soundtracks." *Sydney Morning Herald*. July 27, 2015. http://www.smh.com.au/entertainment/music/from-beethoven-to-bleeps-and-bloops-the-symphony-of-video-game-soundtracks-20150723-giim12.html (accessed December 2, 2016).

Thomson, Philip. *The Grotesque*. London: Methuen, 1972.

Thomson, Virgil. *The State of Music and Other Writings*. Edited by Tim Page. New York: Library of America, 2016.

Timberg, Scott. "Halt, or I'll Play Vivaldi!" *Los Angeles Times*. February 13, 2005. http://articles.latimes.com/2005/feb/13/entertainment/ca-musichurts13 (accessed August 7, 2014).

Tobias, Evan S. "Let's Play! Learning Music through Video Games and Virtual Worlds." In *The Oxford Handbook of Music Education*, vol. 2, edited by Gary McPherson and Graham Welch, 531–548. Oxford: Oxford University Press, 2012.

Toplin, Robert Brent. "The Filmmaker as Historian." *American Historical Review* 93 (1988): 1210–1227.

———. *History by Hollywood: The Use and Abuse of America's Past*. Urbana: University of Illinois Press, 1996.

———. *Reel History: In Defense of Hollywood*. Lawrence: University Press of Kansas, 2002.

van Elferen, Isabella. "The Gothic Bach." *Bach Perspectives* 7 (2012): 7–20.

Yang, Mina. *Planet Beethoven: Classical Music at the Turn of the Millennium*. Middletown, CT: Wesleyan University Press, 2014, 29–38.

Walker, Alexander, Ulrich Ruchti, and Sybil Taylor. *Stanley Kubrick, Director: A Visual Analysis*, Rev. ed. New York: Norton, 2000.

Wallin, Mark Rowell. "Myths, Monsters and Markets: Ethos, Identification, and the Video Game Adaptations of *The Lord of the Rings*." *Game Studies* 7, no. 1 (2007). http://gamestudies.org/07010701/articles/wallin/.

Walton, Whitney. "Gender and Genius in Postrevolutionary France: Sand and Chopin." In *The Age of Chopin: Interdisciplinary Inquiries*, edited by Halina Goldberg, 224–243. Bloomington: Indiana University Press, 2004.

Waugh, Patricia. *Metafiction: The Theory and Practice of Self-Conscious Fiction*. London: Routledge, 1984.

Wildgoose, David. "From Poetry to Playability: How Visceral Games Reimagined Dante's *Inferno*." *Kotaku*. February 2, 2010. http://www.kotaku.com.au/2010/02/from-poetry-to-playability-how-visceral-games-reimagined-dantes-inferno/ (accessed July 20, 2014.)

Wilson, Devin. "*Frederic—Resurrection of Music Complete Review*." *Slide to Play*. February 17, 2012. http://www.slidetoplay.com/review/frederic-resurrection-of-music-complete-review/ (accessed October 1, 2015).

Winton, Calhoun. *John Gay and the London Theatre*. Lexington: University Press of Kentucky, 1993.

Zipes, Jack. *The Irresistible Fairy Tale: The Cultural and Social History of a Genre*. Princeton, NJ: Princeton University Press, 2012.

Index

Note: Titles of classical works are listed under the composer's name, and individual movements are identified by the larger work. For example, "In the Hall of the Mountain King" is identified under "Grieg, Edvard, *Peer Gynt*." Games in a series are listed under the general title of that series. *Zelda II: The Adventure of Link*, for instance, can be found under "*The Legend of Zelda* (series)."